Postcolonial Indian Fiction in English and Masculinity

Edited by
Rajeshwar Mittapalli
Letizia Alterno

ATLANTIC
PUBLISHERS & DISTRIBUTORS (P) LTD

Published by
ATLANTIC
PUBLISHERS & DISTRIBUTORS (P) LTD
7/22, Ansari Road, Darya Ganj,
New Delhi-110002
Phones : +91-11-23273880, 23275880, 23280451
Fax : +91-11-23285873
Web : www.atlanticbooks.com
E-mail : info@atlanticbooks.com
Branch Office
5, Nallathambi Street, Wallajah Road,
Chennai-600002
Phones : +91-44-64611085, 32413319
E-mail : chennai@atlanticbooks.com

ISBN 978-81-269-1098-4

Printed in India at Nice Printing Press, A-33/3A, Site-IV, Industrial Area, Sahibabad, Ghaziabad, U.P.

Preface

Indian civilization began with matriarchy as its ruling principle. Several scholarly studies have corroborated this fact. Woman was viewed as the life-giver and therefore worthy of worship. This explains the Hindu practice of worshipping female deities—a practice which does not obtain in any other major religion of the world. It looks like when men discovered their own contribution to bringing life into being the balance started tilting in their favour. This resulted in the worship of the phallus of Shiva, *adideva* or the first god according to the Hindu cosmos. This development, together with the consolidation of the concept of private property and the culturally constructed need to continue the family line so that property and privileges could be passed on to the next generation, most definitely originated the patriarchal social structures that privileged men and marginalized women in the social and political spheres.

Subsequent social developments and religious/moral discourses institutionalized men's power and privileges. The religious myths, for example, have men—and the romantic notions of valour and physical prowess associated with them—at the centre of their fictional interest. They culminated in the projection of the super-masculine image of Krishna (often described as *purushotama* or the greatest of men) who has eight wives and a large but unspecified number of lovers called *gopis*. This mythical figure has been endowed with such super-masculinity that in the Vaishnava *bhatki* tradition even a male devotee treats himself as the beloved or mother of Krishna in what appears to be some form of willing feminization of the self. On the same lines, Shiva too has been ascribed super-masculinity. According to some cultural traditions prevalent in the rural areas of south India women, any number of them, can enter into a ritual wedlock with Shiva and stay married to him all their lives. Indian men often followed the example of their gods, and their kings down on the earth, and found it a convenient way of asserting their hegemonic masculinity, among other things, by marrying a number of women when they could afford it.

Indian masculinity, so constructed, did not stay on high pedestal and remained unchanged over the centuries. It took a severe beating during the successive invasions from across the border since the beginning of the last millennium. During the pre-British era Indian men came to see themselves as a submissive lot, incapable of protecting their pride and the honour of their women, in the face of an overwhelmingly powerful aggressor. Ashis Nandy has theorized that the British colonial masters sought to feminize the Indian men by setting themselves up as a 'hyper-masculine' race. However, it is difficult to subscribe to this view because the British colonial rulers were never on intimate enough terms with the natives in order to compel them to experience their perceived effeminacy. Even at the height of the British rule there were just about one hundred thousand white people in India and a large majority of the common people of India never even got to see a white man all through their lives. It was thus not really possible for the British rulers to project themselves as a hyper-masculine race in the imagination of the common Indian men, and conversely for the Indians to respond with effeminate behaviour. In fact, the British rulers' own masculinity was occasionally under attack with the native princes frequently marrying a number of white women and adding them to their already large harems. There is a further point which commentators fail to note: the British did their best to rehabilitate Indian masculinity—the romantic variety hinged upon physical prowess and military exploits—after the Revolt of 1857 by tapping the fighting potential of the martial races.

In the postcolonial era several factors combine to render Indian masculinity interesting and problematic. Freedom from the colonial yoke heralded for Indian men, on the one hand, the possibility of regaining their lost confidence in themselves, and on the other hand, the peace mantra preached by Gandhi together with India's grinding poverty that robbed people of their sense of dignity; the still very strong caste system which obliged the members of the lower castes to be subservient; the growing assertiveness of Indian women which resulted in the loss of some of the social and economic space men had previously occupied; and, above everything else, the series of gender biased laws[1] enacted by the Indian parliament, have all had their profound implications for especially the middle class urban men who incidentally populate the novels studied in this volume. These post-Independence developments have thrown Indian masculinity into a crisis and caused intense psychological turmoil in men. But instead of addressing the issue in the spirit of democracy society, the media and the government seem to take only a cynical view of men, and continually goad and coerce them to fit into a predefined, western model, social and psychological frame. These entities appear to be in no mood to acknowledge that for any social or psychological transformation to come about it takes time and that trying to achieve it quickly, and by force, will inevitably have a negative fallout. Caught in this vortex, for which they are utterly unprepared, Indian men experience a split within and the inner conflict sometimes boils over and spills into the social arena in unimaginable, and rarely even in destructive, ways.

The above discussion brings to the fore a simple truth: without a proper understanding of men and without enlisting their co-operation and participation, it will not be easily possible to achieve equality of the sexes. The Canadian novelist Margaret Laurence's opinion holds good in the context of India as well:

> I don't think enough attention has been paid to the problems men have and/or going to have increasingly because of the changes taking place in women. Men have to be re-educated with the minimum of damage to them. These are our husbands, our sons, our lovers.... We can't live without them, and we can't go to war against them. The change must liberate them as well.[2]

But the Indian approach to the issue lacks such inclusiveness. Men are most often portrayed in black and white, treated as undifferentiated mass, and stereotyped as a violent, boorish, emotionally sterile and insensitive lot. While the government indulges in 'excessive legislation' which succeeds more in making men feel guilty of being men rather than yield any tangible positive results, the media seems to go overboard in pleading the women's cause by reserving exclusive, and disproportionately large, space for them. It is surprising that no TV/radio channel or newspaper has anything to offer to boys and adolescent men by way of advice, counselling, social education and awareness-raising. It is as if there has been a complete reversal of what used to obtain in the past. While in the past all the discourses—the *shastras*, moral codes, etc.—were aimed at 'educating' men (and thus helping the institutionalization of patriarchy) modern discourses are aimed at women to the total exclusion of men and their genuine concerns. Young boys who regularly read newspapers and watch TV programmes are very likely to grow up believing that they are somehow unwanted and that the world is unconcerned about them. It is true that families still valourize boys in numerous ways, but appreciation earned out in the world is a lot more valuable for men than the constant reassurance of their worth at home.

Given the fact that boys and young men have hardly any reliable source of information, guidance and counselling for self-improvement and to sensitize themselves to the needs of the women around them, and having been negatively reinforced by Indian films, they either follow the dictates of their instincts (which is detrimental to the interests of women anyway) or copy the behaviour of the men around them (which is of not much help either) than develop personality traits friendly to women and in the process put themselves on a collision course with the forces seeking to impose the restructured social norms and standards on them.

It thus happens that there is a multitude of factors responsible for the confusion Indian men have been experiencing in the postcolonial period. Patriarchy, with all the attendant evils, comes first. Contrary to the popular perception, in modern India, men are equally the victims of the patriarchal ideology as women even if they have traditionally benefited from it (the so-called patriarchal dividend). To begin with, when they are young children and are not yet equipped with the intellectual resources to resist psychological conditioning patriarchal moral codes are planted in their heads and since the formal education system too does little to foster gender equality these ideas get fossilized and are put into practice when the boys come of age. Patriarchal ideology which romanticizes men's achievement of higher cultural aims, such as success at work, takes its toll on their lives by obliging them to adopt risky lifestyles, do potentially dangerous things, diminish their concern for health and personal well-being and in the process subject themselves to tensions and psychological pressures. Their stiff upper lip attitude, which patriarchal ideology compels them to maintain, makes them silently suffer emotional crises, earns them the accusation of being inarticulate, alienates them from their immediate family members and robs them of the chance of enjoying their love. Consequently they live far shorter lives than women. Again in pursuit of cultural aims, such as higher education and well-paid jobs, especially the middle class urban men postpone marriage until they are past their sexual prime and that way forgo the chance of sexual pleasure when they biologically peak. It would thus make a lot of sense to fault the ideology that governs people's lives and strive to revamp it rather than target men *en mass*, especially when they are under-organized, confused, divested of their traditional support systems and have been offered no alternative philosophical framework of equal practical value. After analyzing some of these issues in her book *The Indian Man: His True Colours* Sandhya Mulchandani concludes:

> Entangled in changes that have not been at their call or initiative, forced to make changes that go against the grain of masculine tradition, [Indian] men are increasingly caught between what they recognize as being politically correct and their own self-interest.[3]

Curious as it may look, and obviously unconsciously, women too contribute to the continued prevalence of the patriarchal philosophy. Indian mothers, for example, routinely encourage their sons to fight every step of their way to dominant social positions and in the process turn them into aggressive oppressors. Aggressive behaviour which is encouraged to be cultivated by all at home, including the women, will not be limited to men's behaviour outside home. It will eventually percolate through to their relations with their wives, daughters and even sons and other male dependents. Statistics are often cited to prove men as 'domestic terrorists' and to establish that women bear the brunt of their violence. While there is no gainsaying this, an important fact needs to be mentioned here: more severe forms of men's violence—such as torture, maiming and murder—are often reserved for fellow men.

Thus it is in the interest of both men and women to evolve non-violent masculinity by discarding the patriarchal ideology. Mangesh Kulkarni, one of the very few scholars who have written on the issue of Indian masculinity, avers:

> ...traditional forms of masculinity, which valorise self-centred, unemotional, competitive, aggressive and sexually promiscuous behaviour, require serious reevaluation for enhancing the wellbeing of both men and women. In the West, this ferment has led to the development of Men's Studies.... [R]esulting investigation of masculinity from historical, political and socio-psychological perspectives has yielded a rich harvest.[4]

But this re-evaluation is fraught with great difficulty in the Indian context. Patriarchal ideology cannot be easily isolated from the traditionalism, conservatism and the general philosophy that rules the lives of Indians. For instance, when people accept and worship gods who have married many times over, or expelled their wives on mere suspicion, how can they have spiritual/moral strength to question similar practices obtaining in real life? When they uncritically observe ritual practices that are loaded heavily against women how can women question the exercise of masculine power over them?

Another instance of traditionalism is the widespread son preference which is often blamed for female foeticide and adverse sex ratio. Son preference has its origin in the concept of *punnama naraka* (the part of the Hindu hell reserved for those who die without a son). The practice of dowry and lack of a strong social security apparatus further contribute to the preference for sons.

Finally, there is the Indian society itself, with all its contradictions and imperfections, which has stubbornly remained conservative and rigid all through the postcolonial period. While on the economic and political fronts there are now greater choices and opportunities, thanks to liberalization and democratization, in matters such as caste, religion, love and marriage the choices have not expanded. There has been no corresponding liberalization and democratization of the social institutions. Indian men and women thus find themselves in a dilemma—facing, on the one hand, rapid modernization and democratization on the economic and political fronts and, on the other hand, conservatism, rigidity and lack of choice on the social front. The Indian man for whom change means a lot more than change in his relations with women, finds it difficult to juxtapose these two worlds and therefore experiences anxiety and angst. If acting out the traditional man assures him of a modicum of peace and earns for him greater social approval he would be more readily inclined to conform rather than resist. Is there still any hope for practising what men might think is right, including the principle of equality of the sexes? Tradition muffles men's voice, as much as it does women's, and puts symbolic manacles on their minds.

Individualism is a possible answer to this problem because it views men and women as individuals with distinct identities rather than as parts of a larger whole, and sex as a mere biological marker rather than as a social signifier. However, practising individualism in India is not easy because Indian society continues to be extremely conservative and is quick to interpret self-assertion as defiance of tradition rather than as a sign of progress. The group mentality of Indians, actively reinforced by such social institutions as caste, seems to prevent the growth of individualism in India. Indian women, for that matter Indian men as well, are not exactly free to assert themselves in such matters as the choice of a marital partner. Young men and women are not allowed to move freely by the Indian society. They are actively discouraged from establishing meaningful emotional relationships by society, right wing religious outfits and sometimes even by the state. Indian society practises an invisible *purdah* system that seeks to strictly and systematically segregate men and women since their childhood itself and this leads to widening of the psychological chasm between the sexes. Lack of sustained and supportive interaction between the sexes contributes to the development of stereotypical views about men as well as women. In the Indian context, in a large majority of cases, men and women are allowed to come together only after they get married on the basis of a few minutes of 'bridal interview.' Then they are asked to live happily ever after! Where then is the chance for them to get to know each other, fall in love and admire each other, defy the retrograde traditions and assert their individuality? Arranged marriages may be durable, but most of them are devoid of love (since they are not founded on love), and for that reason they often suffer a symbolic death in less than half a dozen years. When there is neither love, nor the immediate possibility of divorce, the chances of domestic violence—both physical and psychological—are far higher. Men alone cannot be faulted for this scenario; it is a very complex social and psychological issue. The entire gamut of Indian philosophy, the prevailing ritual/moral/social practices and even the belief systems need to be re-examined and harmonized with the ethos of the age. The approach to the issue should thus be nuanced and comprehensive and aimed at ringing in gender justice and not merely at essentializing, reviling, blaming and shaming men for all the evils under the Indian sun.

Much has already been said from the women's point of view, and it was good that it was said, because their world view now finds wide acceptance. They have come to be understood in a far better light than a century ago. Like women, as adumbrated already, men too have been stereotyped and much has been uncritically assumed for them. While facing the challenges posed by the postcolonial India, men too find their problems multiplied. They too feel that they have a right to be heard and be given a chance to present their point of view. There is now a growing awareness that men's legitimate rights are being violated as a matter of routine and without the least regret. It is certainly not desirable to secure for women rights and privileges at the cost of men's rights. It is like going to the other extreme and therefore will amount to upsetting the fine balance that should prevail between the sexes at all times for the health of society.

One way of achieving this balance in India is to discuss masculinity as an academic subject. But there is an acute dearth of studies on masculinity while there are studies aplenty on women's issues. Masculinity studies and women's studies need not be at cross purposes. In fact, they can eminently complement each other and foster understanding between the sexes. Studying the depiction of masculinity in Indian fiction in English can be a good beginning for understanding Indian masculinity and its changing contours in the postcolonial period because this branch of literature faithfully reflects the new social mores, everyday ideology and popular psychology of the ever expanding urban middle class. Indian fiction in English is the only body of Indian literature which is pan-Indian in its conception and appeal. This fiction, especially of the postcolonial period, is produced by writers who are equally familiar with the East and the West and are largely free from cultural, linguistic and regional prejudices. Moreover, these writers indubitably have the ideological commitment, range of vision and intellectual honesty to address issues frankly and boldly. It is because of this open-mindedness and receptivity to new ideas that Indian fiction in English has been at the forefront of treating unconventional themes including masculinity.

This volume comprises scholarly essays that explore from multiple perspectives postcolonial Indian masculinity (more correctly, masculinities) as portrayed in Indian novels in

English. It attempts to draw critical attention to Indian masculinity and its imaginative treatment in literature. Every essay has an abstract prefacing it; therefore, it has not been felt necessary to offer a foretaste of what the essays discuss. Instead, we thought it would be more helpful to treat the readers to the above account of the religious, social and psychological background of Indian masculinity and thus adequately equip them with ideas for the appreciation of the material presented in this book. We conclude by pointing out that not all the contributors are in agreement with our views on Indian masculinity.

Rajeshwar Mittapalli
Letizia Alterno

Notes and References

1. Section 498A of the IPC, Dowry Prohibition Act, 1961, Domestic Violence Act, 2005, etc.
2. Margaret Atwood, "Face to Face," *A Place to Stand On: Essays by and about Margaret Laurence*, ed. George Woodcock (1974; Edmonton: NeWest Press, 1983), p. 23.
3. Sandhya Mulchandani, *The Indian Man: His True Colours* (New Delhi: Picus, 1999), p. 177.
4. Mangesh Kulkarni, "Reconstructing Indian Masculinities," *Gentleman* (May 2001).

Contents

1

A Reading of G.V. Desani's *All About H. Hatterr* as Queer Autofiction

Geetha Ganapathy-Doré

Abstract

Indian Independence movement was closely linked to Indian women's liberation. Apparently not much attention was paid to male anxieties with regard to the new identity they were being obliged to forge. G.V. Desani's *All About H. Hatterr* not only deals with the question of postcolonial language but also with what may be termed the queer identity of the modern Indian hero. Such a reading provides by the same token a key to unlock the difficult to decipher Desani code. The protagonist whose name H. Hatterr could be diversely interpreted constantly vacillates between the position of the author and that of the reader, the knowledge of the Empire and the wisdom of the East. H. Hatterr writes his novel in London during his exile and at night for the benefit of his lady love left in India. However, the narrative describes his gradual distancing from female relationships towards masculine friendships either sought for or rebuffed, first in the city's club and then in the villages of India with all sorts of rascals and holy men. Is this perpetual wandering an individual destiny or a case of "virility" trying to find sublimation in celibacy? In which measure does the hybrid and subversive language participate in the queer autofictional discourse? The article relies on the constant modulation of his text by Desani, his discussions on the genre of the novel and the very form of his novel to show how he uses Buddhist logic to write his sexual difference in a western literary form.

Desani's one and only and one-of-its-kind novel, first published in 1948, enjoys a cult status among postcolonial readers. Salman Rushdie had acknowledged many years after the publication of his own epoch-making novel *Midnight's Children* that he learnt a trick or two from Desani and that "*Hatterr*'s dazzling, puzzling, leaping prose is the first genuine attempt to go beyond the Englishness of the English language" (Rushdie xviii). Gayatri Spivak had earlier pointed out the uniqueness of *Hatterr* as a "virtuoso novel where 'English' attempts to claim its status as one of the Indian languages (belonging to a national underclass) through the techniques of sustained literal translation of the vernacular rather than islands of direct monstrous speech in a sea of authored standard English" (Spivak 240). But as Chelvanayagam Kanaganayakam remarks, "the novel remains very much a resistant text" (Kanaganayakam 69). The Desani code is difficult to crack.

Peter Russell's and Khushwant Singh's interpretation, which was chronologically close to the text's publication, situates the work in the context of English literature and looks upon Desani's Faustian enterprise as an attempt to make a heaven out of the earthly hell of human existence. This approach is quite justified in view of Desani's own allusions to William Blake. Anthony Burgess has praised the gloriously impure language of Desani whom he compares to Shakespeare and Joyce. Jacqueline Bardolph tries to decipher Desani's language madness in the light of Lewis Carroll's philosophy of non-sense. Molly Daniels considers Hatterr to be a combination of both Alice and the mad hatter. Kanaganayakam elaborates on the parallels between *Hatterr* and *Alice in Wonderland*. "The fairy tale jettisons the logic and problematizes the relation between language and reality. Similarly, caught in a world he does not understand, Desani's character is forced to recognize that language creates its own reality and identity is indeterminate" (Kanaganayakam 55). Sunanda Mongia relies on psychoanalysis to comprehend the text given the confessional form of the narrative and its references to "Doktur Med. Freud and Herr Jung" (67). Taking the cue from Burgess, Srinivas Aravamudan has studied the postcolonial affiliations between Joyce's *Ulysses* and *All About H. Hatterr*. Gerhard Stiltz, on the other hand, has stressed the postmodern aspect of the novel by highlighting its semantic, logical, aesthetic and cultural pluralism. Desani himself seems to have anticipated Edward Said's theories on Orientalism by making his protagonist remark: "Damme this is the oriental scene for you" (41).

Having worked with the BBC where he might have met George Orwell,[1] Desani possessed an intuitive awareness of the global village that Marshall McLuhan conceptualized in 1962. Desani's imagined fusion between *Paris Soir* and *Time Magazine*, between *New York Times* and *Frankfurter Zeitung* and premonition of the world circus whose "great kingpin" (68) will be the clown Bill Smythe make his novel a narrative of globalization ahead of its time. But it is Amitav Ghosh who renders full justice to the pioneering status of Desani's novel in the homage he paid to the author at the time of his death. According to Ghosh, "Hatterr" is, in fact, "a sustained and complex interrogation of modernism; by the same token it is also a profoundly resourceful defence of certain non-Western spiritual and metaphysical ideas" (Ghosh home page). Desani deals with the theories of Marx, Freud, Darwin and Einstein in an absolutely irreverent manner before coming up with his theory of contrasts inspired by Havelock Ellis's ideas. Amitav Ghosh interprets Desani's strategy of evasion as an attempt to "question and undermine the presuppositions of a certain kind of totalising modernity."

Ghosh's remarks prompt us to unravel the travesty of identity in Desani to examine whether *All About H. Hatterr* could be a queer autofiction. This paper[2] attempts to read Desani in the light of autofiction and queer theories to show that this interference enables the signifiers to confront each other releasing some meaning and making the text more "writable" in the Barthesian sense of the term. Such a theoretical and generic shift does not reduce it to a two dimensional and caricatural flatness. On the contrary, it adds to the confusion.

Applying theoretical developments of the 1990s to a text published in 1948 may appear as a queer task in itself. Desani's aesthetics which is an aesthetics of overturning and reversal leaves space for an irrelevant, indeed even erroneous reading. Formal textual proofs help us posit that the author's fictional double, H. Hatterr, is a queer who is not aware of his queerness rather than an eccentric who asserts himself as such. It is *Hali*, the play that Desani wrote which provides the key to the ambivalence in the identity of Harry (the first name abridged to H in the novel), for Hali is a boy disguised as a girl by his mother who chooses to call him by a female first name, Girija (Desani, 1991: 3). In this collection, we encounter another strange passage written in the first person about an impudent young man called Muglai.

> He was about thirteen. And judged by *any* standard, he was an entirely attractive person. I liked him very much.... When I first saw him, I caught myself wondering about the heartaches so much charm could cause a young possessive girl, in the days to come. The girl angle was a part of my thinking in those days. If I may say so, it still is, gentlemen. (Desani, 1991: 53)

Desani's protagonist Hatterr betrays similar emotions when he meets Sadanand, a young recluse:

> He was tall, just over six-foot, most pleasant to look at—his young face covered with a fine down—and he had a youthful beard: altogether a handsome body of man. (119)

The male narrator's female gaze is nothing shocking to the Indian public which is used to the role playing modes of Chaitanya's love for Krishna. When such bisexuality is openly expressed in English, it sounds queer.

The term "queer" in its primary sense of strange or bizarre is used thrice in the novel: to refer to Hatterr (64), to describe the clinical aspect of a situation in which he serves as a living plate to a hungry circus lion (82) and finally to denote his wife Kiss Curl (226). Let us call to mind that Alice uses the word queer many times in Lewis Carroll's novel. The word queer was used by groups of men in the New York of 1910s and 20s in order to endorse their homosexual desire rather than their effeminate bearing. Desani might have come across such Americans among the allied soldiers who frequented the London milk bars during the war. In Desani's text, unbridled masculine sexuality can be perceived not only through the lexical and semantic intimacy between two or more languages and the joyful quiver of the sentence structure but also through a spectrum of adjectives and nouns disseminated in the text which are generally associated with homosexuality and its attendant gaiety—dandy, gay, jolly, merry, rummy, frolic, mirth. Though the book was initially designed to appeal to the attention of a woman called Kumari, it is dedicated to a man, Kanhayalal Savaldas who is supposed to be the real life double of Bannerrji, the brother in arms of H. Hatterr in all his misadventures. Besides, biblical and literary references to the friendship between David and Jonathan, sonnets 128 and 140 of Shakespeare, Oscar Wilde's essay "De Profundis" (164), the account of how David Livingston was found by Henry Morton Stanley (195), the fictional and parodic appropriation of the real and almost loving encounter between two highly reputed gurus of India, Ramakrishna Paramahamsa and Swami Vivekananda in Chapter IV (in 1881, Ramakrishna Paramahamsa was moved by the voice of the adolescent Narendra who would later become his disciple), the comparison of the voice of a singer to "an eruption, a vocal lava" (169) are the many clues to the code of homosexual desire incorporated in the text. Above all, the "gesture" affixed to the text by its author in the peritext of warning, though it might constitute an ironical wink at George Orwell who was fond of that word, inscribes it in a performativity and corporeity which shall be dealt with later in the text.

> Damme, this is the medical man's century! Body, man, Doctor the body! (95)

The fact that *All About H. Hatterr* was forbidden in Ireland on account of its indecency[3] shows that the pagan sexual connotations underlying the test were disturbing.

Desani's text shakes the organic stability of the text, the genre of the novel, the form of autobiography, postcolonial subjectivity, masculine sexuality and the English language itself by plunging the reader in a delicious in-betweenness. The conditions in which Desani wrote the novel were sufficiently Beckettian. Desani wrote alone in the night, poor and exiled in

London during the years of war. Though the windows of his room were shut, the air had become irrespirable. However, initially no Beckettian melancholy awaits the reader, the guardian of literary conscience, but rather a Vaudevillesque and Shakespearean greeting, especially if he has been wise enough to resist the author's initial appeal not to read his anonymous letter of a text. This flight of the author in front of the reader continues in the constant rewriting of the text. Though my paper relies on the first Indian edition by Arnold Heinemann in 1985, the consultation and comparison of different editions are necessary for a genetic textual research proper. In order to have an idea of the hide and seek game that Desani plays with the reader, the publisher, history and geography, let us simply note that the text was first published by Aldor in 1948 and reprinted in 1950 by Saturn Press. A revised edition was published in the United States in 1951 by Farrar, Strauss and Young. A further revised edition with an introduction by Anthony Burgess is jointly published by The Bodley Head in England with Farrar, Strauss and Grioux in the US in 1970. Desani had not done with it yet. He brought more modifications and added a supplementary chapter and got his novel published again by Lancer Books in the US in 1972. The history of the struggle for the addition of this appendix is narrated in the later versions of the text in the form a nightmare in which H. Hatterr begs his surgeon not to cut the appendix. The unconscious identification between the body and the text and the masculine anxieties of castration are obvious:

> Don't take away the appendix, do you hear me?... It is more precious to me than the entire book. (93)

This edition enriched with other editions appeared in England under the aegis of Penguin Books which reprinted it as a King Penguin in 1982. Thus came the editorial consecration. Arnold Heinemann published its Indian version in 1985. The definitive version of the novel was published by McPherson in the US in 1986, i.e. thirty-eight years after its first publication. Considering the same style of language in the article entitled "India for the Plain Hell of it" Desani wrote for the *New*

Yorker in 1997, we might conclude that he had decided to fix his text truly in 1986.

As if the indeterminacy concerning the body of the text did not suffice, Desani confuses the clues as to the identity of the author and the genre of his text with a view to undoing the unity and solidity of the subject on the one hand and the logic of the mercantile culture that ensures the circulation of the book, on the other. Before accessing the novel's text properly speaking which is entitled *H. Hatterr by H. Hatterr* and which slightly varies from the official title *All About H. Hatterr,* the reader has to go through an auctorial peritext (Gasparini 62) where Desani reveals the conditions of emergence of his text. In spite of the author's confession that he tells nothing but the truth and who signs this preface with his true name, the immediate detachment from this avowal by the warning "what follows is wholly H. Hatterr, his work" unveils the fact that the true queer self prefers to keep the mask of the hetero-normative false self. This masquerade nevertheless serves the purpose of telling the reader that the narrator is but a puppet of the ventriloquist author. The "artificiality" of Desani's humour to which Kanaganayakam draws our attention often is a sign of this falseness (Kanaganayakam 57). At the same time, the author demystifies the act of writing when he informs the reader that thirty words commencing by Z had to be deleted from the manuscript because his typewriter had lost its Z key. The narrator for his part gives a sample of reader responses which he calls laughter-response at the end. Self-deprecation reaches a higher level when H. Hatterr introduces himself.

> Biologically I am fifty-fifty of the species. One of my parents was a European. From which part of the Continent? Wish I could tell you. The other was an Oriental, a Malay Peninsula-resident lady. From which part of the Peninsula? Couldn't tell you either. (31)

Yet, for him there is no contradiction being born thus. In the presence of the holy river Ganges one Indian night, he perceives the essential unity behind the duality of the creator and the created.

> I felt lost, ego-less, identity-less, like one dead: yet at peace, at great peace, with all creation, all men, and my Maker: Destroyer Lord. (132)

The definition of queer identity given by David Halperin: "an identity without essence" (1995: 62), a notion which could be compared to the Buddhist concept of *sunya*, is illustrated in the above discourse. Desani deconstructs the enunciative presuppositions of the English speaker in order to sketch the fluctuating and plural identity of H. Hatterr in the form of a conundrum where multiple and totally incoherent meanings enter into competition. H. Hatterr stands for Hindustaniwallah Hatterr, an average Indian who wears a cap (the leaders and followers of the Congress party used to wear a white cotton cap, called the Gandhi cap ever since) and may be suffering from a mental disorder. But his wife calls him Harry. Harry as in Tom, Dick and Harry, in other words, anyman and everyman.

> Everyman, I will be thy guide. (31)

This disindividualization makes Hatterr's autobiography, however singular it may be, the biography of each one of us. One of the characteristics of queer autobiography is that it is mostly read as a collective autobiography. The initials H.H. referring to His Highness or His Holiness translate the high opinion one might have of one's self. If the reader is as inventive as the author, he or she could discern in the doubling of the consonants H, T, R the sound structure of the German greeting Heil Hitler especially if he or she has in mind the allusion to *Mein Kampf* in the book. H. Hatterr is like Charlie Chaplin's barber, the caricatural anti-hero, a "Hitler Hater" who delivers the following message through his attorney Rambeli:

> It is not nice to drop bombs on ladies and gentlemen and their innocents below. (316)

The structure of the novel pursues the defamiliarization tactics by throwing overboard the conventional novelistic plot with a beginning, a climax and an end. It consists of a warning, a preface, a different title page, a contents page, another warning, a mutual introduction, seven chapters and an apology. In another register, Desani destabilizes the reader used to dilemmas and trilemmas by proposing him the tetralemma inspired by Buddhist *Tharka* model. Each chapter is therefore composed by a digest, instruction, presumption and life encounter.

The best way to combat mercantile culture according to Desani is the homeopathic method. One way to achieve this is to render the referent suspect. Therefore his text will be labelled gesture (subversively) or novel (conservatively) according to the demands of the market. With Desani, what you see is not what you get. The purpose of his "counterrealistic, digressive and fragmented narrative" is to present a "subversive version of spiritual India" (Kanaganayakam 65) and by the same token initiate the reader into an alternative sexuality.

The title of the novel which starts with "All About" harks back to at least two worlds. The first is the sulphurous world of the tabloids in which all the truth is divulged as in the film *All About Eve* (1950). In colonial India, this kind of revelations about the intimate life of sahibs was made in the "vernacular rags" (47 & 151). Desani's narrative is a case in reversal in the sense the English reader learns all about an Oriental gentleman therein. The other is the self-taught universe of the Everyman series. Desani had quit school thrice because he could not stand its sterile formalism. His novel is an instruction manual for the school of life in which wisdom acquired through experience claims to substitute the constructed knowledge of the Empire.

Early on, *H. Hatterr by H. Hatterr* is designated as a biography. Desani gives a stunning list of biographies of renowned or depraved people such as Saint-Augustin, Benvenuto Cellini, John Bunyan, James Boswell, Cardinal Newman, Jean-Jacques Rousseau, Thomas de Quincey, Giacomo Girolamo Casanova and Adolph Hitler. He also cites other authors such as Samuel Pepys, Edward Gibbon and Rudyard Kipling who had used some subgenres of the biography such as the diary, memoirs, autobiographical novel and travel writing in order to underscore the elasticity of the autobiographical genre. At the same time, Desani deconstructs the reader's horizon of expectation by giving a multiplicity of possible definitions of his text as a joke, a big lie, an apology, a homage, a literary suicide, a song, a mosaic-organon, a medico-philosophical grammar, a horseplay, a design for diamond-cut-diamond, a model of discipline for the body, a mills and bomb,[4] a time bomb, a scenario, etc. By appropriating both the definition of autofiction by Serge Doubvrosky as "the language of an adventure confided to the adventure of a language set free" and that of queer identity by Lee Edelman as "a zone of possibilities," Desani's narrative could be decoded as a queer autofiction.

Queer autofiction reverses the supposed exemplarity of individual lives narrated by narrating the life of an ordinary and anonymous person who sets a bad example. "The Confession of the Greatest Splendid Failure" (83). In queer autofiction, the one who confesses is not so much the author but the reader who is made to recognize the part of strangeness in him. A life story that at the outset announces the death of the protagonist and stages it is certainly weird. By doing so, queer autofiction, at least in Desani's case, isolates life from its consubstantiality with beings to make it an object of philosophic contemplation, "this life" in the manner of the Vedantic explanation "tat tvam aci" (thou art that).

In *Culture and Imperialism*, Edward Said criticises the empire for having produced "more refugees, migrants, displaced persons and exiles than ever before in history" (Said 332). The picaresque wandering of H. Hatterr in the seven[5] imperial cities of British India has invited comparisons with Don Quixote and Tristram Shandy, while the H. Hatterr and Banerrji couple could be viewed as a recast of the Lama and Kim in Kipling or Laurel and Hardy in cinema. But so far no textual analysis has drawn our attention to the progressive moving away of shy Harry from his relationships with women including his wife Kiss Curl née Rialto, the unknown dhobi woman, he kisses and the acrobat Rosy whose "total lack of femininity" (71) he finds attractive towards masculine friendships searched for or spurned, first in the town's club and later in the villages of India, with all sorts of rascals and wandering holy men.

The colonial encounter constituted a moment of intense challenge to one's identity, especially sexual identity. Prem Chand's short story "The Chess Players" which was later made into a movie by Satyajit Ray contrasts the rigidity of the English General Outram with the bedecked Indian poet King Wajid Ali Shah. India itself was considered to be a vast outdoor playground for Western men. Whiteness had become equated with male superiority and blackness with female subjugation. Mahatma Gandhi's *My Experiments with Truth* advocated his belief in self-restraint through celibacy and vegetarianism. It has been alleged that he slept with young girls to put his self-control to test. This aspect of Gandhi's life has always intrigued commentators. But in Indian philosophy the vanquishing of desire and not the conquest of its object is considered the ultimate victory. If some renounced their sex life, others were even ready to go to the extent of performing the last *sadhana*. But nothing frightens H. Hatterr as much as the status of the "Celibate-Castrate" (149).

Gandhi perfected his moral courage by waging a war of the mind over his body. G.V. Desani was not an unconditional admirer of Gandhi. He had satirized the man who did not want to be enslaved by his desire by literally translating his name into English as Fascination-Slave-Action-moon Grocer" (312). Hatterr, who is an outsider in the sense he is a half caste, is not able to reconcile himself to becoming an uncritical disciple of the nationalist guru. The first chapter in which Hatterr makes merry by drinking toddy, strips his Western dress and performs an almost tribal dance can be read as a shameless exhibition of his body for the voyeuristic pleasure of the English reader, for his Indian onlookers are quite nonchalant about it and are involved in the business of recycling second hand clothes. But it is a satire of the nationalists as Kanaganayakam rightly surmises (Kanaganayakam 66). Gandhi exhorted Indians to be teetotallers and wear homespun garments to counter the import of milled cotton from Manchester. He himself decided to give up his Western ways of dressing and bared his body to resemble the Indian peasant which prompted Winston Churchill to despise him as a half-naked fakir. Desani decides to offer the English reader not one but

> Two naked fakirs on a dust-heap! (216)

In the wrestle that ensues, the indecent future of the postcolonial Indian becomes clear.

> In a trice, I am holding in my hand the chap's slip.
> He has my loincloth.
> Then, it is every man for himself. (217)

H. Hatterr is initially embarrassed to undress before another man, a rite of passage in becoming a man, but affirms that he is no "Harvard sissy" (132). Male body is on display in Chapter III (133). A character whom Hatterr called the bishop commands all the members of his group to apply mustard oil before plunging into a river. Hatterr, who was not used to this local irritant, feels like a "cat on hot bricks" (133). His pathetic jive amuses the onlookers. He is terribly self-conscious about his looks even when he is beaten up and black eyed.

> He made me touch up the eye-lashes, too, with a pinch of ash, as might any Paris-London-New York society belle-femme. (141)

One of the reasons that propel H. Hatterr towards Giri-Giri is the fact that he possesses Hapsburg lips (166). Hatterr is mesmerized by the handsome Giri-Giri.

> His entire person was pure charm. I am yet to encounter a female to match that chap's pagan attraction. (167)

The night he spends in the company for Giri-Giri is not ticklish as the name indicates but gets sadomasochistic instead.

> He decides to treat me like a hobby horse.... Giri-Giri was mounted on my back, and telling me to get cracking, *gee-up!...* More than once I told him not to kick me with his heels. (178-79)

Hatter's self portrait as a consecrated Indian scholar in Chapter VI is completely queer.

> I was in the semi-nude required of me by the *abhisheka* occasion: the orange coloured silk square, worn as a loincloth, and the apricot turban to add to the gay note. (238)

The masculine undergarment, be it in the form of 'yellow fancy' or slip or loincloth seems to obsess him in his wavering between "shirtdom" and "skirtdom" (251). Well before Judith Butler, H. Hatterr alias Desani wants to put forward the idea that sexual identity springs from social convention rather than biological determination through the humorous episode of a Hindu boy who could not "tell boys from girls unless they were conventionally dressed" (310).

Hatterr's ego measures itself against European men as well. When William the Oxford student vacationing in Cambridge proposes to exchange his original Chippendale for Hatterr's Missionary Society stereoscope, he is not duped.

> I may be tiddly by the Cantab. and Oxon standards, but damme, I can tell a 'cello, if it's a genuine Chip!' (194)

However, his inferiority complex surfaces in front of his wife's friend Appadine-Sinclair's "Varsity Bleat" (248).

The most striking aspect of *All About H. Hatterr* is naturally its hybrid language. Desani's mixed style draws inspiration perhaps from *Fasana-i-Azad*, a picaresque novel in Urdu written by Rathan Nath Sharshar in 1880. The postcolonial aspect of Desani's writing back to the empire that violently transforms the language of the colonizers and announces the birth of a new crosscultural subjectivity is obvious.

> I write rigmarole English, staining your goodly, godly tongue, you may be. (37)

The idea of palimpsest, filigree, trace, dual language, interlingua that Chantal Zabus mentions in her study of Europhone African literature and the concept of "whole language" that Anthony Burgess advances in the introduction to Desani's book prove very useful in understanding the linguistic cutting and pasting that Desani performs. Notable among his word play is the double entendre[6] which seems to transpose both the author's sexual ambivalence and his scepticism with regard to the new nation whose past proves as elusive to grasp as Shivaji's treasures that Hatterr sets out to unearth. Nevertheless, T.S. Eliot's observation that it is amazing that anyone should sustain a piece of work in this style and tempo at such length (quoted by Burgess 8) must steer us towards the exploration of what Eve Kosofsky Sedgewick calls the "fractal complexities of language" (Sedgewick, 1993: 9). More than the verbal pyrotechnics and the inexhaustible inventiveness of Desani, it is the oral nature and the hyperactivity of the linguistic performance that strike the reader. Body and sexuality irrupt into the textual surface. Peter Russell and Khushwant Singh evoke an "endocrine enslavement" in *H. Hatterr* (Russell & Singh 19). If Indian philosophy tries to channel sexual energy in the paths of *bakhti*, *karma*, *yoga* and *jnana*, H. Hatterr experiments with what he calls the way of the libido, pouring his overwhelming masculine sexuality into the language.

The narrator's wish to sublimate his virility in celibacy in the yogic tradition may have something to do with the twist of fate that the old palm reader predicts to Desani saying that he will die assassinated. But far and above a particular destiny, this wavering between two genders hints at a movement of flight from the original shadow of the mother.[7]

> Sometimes like I remember her. Sometimes just her skeleton.... Wounds, lacerations, and bites all over her; As if she had been savaged? (222)

The mother tongue is here a synecdoche for the flesh and blood of the mother's body in Desani. The unbearable lightness of being and the laughter therapy he proposes are in fact the lopside of a profound tragedy and deprivation of love.

> I am a most poor man and a stranger.... I am lonely. (37)

This is a twisted quotation from Shakespeare's Henry VIII where Catherine of Aragon tells the English king that she is "a most poor woman and a stranger." Amitav Ghosh attributes the incommensurable gap between what Desani wanted to say with the language he was saying it in to the postcolonial predicament of having to express oneself in a foreign tongue.

However, it might be interpreted as a sign of Desani's not daring to "come out." Desani's queer attitude which is expressed in the following absurd formula—

> We are all bound to be hanged and therefore will never drown. (291)

—is reminiscent of Buddhist philosophy where death constitutes the only certainty and where the point of equilibrium between polarities whether they be ethical or gender-based is conceived in the neti-neti neither...nor, midway between sexuality and spirituality, half honourable like H.H. This reading could satisfy both the homosexual reader initiated to the queer dharma and the heterosexual reader who knows Indian philosophy. In spite of the initial difficulties that it has known in a society imbibed with prudish Victorian values but which had conceived at the dawn of its civilization the hermaphrodite identity of Shiva, gay identity has at least one magazine[8] fully dedicated to it and several websites, novels and films in both English and regional languages in contemporary India whose culture is being globalized by paradoxically embracing and at the same time resisting American culture.

Notes

1. There is a slight resemblance between Hatterr's main story and *Burmese Days*. Both involve a European having sexual relations with an indigenous woman and the consequences of it.
2. A former version of this paper has been published in French in *QUEER: Ecritures de la difference*, vol. 2, *Représentations: Artistes et Créations*, ed Pierre Zoberman (Paris: Harmattan, 2008) 95-110.
3. Quoted from a facsimile of the inside of the cover of *H. Hatterr* reissued in London in 1950 in Russell & Singh's *G.V. Desani* 31.
4. A pun on Mills and Boon, publishers of pink romantic novels. Desani's queer romance is a 'bomb' and not a boon in so far as its purpose is to shock.
5. Note the mysticism of numbers in Desani's writings. Allusions to the seven stars of the constellation of the great Bear known in India under the name of the *Saptarishi* (seven sages), to the seven ages described by Shakespeare and the seven seals of Adventists.

The number of chapters in his book, the prefacing ritual, the auctorial peritext and the allographic epitext seem to have derived from tantric esoteric practices.

6. Ex: Ali Bee/alibi (40), You Essay/USA (88).
7. Desani's mother's name was Rukmani Chabria Desani. He did not carry his father's family name Manguirmal. For more details on Desani's biography, cf <http://www.desani.org/>.
8. *Bombay Dost.*

Works Cited

Aravamudan, Srinivas. "Postcolonial Affiliations: *Ulysses* and *All About H. Hatterr.*" Ed. Karen R. Lawrence. *Transcultural Joyce.* Cambridge: Cambridge UP, 1998. 97-128.

Bardolph, Jacqueline. "Language Madness in G.V. Desani's *All About H. Hatterr.*" *Commonwealth, Essays and Studies* 8.1 (1985): 1-13.

Burgess, Anthony. Introduction. *All About H. Hatterr,* by G.V. Desani. New Delhi: Arnold-Heinemann, 1985. 7-11.

Butler, Judith. *Gender Trouble: Feminism and the Subversion of Identity.* New York: Routledge, 1990.

Daniels, Molly A. *G.V. Desani: Writer and Worldview.* New Delhi: Arnold-Heinemann, 1984.

Desani, G.V. *All About H. Hatterr.* 1948. New Delhi: Arnold-Heinemann, 1985.

____. *Hali and Collected Stories.* New York: McPherson & Co., 1991.

____. "India, For the Plain Hell of It." *The New Yorker* 30 June 1997: 62-69.

Doubvroski, Serge. *Fils.* Paris: Galilée, 1977.

Edelman, Lee. *Homographesis: Essays in Gay Literary and Cultural Theory.* London: Routledge, 1994.

Gandhi, M.K. *The Story of My Experiments with Truth.* 25 March 2008. <http://www.nalanda.nitc.ac.in/resources/english/etext-project/biography/gandhi/>.

Gasparini, Philippe. *Est-il je? Roman autobiographique et autofiction.* Paris: Seuil, 2004.

Ghosh, Amitav. Official website. 25 March 2008. <http://www.amitavghosh.com/essays/essayfull.php?essayNo=45>.

Halperin, David. *Saint Foucault: Towards a Gay Hagiography*. New York: Oxford UP, 1995.

Kanaganayakam, Chelvanayagam. "H. Hatterr and Sauce Anglaise: G.V. Desani." *Counterealism and Indo-Anglian Fiction*. Ontario: Wilfrid Laurier UP, 2002. 51-74.

Landry, Donna and Gerald Maclean, eds. *The Spivak Reader: Selected Works of Gayatri Chakravorty Spivak*. New York: Routledge, 1995.

Leyland, Winston, ed. *Queer Dharma: Voices of Gay Buddhists*. San Francisco: Gay Sunshine Press, 1998.

Mongia, Sunanda. "Paan juice stains the goodly godly tongue." *Biblio* 4.1-2 (1999): 12.

Rushdie, Salman and Elizabeth West, eds. *The Vintage Book of Indian Writing*. London: Vintage, 1997. The quotation in my article's first page is taken from Rushdie's introduction to the anthology.

Russell, Peter and Khushwant Singh, eds. *G.V. Desani: A Consideration of his All About H. Hatterr* and *Hali*. London: Karel Szeben, 1952.

Said, Edward. *Orientalism*. London: Vintage Books, 1979.

____. *Culture and Imperialism*. New York: Alfred Knopf, 1993.

Shrader, Sabine. "L'écriture autobiographique gay et lesbienne au XXe siècle—l'invention des moi(s) homosexuel(s) dans la littérature française." Paper presented on May 28, 2005 at the 'Queer Strategies' colloquium organised by CENEL at the University of Paris 13.

Sedgewick, Eve Kosofsky. *Tendencies*. Durham: Duke UP, 1993.

Stilz, Gerhard. "'Truth? Hell, you will get contrast, and no mistake!' Sanitizing the intercultural polyemma in G.V. Desani's *All About H. Hatterr* (1948/72)." *Hybridity, Postcolonialism and Modern Indian Literature*. Ed. Monika Fludernik. Tübingen: Stauffenburg, 1997. 79-101.

Zabus, Chantal. The African Palimpsest: Indigenization of Language in the West African Europhone Novel. Amsterdam: Rodopi, 2004.

2

Marriage, Sexual Violence and Indian Masculinity: A Study of Shashi Deshpande's *The Dark Holds No Terrors* and Anita Nair's *Mistress*

Aparna Sundaram

Abstract

Indian masculinity is a complex idea that is deeply entrenched in generations of social conditioning in a tradition bound cultural setup. Masculinity cannot be studied in isolation but only in relation to the feminine as one construct cannot exist without the other. The relationship between the two sexes has been, over the ages, one of power struggle and it is more so in modern India in which women are educated, assertive and self-reliant to some extent. In this scenario, the male has to redraw the boundaries to assert his superiority even within the marital relationship. This paper endeavours to focus on the act of marital rape as a tool used by men to reaffirm their 'superior position' within marriage and to wrest power as portrayed in the novels *Dark Holds No Terrors* (1980) by Shashi Deshpande and *Mistress* (2005) by Anita Nair.

"May you be the mother of a hundred sons" is a blessing that Indian women receive from elders (Bumiller). A majority of Indians firmly believe that to give birth to a son is a blessing and to a daughter is a curse. In a context such as this, the Indian male's ego has been overfed and his image blown up many times over giving each one a much-heightened sense of self and a free hand to rule over women. Male supremacy cannot be attributed just to physical superiority alone as Kate Millet suggests in *Sexual Politics*: "Male supremacy, like other political creeds, does not finally reside in physical strength but in the acceptance of a value system which is not biological" (27). Indian masculinity is a complex idea that is deeply entrenched in generations of social conditioning within a tradition-bound cultural setup. Mick Leach supports this claim when he says: "Unlike the biological state of maleness, masculinity is a gender identity constructed socially, historically and politically. It is the cultural interpretation of maleness, learnt through participation in society and its institutions." Masculinity cannot be studied in isolation but only relative to the feminine as one construct cannot exist without the other. The relationship between the two sexes has been, over the ages, one of power struggle and it is more so in modern India in which the woman is educated, assertive and self-reliant to some extent. In this scenario, the male has to redraw the boundaries to assert his superiority even within a marital relationship. This paper endeavours to focus on the act of marital rape as a tool used by men to reaffirm their 'superior position' in a marriage and to wrest power as portrayed in two profound and important novels of modern India namely *The Dark Holds No Terrors* (1980) by Shashi Deshpande and *Mistress* (2005) by Anita Nair.

Through the ages men have considered themselves and their experiences as central to life and women and their experiences were perceived as peripheral and insignificant and thereby establishing themselves as 'self' and women as the 'other.' Simone de Beauvoir says, "History has shown us that men have always kept in their hands all concrete powers; since the earliest days of the patriarchate they have thought best to keep women in a state of dependence; their codes of laws have been set up against her; and thus she has been definitely established as the Other" (171). This idea is further discussed by Seemanthini Niranjana when she talks about specific roles than both the genders play that has led to "dichotomies like home/world = female/male" (22). Gender status is determined by the cultural, religious and social ethos prevalent in a society, which may or may not be conducive to attaining gender equality. Even in today's world, any society cannot claim to have attained gender equality as the male always has an upper hand at some level. India is no different being a rigid and tradition-bound society that is unwilling to shed many of its age-old practices including a lopsided gender equation which Elisabeth Bumiller aptly sums up: "Indian men may beat their wives but they worship their goddesses" (10). A look at the cultural and religious history of India and its people would put the image of the Indian male in perspective.

Hindu mythology is a vast repertoire of stories that have been handed down through generations from which people have derived beliefs and found role models. Hindu mythology is found on the mighty triumvirate male gods namely Brahma, the creator, Vishnu, the preserver and Shiva, the destroyer and among the three, the fate of the universe rests. All the important mythical characters are reincarnations of these three gods. In Hindu mythology, women are mostly found as consorts to the male gods and do not have their own identity. Among the few exceptions, the goddess Durga, a powerful demon slayer, was supposed to have been created by taking different body parts from the male gods (Kinsley 97). The Indian psyche is strongly influenced by the mythical characters whom they emulate at some unconscious level. The ideals that men have to emulate are powerful and sometimes even violent whereas women have submissive, self-sacrificing and passive characters to idealise. Shashi Dephpande feels that myths originated with men and hence they are the point of view of men ("Telling Our Own Stories" 89). *Manusmriti*, an ancient text that laid down laws which were instrumental in shaping the characters of the Indian male and female, but ascribed a superior role for men. Indian masculinity can be understood thus as a construct that arose out of a deep-rooted sense of superiority in relation to women who were subjugated and oppressed.

Creation of any identity—masculine or feminine—rests mainly upon the patterns of power structures that exist in a society. The Indian male is largely exposed to a set of beliefs in which male supremacy is unchallenged and female subjugation is taken for granted. The male identity is mainly constructed through personal possessions and achievements. A man identifies himself with his occupation and the wealth he has acquired and women sometimes figure on his list of possessions. Men are always in a position to oppress women in any familial role they play like son, father, husband and brother. Another important aspect of the masculine identity is his sexuality. The male sexuality is seen as a sign of strength whereas the female sexuality is considered a taboo (Arora 122). The male identifies greatly with his sexual prowess and it plays an important part in creating the collective as well as individual male identities.

Modern times however have upset this unbalanced gender equation with more and more women being emancipated through education and careers. In this changing scenario, it is natural that the mindset of the male also transform into a tolerant and inclusive one giving space for women to find their own strength. The reality is quite different though, as the changing times have put the Indian male in a very complex situation in which he is obliged to embrace the new ideas but is unable to reject the old ones. The Indian male is caught in the midst of a rapidly changing social setup with empowered women vying for space in his professional and personal arena.

It is in this context that Shashi Deshpande and Anita Nair discuss marital rape perpetrated by the modern Indian male in their novels. Shashi Deshpande (1941-) is an acclaimed Indian novelist who has earned an enviable place for herself in the literary milieu of the country with her powerful depiction of women's lives. She has to her credit many novels: *The Dark Holds No Terrors* (1980), *Roots and Shadows* (1983), *The Binding Vine* (1988), *That Long Silence* (1988), *A Matter of Time* (1996), *Small Remedies* (2000) and her latest *Moving On* (2004). She has also authored many short stories, collected in volumes such as *Intrusion and Other Stories* (1993), and *The Stone Woman* (2001). Many of her novels have been translated into Indian as well as foreign languages.

Anita Nair (1967-), a recent entrant into the Indian English literary field, brings a refreshingly frank and straightforward narrative style to her works. Her body of work includes novels like *Better Man* (2000), *Ladies Coupe* (2001), and *Mistress* (2005). Her other works include *Where the Rain is Born—Writings about Kerala* (2003) which was edited by her, *Puffin Book of World Myths and Legends* (2004) and *Adventures of Nonu, the Skating Squirrel* (2006). Anita Nair's works reflect a wide range of interests making her a multi-faceted writer of the present generation.

Rape is a sexual act that is seen as a potent tool to overpower, control and 'put women in their place' by men. Men have been using sexual violence and rape as a means to wield control over women from time immemorial and across cultures. Fran Hosken says that violence against women is perpetrated "with an astonishing consensus among the men in the world" (qtd. in Mohanty 178). When it comes to marital relationships, many men consider themselves the sole owner of their wives and their bodies and would go to any extent to assert their right. There are many untold stories of marital rape happening within the four walls of seemingly happy homes in India which most of the time are not even construed as rape as it is thought that men have only taken what is rightfully theirs, while women remain mute spectators robbed of their dignity in their own homes.

In *The Dark Holds No Terrors*, Deshpande tells the story of Sarita who is a successful paediatrician quietly grappling with the horrifying truth about her husband who turns a rapist every night. His sexual sadism is attributed to his inability to rise to the level of his wife professionally. In *Mistress*, Nair discusses the act of marital rape in one instance when the protagonist Radha's husband forces himself upon her in order to assert his position as her husband, when she is drawn to another man. The paper will now discuss each of these characters, namely Manu in *The Dark Holds No Terrors* and Shyam in *Mistress*, in detail in the context of sexual violence within marriage.

The Dark Holds No Terrors is narrated from the point of view of Sarita its chief protagonist. At the pinnacle of her success as a doctor, she finds herself confused and battered as her husband Manu attacks her every night with sexual brutality. She is filled with dread and shame at being abused by her husband whom she has married against the wishes of her parents. The reader is introduced to Manu as a third person and is not privy to his thoughts. The novel opens with a prologue uttered in first person by Sarita:

> Now there was no waking. The dream, the nightmare, whatever it was, continued. Changing now, like some protean monster, into the horror of rape. This was not to be death by strangulation; it was a monstrous invasion of my body. I tried to move, twisting my body under the weight that pinned it down. It was impossible. I was pinioned to a position of an abject surrender of my self.
>
> ...It was more as if my mind had deserted my shamefully bruised body, disowning it, making it insensate.
>
> And then the two came together. I knew where I was and what had happened. Panic and sensation came back simultaneously. I turned my head slightly, fearfully, and saw him beside me, snoring softly. No more a stranger, but my husband. (11-12)

The above passage from the prologue that describes Manu's sexual attack sets the tone for the novel, which traces the journey of Sarita to her estranged parents' home where she finds renewed strength to face life.

Deshpande creates an almost perfect man in Manu when Sarita met him in college. He used to be the heartthrob of many women in college participating in dramatics and literary events. After they were married, the charm with which he used to recite poetry to Sarita, something that drew her to him in the first place, could not help him succeed professionally. While Manu was a poorly paid college professor, Sarita surged ahead of him with her career as a doctor.

Given the image of the Indian male as a superior being, Manu is unable to accept a lower position in his life even though Sarita has never tried to slight him. In an interview to Bumiller, actor Shabana Azmi remarked: “Women particularly in India feel very guilty about being successful. There is a feeling that somewhere you are losing out on your femininity, so the woman tries to compensate in the home by playing second fiddle to everybody because she’s guilty of being successful” (199). A casual remark, “How does it feel when your wife earns not only the butter but most of the bread as well?” (*The Dark* 200), made by a journalist who interviewed Sarita had acted as a trigger for Manu to launch his attacks and transform him from a seemingly normal man to a monster at night.

Manu begins his nightly sexual assaults because of his sense of worthlessness and powerlessness. He feels as though he is robbed off his manhood by not earning more than his wife. Since he is unable to match her or supersede her professionally, he does what men have been doing for ages to assert their power over women. He resorts to rape night after night as though to affirm who is more powerful or who the ‘man’ is in the relationship. S.P. Swain comments on Manu’s actions: “His masculinity asserts itself through nocturnal sexual assaults upon Saru. Thus the benevolent, cheerful husband by day turns a lecherous, libidinous rapist at night. Saru becomes a mute sufferer, wallowing in self-pity and choked in silence” (36). In a battered and bruised Sarita, Manu achieves his goal. While she endures his assaults, she describes her state of mind thus: “There is this strange new fear of disintegration. A terrified consciousness of not existing” (22). In Sarita’s weakness and vulnerability he finds his strength, in her powerlessness he finds power and by overpowering her he finds his manhood.

The Indian male as established earlier creates his identity around his profession and his possessions. In Manu’s case, the absence of both leaves him with a feeling of being castrated. His profession does not give him a valid identity and his wife snatches from him what is traditionally due to his ilk—to be financially superior and independent. Sarita herself tries to understand Manu’s character when she says: “Perhaps there is something in the male that is whittled down and ultimately destroyed by female domination" (*The Dark* 85). Later in the novel, Sarita also goes on to say, to maintain a happy marriage—

> A wife must always be a few feet behind her husband. If he's an MA, you should be a BA. If he's 5' 4" tall, you shouldn't be more than 5' 3" tall. If he's earning five hundred rupees, you should never earn more than four hundred and ninety-nine rupees. That's the only rule to follow if you want a happy marriage.... Women's magazines will tell you that marriage should be an equal partnership. That's nonsense. Rubbish. No partnership can ever be equal. It will always be unequal, but take care that it's unequal in favour of your husband. If the scales tilt in your favour, God help you, both of you (137).

The above passage defines the lopsided gender equation, discussed earlier in this paper, within the context of urban marital relationships.

Manu, the man, is a complete failure according to the idea of Indian masculinity. In order to restore his manhood and to assert his power, he sexually assaults his wife. Here it is imperative to note the importance men give to money and wealth and their role in the construction of a masculine identity. It is only when the foundations of his identity are challenged that Manu uses rape as a weapon to rein in his wife and show her, her rightful place within marriage. Manu thinks very little about the consequence of his actions as he is gravely affected by his hurt male ego and as a result, he jeopardizes his marriage and his life.

Nair's *Mistress* revolves around the life of Radha, Shyam and their morbid marriage against the backdrop of the narratives of Radha's uncle, Koman, who is a Kathakali exponent. The novelist uses some interesting techniques in the novel interweaving the dance form of Kathakali, its mythical characters and the story of Radha. Her unhappy situation in the ill-matched marriage drives her into the arms of Chris, an American writer. The novel culminates in Radha finding her own voice and deciding to live independently.

The most remarkable part of the novel is the characterisation of Shyam, which is a perfect mould of a modern, educated, tech-savvy Indian male who finds it hard to shed his traditional role as a man. Nair has given Shyam his own voice through his first person narrative and thereby taking the reader straight into his mind. If Manu is a character created in the eighties personifying the ethos of the time, Shyam is a twenty-first century Indian male through and through. Unlike Manu, Shyam is extremely successful in his business, which is his undoing in a sense. He is never reluctant to turn any opportunity into a money making venture. His only failure perhaps is his inability to understand his wife and treat her as an individual who has a mind of his own. To him Radha is another possession, which he is proud of, like he is of his business ventures. He repeatedly refers to her in the novel as "my Radha" as if to affirm his ownership. In place of an understanding and meaningful relationship that marriage can be, Shyam wants an unequal relationship that would make Radha his proud possession. Simone de Beauvoir speaks about this masculine trait in *The Second Sex*:

> ...subordinated economically and socially to her husband, the good wife is the man's most precious treasure. She belongs to him so profoundly that she partakes of the same essence as he; she has his name, his gods, and he is responsible for her. He calls her his 'better half.' He takes pride in his wife as he does in his house, his lands, his flocks, his wealth and sometimes even more; through her he displays his power before the world: she is his measure and his earthly portion. (207)

The idea of possession, discussed earlier on in this paper, is an integral part of Shyam's identity and his stature grows in proportion to his wealth.

Shyam's idea of marriage is to keep a pretty wife, indulge in her wishful fancies and make her dependent on him. He does not want an assertive woman as a wife. Radha and Shyam are incompatible in many ways and Radha feels suffocated in her marriage. She compares herself to the butterfly she caught and pinned to a board as part of biology projects in school and feels that "somewhere within a little heart beat, yearning to fly" (Nair 54). When Radha meets Chris, she finds her match because he shares her sensitivity and her taste for art and literature. As Shyam suspects Radha's affair with Chris, he is consumed with jealousy. Shyam knows that he cannot reign over Radha's mind and hence decides to reign over her body. Overcome by frustration and blinding anger, he forces himself on Radha, and offers an explanation himself:

> The resentment I felt for being tolerated rather than loved, the yearning I had suffered, the loneliness of these eight years, all fused to become a consuming desire to possess her. To make her mine. To reach within and tear down that film of indifference that coated her eyes each time I took her in my arms. (163)

Later he feels rather satisfied with what he has done and arrogantly says, "Women like to be made to feel like women, dominated and put in their place. Even my Radha. So I wasn't wrong, after all (164).

By a single act of sexual transgression, Shyam robs Radha of her dignity, her control over her body and her right to say "no." Radha is left shocked and bruised after Shyam's attack on her body. After the incident Radha says, in a state of shock:

> Two nights have passed since Shyam plundered my body, seized and took away my right to say no. Time hasn't made it better, only worse....
>
> There are no categories of rape. Rape is rape, even when sanctified by marriage. And the rapist doesn't have to be a stranger emerging from the shadows. He could be your husband. What Shyam did was to rape me.
>
> I close my eyes, willing myself to forget. But I cannot shut my mind to the expression in his eyes as his body bucked and heaved over mine. His eyes seared and burnt. They said: you are mine, you are mine. Shyam's eyes branded me more than his body did. (164-65)

To understand the character of Shyam, it is important to reiterate the fact that Indian men, or for that matter, men from other cultures, look at women in their lives as their property.

When a woman is indifferent to her husband and turns to another man for love or sex, it directly questions the virility of the husband. In this case, Shyam needed to reassert his ownership of Radha and 'mark his territory.' He wanted to prove that he is the husband and he has complete rights to his wife's body whether she welcomed the intrusion or not. The very description of the act in the novel shows Shyam with an almost animal like drive to prove his virility and assert his position as the husband. His one act of rape leaves a deep scar on Radha whereas, he is quite satisfied with what he has done without an iota of remorse.

Shyam resorts to rape to assert his identity as a husband and as a virile man. He is blind in his pursuit and does not care for Radha's feelings. Nair also discusses another important issue with regard to Shyam in the novel, which is his sterility. When Shyam comes to know that he is the reason for Radha's not becoming pregnant, he keeps it from her. Shyam thinks: "How can I have an infertility problem? [...] Women were infertile not men" (Nair 204). He wants Radha to look at him as a "full-bodied, red-blooded alpha male capable of fathering a hundred and one children" (Nair 205). Here again an Indian male would feel less of a man if he is unable to sire a child. It is only towards the end of the novel when Radha decides to leave him that he reveals the fact to her.

At the end of the novel, Shyam does evoke a sense of sympathy from the readers as he loses his most important possession in life, namely Radha. This perhaps poses the question as to whether Shyam is a victim of social conditioning as discussed earlier. It may be true that a character like Shyam could be conditioned to believe that he is superior to women and hence his high-handed behaviour but it cannot be overlooked that he fails as a civilised human being.

Taking the characters of Manu and Shyam created by two women writers of contemporary India, one can see how modernity has seeped through the Indian male only to a very shallow level, because deep down they still hold on to traditional beliefs of the superiority of men and subjugation of women. The characters, Manu and Shyam, perpetrate acts of sexual violence against their wives, even though for different reasons, to achieve a similar end—assertion of power. Both these characters have scant regard for their wives' feelings and do not for a moment think of the consequences of their actions, which leads to the failure of their marriages. Shyam's marriage would have failed anyway but the end of Manu's marriage could be attributed to his sexual assault on his wife.

If the two characters, Manu and Shayam, can be considered representatives of the modern Indian male, one can definitely draw certain conclusions. The fact that the modern Indian male has not completely shed his traditional garb is obvious. It is also apparent that the construction of the Indian male identity rests largely on the wealth he acquires and the status he attains on the basis of it. His relationship to women is far from being equal even though in public spheres one can see men talk of gender equality. The Indian male is threatened by the great strides that women have taken in the recent time. At the same time it would be unfair to generalise marital rape as a means to an end adopted by men to maintain dominance, but to think that it never happens would be too naïve. Leach suggests that all men are not rapists but "dominant modes of masculinity are integral to the maintenance of sexist cultures which benefit most men in some way. The logic of sexism is ultimately one of objectification and dehumanisation. If rape culture is an exaggeration of sexist culture, then it is a slight one."

Deshpande and Nair have brought to the fore the issue of marital rape, which is often not discussed in public and which does not necessarily amount to violence under the law because it is the husband who is the perpetrator. Women have been living in pain and silence for ages as victims of male dominance and sexual violence. The idea that rape can be used as a tool to control women reaffirms the fact that male sexuality has a great influence on the creation of masculine identity. As discussed earlier male sexuality is regarded as a symbol of power and strength whereas female sexuality is considered passive and something to be ashamed of. These two novels bring into focus the issue of domestic sexual violence making them, in the process, important documents for the understanding of gender relations in modern India.

In today's world, which is increasingly intolerant, violent and war torn, women are victims of gross sexual violence. In many war torn African countries one hears constantly of gang rapes of women and children by militiamen, traumatising and scarring them forever. In rural India and neighbouring Pakistan, women are gang raped as punishment for the wrongs committed by the men in their families. Even in urban centres, women are sexually harassed in public places, work places and educational institutions. Passage of time has done little to change the way men perceive women—as sexual objects that can be controlled and dominated.

However, it is also important to acknowledge the attitudinal changes that are beginning to happen among educated urban Indian men who have learnt to respect women and treat them as individuals with their own minds. It is certainly a positive trend that promises to spread widely. Everyone is a victim of some form of social conditioning or the other but it is important for people in a civilised society to reject practices and beliefs that would oppress other human beings. A society must work towards a balanced gender equation in which both men and women are able to find their own rightful place. It would be apt to conclude in the words of Shashi Deshpande: "A world without frightened, dependent, trapped, frustrated women is a better world for all of us to live in" ("Why I am a Feminist" 85).

Works Cited

Arora, Anjali. "The Middle-class Indian Woman: Social Rules, Societal Status." *The Other Revolution: NGO and Feminist Perspectives from South Asia.* Ed. Renuka Sharma and Purushottama Bilimori. Naari Ser. on Women Studies No. 3. New Delhi: Sri Satguru Publication, 1999. 108-29.

Bumiller, Elisabeth. *May You Be the Mother of a Hundred Sons: A Journey Among the Women of India.* New Delhi: Penguin, 1991.

de Beauvoir, Simone. *The Second Sex.* 1953. Trans. and ed. H.M. Parshley. Middlesex: Penguin, 1972.

Deshpande, Shashi. *The Dark Holds No Terrors*. 1980. New Delhi: Penguin, 1990.

____. "Telling Our Own Stories." *Writing from the Margin and Other Essays*. New Delhi: Penguin-Viking, 2003. 86-100.

____. "Why am I a Feminist?" *Writing from the Margin and Other Essays*. New Delhi: Penguin-Viking, 2003. 82-85.

Kinsley, David. *Hindu Goddess: Vision of the Divine Feminine in the Hindu Religious Tradition*. 1986. Berkeley, LA: U of California P, 1988.

Leach, Mike. "The Politics of Masculinity: An Overview of Contemporary Theory." *Social Alternatives* 12.4 (Jan. 1994): 36-37. *xyonline*. 2 April 2008. <www.xyonline.net/ politicsofmasculinities/shtml>.

Millet, Kate. *Sexual Politics*. New York: Doubleday, 1970.

Mohanty, Chandra Talpade. "Under Western Eyes: Feminist Scholarship and Colonial Discourses." *Contemporary Postcolonial Theory: A Reader*. Ed. Padmini Mongia. New Delhi: OUP, 1997. 172-97.

Nair, Anita. *Mistress*. New Delhi: Penguin, 2005.

Niranjana, Seemanthini. "Discerning Women: Variation as the Theme of Gender—A Review." *The Other Revolution: NGO and Feminist Perspectives from South Asia*. Ed. Renuka Sharma and Purushottama Bilimori. Naari Ser. on Women Studies No. 3. New Delhi: Sri Satguru Publication, 1999. 18-41.

Swain, S.P. "Shashi Deshpande's *The Dark Holds No Terrors*: Saru's Feminine Sensibility." *Indian Women Novelists*. Set III. Vol. 4. New Delhi: Prestige, 1995.

3

Beyond the Phallic Axis in Vikram Chandra's *Sacred Games*

Adalinda Gasparini

Abstract

Postcolonial literature is more than a bridge between the settler and settled cultures. It is a new kind of space that does not establish boundaries: it dissolves them. More a way than a place, it looks familiar to a psychoanalyst eye. Vikram Chandra writes about illusions whose fading does not unveil a new ideology nor an impotent cynicism. In his *Sacred Games* we notice the irreversible weakening of the phallic identity. Gaitonde, a major gangster, and Jojo, a procuress, defend their identity playing the favourite strife between men and women, the same represented by Carmen and Don Josè in the famous lyric opera by Bizet.

1. 'Don't you understand?'

Ganesh Gaitonde, the wealthy head of one of Mumbai's most powerful criminal gangs, has secretly collaborated with the Indian secret services, and has had as his spiritual guide an internationally famous guru. He has discovered that his Guru-ji has organized, with his help, an atomic attack that will destroy the city, in order to attribute responsibility to an Islamic terrorist organization that has been created for this purpose. The aim of his spiritual guide, whom he had regarded as the caring father that he had never known, is to bring about a pure India, cleaner and more orderly even than Singapore. Ganesh Gaitonde has unsuccessfully tried to stop the attack, and is now waiting in the atomic bunker at Kailashpada, where he will survive the city's destruction.

He is very lonely, however, and his identity has nothing left to support it: only Jojo Mascarenas, to whom he is linked by the understanding experienced in so many telephone conversations over the years, is able to stop his being slipping endlessly away.

> We were so small, and this world was so vast. Without her voice in my ear, I was smaller still.
>
> I had to bring her in. (Chandra, *Sacred Games* 805)

Jojo Mascarenas had once tried to become an actress, and then became a success procuring models and aspiring actresses for rich and powerful men. The most important of these is a former Miss India who has become a famous actress, Zoya Mirza. Jojo has proposed that she become Ganesh Gaitonde's lover, and has thus found her the financier for her cinema career and for the plastic surgery that has made her perfect. The gangster first tries to convince his friend, whom he has never met in person, to join him in the bunker. Meeting with no success, he brings her there by force. She tries to convince him to let her go, but Gaitonde is unbending:

> 'Don't you understand? I can't stay like this. I can't. I have to go out. You can't keep me in this jail.'
>
> 'Don't you understand? Up there you'll die.'
>
> 'So what? I would rather die than stay in this hole.' (Chandra, *Sacred Games* 813)

Gaitonde forces her to stay in the modern bunker, which is supplied with every luxury, as an expression of the force that allows her to save herself. For Jojo it is an unbearable prison. In this confrontation, their understanding, thanks to which each had been able to understand the other's mood just from hearing their voice on the telephone, vanishes. Gaitonde is unable to take Jojo's words seriously, and tries to impose himself, maintaining that what she is saying is nonsense: he, unlike her, knows what she needs.

> 'That is complete nonsense. You're crazy right now. You know that's not the truth. You don't want do die.' (Chandra, *Sacred Games* 813)

Why does Gaitonde not try to understand her, why does Jojo not take into account the fact that Gaitonde cannot remain in a situation that puts his back to the wall? '*Don't you understand*?' they ask each other as if in mutual incomprehension. Jojo Mascarenas should put her pride to one side to allow him to show his virility and should bear witness to the only truth that he can manifest: only I can save you, and if I hurt you it's for your own good. She could manage to understand that his unstoppable blind determination is the only form of love that he can give her. She could at least pretend to listen to him to save herself.

But Jojo is unwilling or unable to play the game between men and women that accepts ancient limits, which seems ridiculous to her. Her aim is not to be subjected, but to challenge him.

> 'Shall I tell you the truth, Gaitonde? You are a coward. You used to be something, you used to be a man, but now you are a trembling little madman hiding in a pit.' (Chandra, *Sacred Games* 813)

Jojo knows that his reaction will be violent, and is not surprised when he responds with a violent backhander and follows her, shouting words that could very well emerge from the mouth of a sexual abuser.

> 'Randi.' I followed her around the room as she staggered back. 'You want to see what kind of man I am? Let me show you. No, come, come. Here, you want some more? Who's trembling, han? Who's shaking?" (Chandra, *Sacred Games* 813)

Her mouth bleeding, Jojo laughs: he has not shown her anything, he cannot shock her, stop her, master her, silence her. The mirror that Perseus used to defeat the petrifying Medusa can also be wielded by a woman.

> 'You, you're not a man,' she said. She spat laughter at me, and stood her ground. 'You bought women so you think

> you're a great hero. None of them never liked you, you bastard. Without your cash, you wouldn't even have been able to come near them.' (Chandra, *Sacred Games* 813)

Gaitonde does not want to believe and cannot believe that she is telling the truth, and tries to hit her again, telling her that he wants to save her. Jojo agilely dodges the blow and counterattacks.

> 'Bas,' I warned her. 'Enough. Be quiet. Understand—I am trying to help you. I am trying to save your life.'
>
> 'They laughed at you, gaandu. They made jokes together, about what a pathetic, weak little rat you are. You think you are anything in front of a woman like Zoya? She told us that she never got one good night in bed out of you.' (Chandra, *Sacred Games* 813)

His masculine pride cut to the quick, Ganesh Gaitonde forgets that Jojo is as fragile as he is, and that like him she is afraid. Jojo becomes immense, supported by the mocking choir of all the women that she has procured for him. If he is unable to subject her, if his pride is humiliated, then it is the woman who has taken away his phallic power.

Gaitonde has always been afraid that Zoya Mirza did not love him, that she faked her pleasure with him. Visiting Universal Studios, when Zoya dreamed of working with Arnold Schwarzenegger and winning an Oscar, Gaitonde imagined that he gave her the pleasure that she was looking for and that she faked with him. When Jojo tells him what he has always suspected, she breaks the veil of doubt that protected him from this humiliating truth. Gaitonde is now helpless, like a child caught by his mother whilst doing something wrong.

In order to understand the fascinating and tragic *sacred game* of Ganesh Gaitonde and Jojo Mascarenas, we need to open a psychoanalytic map. The mother has the power to deceive her son into believing that he is her favourite, her only love, and to disillusion him harshly whenever she prefers another, older and more powerful: the father. Equilibrium is needed between illusion and disillusion, without which the debt that the child will incur to preserve his ability to grow up will be so great that his whole life will not be enough to pay it, to free himself from it. We may think of our growing up as a possibility that we obtain on the condition that we accept a debt: we have to believe what our parents say of us, whatever story they tell us. If we are unable to become part of the story that they have prepared for us, we can only close ourselves in a form of autism. It is better to take on the debt with the hope of paying it off with time, once we are grown-ups.

The male character here has a personal history that represents a debt that it is almost impossible to pay. Gaitonde despised his father's weakness, and his mother was unfaithful to his father. One day, his father killed his mother and fled, abandoning him, and his mother supported herself and her child with the help of her lovers. Her son ran away as soon as he was an adolescent, changed his name (as if he were a child of no-one), and went to live in Mumbai, where he became a major gangster. In the chapter that we are reading, *Ganesh Gaitonde Goes Home*, all the power that he has acquired funnels him towards the bunker, where he will meet his destined fate, that very fate that he had been trying to flee.

He wants to have with him the only woman who has ever understood him, a woman who refuses to yield and claims not to need anyone. If now he could save her, make her yield, possess her, he would pay off his debt, feel himself a true man, mitigating thereby his lack of confidence in his identity, which he has managed to keep hidden from everyone else, but not from himself. The maternal feminine power, against which no father has shown himself able to resist, is represented by Jojo and a chorus of high-class prostitutes. This is unfavourable ground for Gaitonde, but he cannot afford to lose this opportunity, and rebuts the claim.

> "That's a lie. Zoya liked me."
>
> She threw her head back and howled. 'Zoya liked me,' she crowed. 'Zoya liked me.' She bent over and put her hands on her knees. 'Zoya liked me.' Blood slipped and tripped on to the ground, but she was only amused. 'Zoya *liked* me.'

> 'She did.' The voice coming out of my throat was strange to me, small and forlorn. (Chandra, *Sacred Games* 813-14)

His voice now reveals that he is losing, but he can no longer stop himself. It is as if his mother were speaking to him like a child: "you're imagining things, you silly fool.... The child no longer has any excuse; he discovers that he has only imagined being his mother's favourite, for she has instead always made fun of him. Gaitonde debates this with himself and fools himself.

> 'The first night we were together, she told me that. She said I was amazing. She did. We did it all night. That's the truth.'
>
> 'Gaitonde, you idiot.' She was triumphant now. 'You fool. She made a chutiya out of you. It wasn't you, you simpleton. She gave you a glass of milk and badams. And in it she gave you a crushed-up Viagra, one full big tablet. She was going to give you two, but I was afraid we'd kill you. I told her, it's okay to want to get ahead, you want to go to the moon, I understand, but don't burst the rocket that's going to get you there. And it worked. It wasn't you, saala. It was the Viagra.'
>
> A blue haze of rage came across my eyes. Through it I saw her, standing straight up, laughing. She was not afraid of me. (Chandra, *Sacred Games* 814)

If Jojo is not afraid of him, Gaitonde is lost, because he has defended himself from his own fragility by frightening others, or dominating them with money and power. He cannot buy her, because she is not for sale; he cannot forgive her, as she has no use for his forgiveness; he cannot save her as she prefers death to salvation by him. Gaitonde is reduced to impotence, and his blue haze of rage is a sort of paranoid madness representing the last bastion of male pride and of the coherence of his identity. Gaitonde must react, as like every human being he values his identity more than his concrete survival. The perception of the integrity of his own being or the hope, however small, of obtaining that integrity allows existence as human subjects, even when burdened by heavy debts or when on the edge of madness or death. If reality were only made up of biological needs and objects suitable or unsuitable for satisfying them, then our world would not be what we experience every day and we would not need to question the suffering and joy we feel, impossible to explain with common sense.

Yet not even Jojo, who appears to be so lucid and self-controlled, is following a sensible plan. If her aim were to conquer him, then she would stop now that he is beaten; instead, she continues to challenge him, tauntingly echoing his words as if they were children making fun of each other. Does she want to conquer or be conquered?

> '*Zoya* liked me,' she said. 'Gaitonde, you fool, you think she was some virgin you impressed with your huge manliness. You chutiya. She had had a dozen men before you, and many afterwards, and you were the most pathetic. You were, you were smallest."
>
> 'Liar. She was a virgin. You told me. She told me.'
>
> 'A virgin?'
>
> 'Yes.'
>
> 'You idiot. How do you think she survived in this city before she came to you? You bhenchod men always pay more for virgins, so she became a virgin for you.'
>
> 'No. I saw the blood.'
>
> She laughed so hard she had to hold on to the side of a table. 'Gaitonde, of all the pompous, gaandu men in the world, you are the blindest. Arre, inside ten miles of here there are twenty doctors who will make any woman a virgin again. The operation takes half an hour, it costs twenty-five, thirty thousand rupees. And in three weeks the renewed virgin can be ready to spread her legs on a white sheet, so some tiny little Gaitonde can see all the blood and think he's big.'
>
> I shot her. (Chandra, *Sacred Games* 814)

The shot closes the bodily struggle that destroys men and women when no one is able to go beyond the mirror-like answerless question: "Don't you understand? Don't you understand *me*?"

Jojo's blood gushes out from a hole at heart level, making the pain of the deceitful blood from the first night with Zoya Mirza disappear.

Gaitonde no longer has any doubt that he is a man; he can rest now, and lies down alongside her. When he wakes up, he discovers that he has slept for more than one day and one night, and sees next to him Jojo's foot as realization returns to him of the fact that he has killed her.

> But what I noticed all new, all keen and fresh and as if for the first time, was how complicated a thing a woman's foot is. It has little pads, and arches, and a convoluted network of muscles and nerves, it has bones, so many bones. It flexes and moves and walks and endures. Its skin takes on the colour of the year it passes through, until the cracks in it form a net as complicated as the life itself.
>
> I held Jojo's foot. I cupped its ankle and held its cold inertia. (Chandra, *Sacred Games* 815)

For the first time, lying next to the body of the only woman by whom he has felt himself understood, whom he has stopped next to him with the gun, Gaitonde welcomes life, which manifests itself in all its complexity in a foot, just as it does in a glance or a lotus vine. Where does this salvation come from to reach Ganesh Gaitonde, and where does it take him?[1]

2. The Favourite Strife

Ganesh Gaitonde Goes Home; in the bunker at Kailashpada he goes to meet his destiny, taking Jojo Mascarenas with him. Their fatal bodily struggle recalls *Carmen*, the story set to music by Georges Bizet (1875). The plot, with some modifications, comes from the short story of the same name by Prosper Mérimée (1845), and it has been retold and restaged so many times that we may consider it one of the great collective dreams of western culture.

The most important difference between the couple in Vikram Chandra's novel and that in Mérimée's story is that the former pair does not have a sexual relationship. As Gaitonde and Jojo meet for the first time in the bunker at Kailashpada, their tragedy is not caused by the erotic attraction of a *femme fatale*. Imputing the tragedy to the diabolic seductiveness of the gypsy Carmen allows an attenuation of the anxiety of the bodily struggle with a justification that appears biological, almost animal.

By not having Gaitonde and Jojo meet sexually, Chandra allows all the disturbing intensity of the extreme bodily struggle between man and woman to emerge for whoever is willing and able to understand.

At the end of the opera, Carmen is about to enter, along with her friends, into the bullring where the toreador Escamillo is to dedicate the corrida to her when Don José, who has deserted and become an outlaw for her sake, comes on stage. Like Ganesh Gaitonde, he has found no space in a consensual male order and now needs a woman to notice his desperation. This desperate and rejected lover is a terrible danger for Carmen, and her friends recommend her to avoid him.

> Frasquita: *Prends garde*!
>
> Carmen: *Je ne suis pas femme à trembler devant lui....*
> *Je l'attends et je vais lui parler.*
> [...]
>
> Mercédès: *Carmen, crois-moi, prends garde*!
>
> Carmen: *Je ne crains rien*!
>
> Frasquita: *Prends garde*!
>
> (*Carmen*, Acte Quatrieme, Scène I)[2]

Carmen stops in front of Don José: *she* does not run away. He implores her, saying that he is not there to threaten her but rather to forgive her and begin a new life together. But Carmen does not want this:

> Carmen: *Tu demandes l'impossible!*
> *Carmen jamais n'ai menti!*
> *Son âme reste inflexible;*
> *entre elle et toi...c'est fini*

Jamais je n'ai menti!
Entre nous c'est fini!

Don José: *Carmen, il est temps encore,*
oui, il est temps encore...
O ma Carmen, laisse-moi
te sauver, toi que j'adore,
ah! laisse-moi te sauver
et me sauver avec toi!
(*Carmen*, Acte Quatrieme, Scène I)[3]

Don José wants to save her notwithstanding the fact that she does not want to be saved.

Carmen: *En vain tu dis: je t'adore!*
Tu n'obtiendras rien, non, rien de moi,
ah! c'est en vain...
Tu n'obtiendras rien, rien de moi!
(*Carmen*, Acte Quatrieme, Scène II)[4]

In order for blood not to flow, woman must here lapse into silence. His word must prevail—is it not in a Man that the Word becomes flesh? Is it not *he* that was created in God's own image and likeness, according to the Old Testament? This truth is affirmed in all possible registers. An Italian proverb in the Venetan dialect that is still quoted today peremptorily summarizes how a woman should be, and I hypothesize that the same thing is said, with minimal variation, in all the world's languages:

Che la piasa
che la tasa
che la staga in casa.[5]

Nobody has ever pretended that women are never to speak. It is enough to think of the great Scheherazade, whose words are enough to make up *The Thousand and One Nights*; the priestess Diotima, who reveals the nature of Eros in Plato's *Symposium*; or the sibyls, who were consulted whenever knowledge other than that commonly accessible was needed. But in the patriarchal order women must close their mouths so that the male word can prevail. Female silence too, if it does not imply submission, is intolerable for men. Scheherazade tells stories every night, but after having asked the sultan's permission, and with dawn she lapses into silence: the sultan can thus go to exercise his power feeling himself fully able to encompass her.[6]

Unlike Socrates' interlocutors, Diotima knows the truth about the nature of Eros, but it is Socrates who reports her words, including her in his own discourse. The sibyls' words were precious, but through their mouths the god Apollo was speaking. The female oracles of antiquity lived apart from the cities, in places that were carefully marked out or hard to reach.

If a woman spoke with her own voice, without accepting male domination, she could only be a character in a tragedy, even if what she spoke was the truth. The soothsayer Cassandra, who had not respected the will of Apollo, lived in the city of Troy foretelling the future, but was condemned never to be believed. Antigone, who had honoured her dead brother's remains against the decree of the king of Thebes, was put to death even though her liberated words had defended one of humanity's oldest and most universal forms.

The male subject in the patriarchal order only exists insofar as his word, his body and his law limit and encompass women, condemning them to death if they refuse to allow themselves to be limited. To defend this patriarchal axis, the Inquisition of Holy Mother Church has sent eight million women to be burnt at the stake as witches in the five centuries of its history.

What huge murderous power is attributed to a woman's independent words and desires, if to manifest them corresponds to tragedy, if her autonomy brings about death for herself and others?

This myth of terrifying female power is nourished by other myths, and is fully present in the unconscious of both men and women, impermeable to modern scientific conventions, equal rights and clear critical thinking. The myth of the wild woman, demonic and damned, wraps around the most external zone of male domination; it is the earth's terrifying edge that forms the base of the *axis mundi*, the pivot of patriarchal culture. Around this upwards-pointing phallic centre is the cultivated and generous earth, wanting only to support it and guarantee that it lasts. It is made up of those women that are lovely and are silent when necessary, welcoming wives and mothers, celebrated by patriarchal culture as much as the heroic male, who liberates the earth from monsters with wars, scientific discoveries and the wielding of power.

In this representation, reminiscent of the Ptolemaic cosmos, the male logos rises in the centre supported by the earth, and all of the demons and phantoms that refuse to be colonized or annihilated are pushed to the margins like the sea monsters on the edges of old sea charts. The demonic female power is the representation of the remainder that culture neither knows how to or is able to dominate, a life force that is unseeing because it is unseen, or removed. What is called demon is a power that does not co-operate with human order, and this naming has the function of pushing it into the most distant space possible.[7] Beyond the borders of the world, or in the heart of its origin, in the female womb: from the body and soul of the woman who does not submit to men lies a danger that overturns everything. This representation is a terrific structure in male and female psychic realities and can be recognized in every human culture.

The hypothesis of a matriarchal society preceding patriarchal society may be considered a myth presenting phallocentric organization as more evolved. In a patriarchy, women must be lovely, be silent and stay *at home*, so that her children and husband may leave her there and find her there as they please. An order assigning to men the right/duty to dominance dates back, perhaps, to the first human records that we have. In Palaeolithic art women are often represented plastically, with monstrously developed breasts, buttocks and vulva, far more than in today's sex symbols. Their extremities are missing and their limbs are only lightly sketched (*Palaeolithic Venuses*), so as to indicate that they have nothing to do with autonomous movement. Male figures, however, are often drawn in movement on cave walls, with stick-figure bodies, well-developed limbs and weapons in their hands. An erect penis often crowns this representation of the male.

The persistence of the myth of masculine superiority, the conviction that the subject of culture is male—the words Man and mankind use 'man' to include both men and women—is still expressed today even in the very moment in which we deceive ourselves that we are looking at it critically. When we believe that the logocentric and phallocentric patriarchy is something desired by men *against* women, all we are doing, men and women both, is attributing to the male part of humanity the responsibility for how culture and the social order *are*: this is an only apparently different way of repeating the supremacy of the male. To talk of a male tendency to prevarication, dominance, arrogance and war and a female tendency to conflict resolution, meekness and peace means changing the terms of the game whilst leaving it intact. The myth is so powerful that we can turn it upside down, not distance ourselves from it, and thus it happens that in Europe we have passed in the space of a century from the certainty that women cannot vote to the affirmation that more women in parliament and government means a guarantee of peace.

What guarantees the permanence of patriarchal culture, the only one of which we have any historical record, is the existence of a phallic *axis mundi*; it would therefore be preferable to grant possession and care of it to women: it is not rare to hear it affirmed that women are considered inferior in order to limit their *real* superiority. In order not to ask questions about the imaginary make-up of the phallic *axis mundi*, we think with laughable naïveté that patriarchal culture has been imposed by one sex on the other.

In my psychoanalytical experience, I have long observed how many women, of every age and socio-cultural condition, demonstrate an unconscious tendency to back up what men say, even when they are fighting him as much as possible on the conscious level.

The myth of a unique centre suggests a reading of the story of Carmen as the violent suppression of female liberty by the male. From this point of view, Jojo Mascarenas is a free woman and Ganesh Gaitonde the representative of a purely male violence. Can we forget that Jojo, who knows Gaitonde well, provokes him to the point of killing her? Can we forget that Carmen could ignore Don José and go to see Escamillo kill the bull for her? When the fanfare and the cries of the crowd go up for his victory over the bull, she is already dead, having preferred to fight Don José. Carmen and Jojo do not want to be limited or stopped by men who want to save them, protect them, love them. Or do they want to be stopped? Don José and Ganesh Gaitonde know the indomitable natures of Carmen and Jojo: why is it them that they want?

Don José lives the same tragedy as Ganesh Gaitonde; like him he has lost every certain reference to a cultural system and has left his family and become an outlaw. But why, like Gaitonde, does he think that only this woman can provide a base for his heart and that only a masterless woman who knows how to tell the truth is able to accept his uncertain soul like a hospitable house? This woman is not maternal, does not want to accept him or give him the time to regenerate himself in her womb. Or does she desperately want to be a life-favouring womb to him but is unable to succeed?

Words reach their maximum violence, and then verbal language gives way and the body enters into action.

Carmen (voulant passer): *Laisse-moi...laisse-moi...*
José: *Sur mon âme,*
Tu ne passeras pas,
Carmen, c'est moi que tu suivras!
Carmen: *Laisse-moi, Don José, je ne te suivrai pas.*
[...]
José: *Non, par le sang, tu n'iras pas!*
Carmen, *c'est moi que tu suivras!*
Carmen: *Non, non! jamais!*
José (avec violence): *Je suis las de te menacer!*
Carmen (*avec colère*): *Eh bien! frappe-moi donc, ou laisse-moi passer.*

(Carmen, cit., Ib.)[8]

This male violence is at one and the same time an expression of impotence and a desperate barrier against that very impotence, felt as it is to be the annihilation of the male subject. If Carmen and Jojo were to understand the weakness of the men confronting them, why should they fight them? Why do they continue to challenge them when they see that they are defeated? Do they want to destroy them or do they want their phallic maleness to demonstrate itself mythically capable and able to contain female destructiveness?

Carmen, like Jojo Mascarenas, does not seem able to bear Don José's weakness, and cruelly lets him know this, challenging his maleness, no matter how great is the cost.

> José (éperdu): *Pour la dernière fois, démon, veux-tu me suivre?*
>
> Carmen: *Non! non!*
> (à demi voix, avec rage) *Cette bague, autrefois, tu me l'avais donnée...*
> *Tiens!*
> (elle la jette à la volée)
>
> José (le poignard à la main, s'avançant sur Carmen): *Eh bien! damnée!*
>
> Carmen recule...José la poursuit...Pendant ce temps fanfares et chœur dans le cirque.
>
> Chœur: *Toréador, en garde!*
> *Et songe bien, oui, songe en combatant*
> *qu'un oeil noir te regarde*
> *et que l'amour t'attend,*
>
> José a frappé Carmen... Elle tombe morte... Le vélum s'ouvre. La foule sort du cirque.
>
> José (se levant): *Vous pouvez m'arréter... c'est moi qui l'ai tuée!*
> *Ah! Carmen! ma Carmen adorée!* (Ib.)[9]

The curtain falls; the fatal bodily struggle has once again been won? She is dead, and Don José gives himself up to the guardians of the law, ready to be executed. He has nothing more to say; there is nothing more to hear.

But in Mérimée's story, Don José has time left to him between Carmen's death and his own, and it is the time in which the story may be told. Just before being garroted, Don José says something to his listener about truth and falsehood that does not cease from making us ask ourselves questions, if we are able to control our fear:

> *Elle mentait, monsieur, elle a toujours menti. Je ne sais pas si dans sa vie cette fille-là à jamais dit un mot de vérité; mais quand elle parlait, je la croyais: c'était plus fort que moi. (Mérimée, Carmen* 38)[10]

3. The Phallic Axis Grows Dim

There are blind antihistorical truths that justify violence. In *Sacred Games*, the truth of fundamentalism is sustained by Guru-ji, who has a huge faithful following all over the world. In order to bring about a pure and perfect India, he does not hesitate to destroy all of Mumbai with an atomic bomb.

The mingling of politicians, or guardians of order, with illegality is elevated to the level of a system. In this latest novel, Chandra relates that though honesty is something that may exist, it has to be spoken of under one's breath. Before the nineteen-sixties, it was improper in Italy to discuss sex; people now hesitate before they speak about doing something because of their ideals. Taking pleasure in doing something that brings with it neither money nor exposure is becoming an intimate act, as Katekar, who has worked with Sartaj Singh for seven years, knows well. He is unable to find a response to a relative of his who asks him why he does not leave his badly-paid job, and reflects to himself:

> Yes, really, *Sadrakshanaya Khalanighranaya*. Katekar knew he could never confess this urge to anyone, much less Vishnu, because fancy talk of protecting the good and destroying evil and seva and service would elicit only laughter. Even among colleagues, this was never spoken about. But it was there, however buried it may be under grimy layers of cynicism. Katekar had seen it occasionally in Sartaj Singh, this senseless, embarrassing idealism. Of course neither of them would ever so much as hint at the other's romanticism, but perhaps this was why their partnership was so enduring. Only once, when they had rescued a trembling ten-year old girl from a shed in Vikhroli, from her kidnappers, Sartaj Singh had scratched at his beard and muttered, 'Today we did good work.' That had been enough. (Chandra, *Sacred Games* 220)

Words like those of the Sanskrit motto of the Mumbai police, *Protect Truth, Destroy Evil*, are part of the grand ideals that in the twentieth century have been used to cover the worst of crimes. It is right to be distrustful of them, but it is impossible to orient oneself in life's labyrinth without giving life a meaning, which functions like Ariadne's clew, and allows us, at least sometimes, to think that we have done good work.

Just as in all of our world, in *Sacred Games* there are rich people who think only of making themselves yet richer, to the point that it becomes difficult to distinguish the morals of the gangster from those of the guardians of order. We hear of people of every faith who suffer persecution and atrocities, but no one thinks to of looking for justice for them. There are young people who, in order to escape from poverty or simply from being invisible, are willing to sell themselves to pimps; there is, above all, the immense city, with its posh areas and its slums, and its beautiful sunsets that are perhaps caused by air pollution.

There are many truths co-existing inside the characters and moving through the city streets like the tendrils of a vine that even winds around itself in the hope of finding something to support it so that it can climb and flower.

In *Sacred Games* the flower is the salvation of Mumbai from atomic destruction, a metaphor for the radical risk that we perceive is faced by this world of ours—so unfair, so full of contradictions, and so rich.

Ganesh Gaitonde, after having held Jojo's motionless foot in his hand, reflects:

> I had slept for more than twenty-four hours.
>
> Get on with it. But get on with what? More money-making, more woman, more killing. I already lived that, I had no appetite for more. So, get on with what? Lying on the ground, next to Jojo, I asked myself that. I felt whole again, delivered from fuzziness and distraction and exhaustion by this long rest on this bloodstained ground. (Chandra, *Sacred Games* 815)

What is this integrity that Gaitonde feels for the first time? How is it possible that a gangster is aware of it after he has killed the friend that he wanted to save alongside himself?

When a part of the meaning of life manifests itself, it has a subdued and invincible force. No religious practice, no ideology, no scientific research, possesses it. It has the indomitable force of a budding leaf, and its nature is the same as that of the *voice of the intellect* that Freud says is *soft* but that insists *until it has gained a hearing*.

> The voice of the intellect is a soft one, but it does not rest until it has gained a hearing. Ultimately, after endlessly repeated rebuffs, it succeeds. This is one of the few points in which it may be optimistic about the future of mankind, but in itself it signifies not a little. (Freud, *The Future of an Illusion* 53)

Something pushes through and only emerges when we renounce trying to dominate life and recognize that all of the knowledge of which we are rightly proud is impotent in the face of pain and love, of a sense of nothingness and of a communion with the whole world. The voice of reason is the radical opening to reality, the discovery of the inevitable limits of our presence: our short time that may be enough.[11] The paradox is that seeking to live ignoring our limits, we only find life by recognizing them.

Now that for the first time he is in control of himself, Ganesh Gaitonde wants to give himself up, and chooses a guardian of the law, like Don José after killing Carmen in Bizet's opera. The only person who comes to mind is the Sikh inspector Sartaj Singh, who was on duty when, years before, he had gone to a secret meeting with Guru-ji.

Sartaj Singh does not know why the gangster has chosen him. The day before he had been called to a man barricaded in his bed room whose wife wanted to kill him and who kept stabbing a kitchen knife into the door panels. During an argument the husband had thrown his wife's white Pomeranian out of the window of their fifth-floor flat. Thinking of the poor little body on the pavement, Sartaj Singh says:

> Love is a murdering gaandu. Poor Fluffy. (Chandra, *Sacred Games* 5)

When Gaitonde calls him the next day to the Kailashpada bunker, Sartaj Singh does not know why. He does not know that he once looked at the terrible head of the Mumbai underworld with humanity; he does not even know that he has met him, as he was disguised. Gaitonde chooses him because he is a guardian of order whose humanity is not cancelled out by his uniform: he is the only person to whom he can give up himself and his story.

Sartaj Singh arrives in the Kailashpada bunker and uselessly tries to convince the gangster to leave it. He remains there, listening to Gaitonde as he tells the story of his first exploits in Mumbai, and at a certain point becomes interested in the story, but when the bulldozer that he has requested manages to make a hole in the bunker's walls he stops listening.

> You're coming in. I'm still talking, but you aren't listening to me any more. Your eyes are afire. You want me, you and your riflemen. But listen to me. There is a whirlwind of memories in my head, a scatter of tattered faces and bodies. I know how they skirl through each other, their connections and their disjunctions, I can trace their velocities. Listen to me. If you want Ganesh Gaitonde, then you have to let me talk. Otherwise Ganesh Gaitonde will escape you, as he escaped every time, as he escaped every last assassin. Ganesh Gaitonde escaped even me, almost. Now, at this last hour, I have Ganesh Gaitonde, I know what he was, what he became. Listen to me, you must listen to me. But you are now in the bunker. (Chandra, *Sacred Games* 817)

What is the purpose of telling the story of a life? Even though Sartaj is no longer listening to him, as he has his work to do, the discovery of the bunker and the two people in it is the start of the foiling of Guru-ji's atomic attack, involving policemen, gangsters and secret agents, people from every religion and faith, ne'er-do-wells and idealists, men and women.... Gaitonde gives himself up to Sartaj, who completes the task of stopping an attack that is so terrifying as to seem only possible in a film. The head of the Mumbai underworld had tried to defeat the fundamentalist Guru-ji, and his defeat is the starting point for the Sikh sardar's success. Gaitonde's bequest is an act of faith without any guarantee, just like any true gift from one person to another. Sartaj's impatience does not stop the gift reaching its destination.

> Under each step of yours, I can see dozens of my years pass. I can see it all together now, from the very beginning to the first house I built for myself, my first home in Gopalmath. (Chandra, *Sacred Games* 817)

In the time required to take a step, a dozen years pass for Gaitonde. Within the pages of a book that only takes up a little less than ten cubic centimetres for all that, like Chandra's novels, it is *big*; a mass of interweaving stories is found, an intricate labyrinth of lives, pain, lost hopes, deaths, heavens, sewers, luxurious rooms.... Vikram Chandra's ability to keep the thread of all these stories together bears ample testimony to his extraordinary power as a narrator. Rather than an omniscient narrator in the classic canonical tradition, Chandra seems to be a listener re-narrating stories without owning them up, but instead taking care of them like a gardener so that they grow and blossom.

Each *Inset* is so rich as to make one think of a rough sketch for a new novel, but although the pages multiply space, Sartaj Singh's investigation and the gangster's story claim the best part of the narrative. No one is listening to him, but Gaitonde goes on speaking:

> Here is the pistol. The barrel fits snugly into my mouth. I think of what Jojo would say: *Bastard, you're scared or what? You want me to do it for you?*
>
> No, Jojo. I'm not afraid.
>
> Sartaj, do you know why I do this? I do it for love. I do it because I know who I am.
>
> Bas, enough. (Chandra, *Sacred Games* 817)

The magical force of literature may still be experienced today: the expanses of time that comes pouring out in a river of words, one person alone narrating, aware of the fact he or she is collecting the words of many people, of all people. There is an interesting coincidence: Chandra's two long novels fall either side of two centuries, two millennia. As in Salman Rushdie's *Midnight's Children* (1981) and *The Moor's Last Sigh* (1995), in *Red Earth and Pouring Rain* (1995) the protagonist is dying and he recounts a whole novel in the first person.

In *Sacred Games* a narrator dies at the end of the second chapter: what does this mean? The chapters that Ganesh Gaitonde narrates in the first person alternate with the events involving the Sikh inspector, reaching thereby almost the end of the novel, and the topological equivalence between Sartaj's footsteps and the dozens of years of life, or chapters, is only announced before the salvation chapter. The person to whom Ganesh Gaitonde's story is addressed both is and is not inside the novel: it is us, the readers, as grasping this topological time Vikram Chandra has been able to listen to it and recount it to us.

In *Sacred Games*, there are large-scale representations of the dramas afflicting our world, the contradictions of history, but the flower blossoms thanks to Chandra's ability to go down into the tiny but infinite drama of the subject: here the world dies, resprouts and is reborn.

There exists a linear, irreversible time and a regular, measurable, space. It is possible to build watches that are ever more precise and to measure things unthinkable a century ago. Knowledge extending beyond the limits of our perception disturbs us, especially when applied to our minds. This is the theme of the Inset *The Great Game*, in which K.D. Yadav, director of the Indian secret service, is dying from a disease that is destroying his mind.

We may consider K.D. Yadav a model of maleness due to his intelligence, ability to command, compassion and love for his nation. His faith is fading, not because he is dying, but because he can no longer distinguish present reality from the long-ago memories.

> K.D. Yadav now has memory, but not sequence. He has elements, but not the distance between them. To him the past is no longer separated from the present by a distinct and comfortable boundary, everything is equally present, all things are connected and are here. Why? What's happened to me? K.D. can't remember. But he can remember. (Chandra, *Sacred Games* 298)

How are two opposing affirmations possible? Can we say that one is true and the other false?

> ...He is in a hospital bed in Delhi, losing his mind. He considers the phrase: to lose your mind. What would be left, if you misplaced your mind? If there is no mind, is there still a self? He remembers the parable, that to know the I there must be another I, an eye that watches the birds of the self feasting on the nectar of the world. But will there still be a watcher if you take these mind-structures away, these façades of language, these foundations of logic, these narratives of cause and effect? What will be left when it all comes crashing down? Bliss, or numbness? A presence, or an absence? 'The spider weaves the curtains in the palace of the Caesars; the owl calls the watches in the towers of Afrasiab.' (Chandra, *Sacred Games* 305-06)

Control eludes K.D. Yadav, and what he understands finds an explanation in parable, whilst his memories crowd uncontrollably.

Where do stories dwell, if they continue when the mind has lost control over reality and self-expression? Stories have one root in dreams, one in delirium; they have roots everywhere in daily reality, allowing our character to emerge with all its otherwise unnameable twists, and can at once hide and unmask our souls. In what part of the mind do stories dwell?

With every one of Sartaj's steps in the Kailashpada bunker, Ganesh Gaitonde remembers a dozen years. Memory is like a book: it is enough to open it and leaf through in order to visit countries and cities, see once again those we love and have lost, feel once more pain and defeat. Memory is immense; it expands and contracts infinitely, but if our brain is switched off then everything disappears.

Writing increases the subject time; it carries its story across generations and allows it to cross borders undreamt of in life. The communication made possible today by the Internet, the immense quantity of information that we can store in a small PC: these things are miraculous, but they are a realization of the same human desire that led to the invention of writing. Our mind accepts and reproduces the immense game of life, and literature is the living mirror of its breath.

Even if Sartaj Singh does not have time to hear Gaitonde's story, it is out of his determination to deliver his story and himself that the investigation is born that will lead to the Sikh inspector's saving Mumbai from the atomic explosion and finding love once again when he meets Mary Mascarenas, Jojo's sister.

4. Another Day

With psychoanalysis, Freud started a radical revolution regarding the question of what the mind is, not only the subjects' psychological life, but also their culture. Contemporary neurology proposes models far more similar to those of psychoanalysis than to those proposed by medicine in Freud's day.

The borders between normality and madness show themselves to be similar to those separating nations or social classes. They exist, but they change with time; no longer representing a certainty, they fade like the *distinct and comfortable boundary* between past and present in K.D. Yadav's mind.

If borders break, we can experience the joy of broadening our horizons, but we must also face the uncertainty of our identity, which loses its traditional signposts and milestones. In his novels Vikram Chandra seems to have contemplated every character, great and small, before telling their story and showing us their faith, simple or complex as it may be: no one is condemned; no one is absolved. There are characters that survive, like Sartaj Singh and Mary Mascarenas; there are others that die, like Ganesh Gaitonde and Jojo, whom we have compared with Don José and Carmen.

We have mentioned Prosper Mérimée's story, in which Don José says that Carmen had always lied, yet he had always believed her: "I believed her: it was stronger than me" (Cit.).

In patriarchy, the domination of women is supported by the attribution to the male sex of a greater reasoning power. Man is born first, as in the Old Testament, and woman is formed from a part of him. It may be remembered that in pre-modern western medicine the sex of the child depended on the temperature of the mother's womb at the moment of conception: if it was not hot enough, then the foetus was able to grow, but the genitalia were unable to emerge and remained inside the body. The child born was thus female, *minus habens* with respect to the male. It may also be remembered that ovulation was discovered at the beginning of the twentieth century: before that, it was thought that sperm contained the *homunculus* and that the woman was to the child as earth is to the seed. A couple's infertility could thus always be attributed to the woman's sterility.

We have to understand how science is based upon cultural myths and how no human thought is possible except within a cultural myth. The primacy of affect with respect to thought processes is ever more evident, even for those who are unaware that Freud provides its first and most decisive theorization.

This understanding implies a suspension of judgement about what is true and false and what is real and what is imaginary. But this does not mean being unaware of the difference between good and evil, because doubting which is the right direction to take in life's labyrinth is not a form of ethical relativism, as if accepting the radical questioning of our epoch were less courageous than choosing sides under the flag.

The phallic *axis mundi*, the pivot of patriarchal culture and support of the dominant male, has been examined over the last century just as much as subquantic physics, and its nature, perceived at first as solid, has been revealed instead as resembling a nebula. No longer does making use of the prospectives opened up in all the sciences imply regressing, as has happened, to forms of fundamentalism that terrify us with their irrational and antihistorical violence.

To speak of maleness today means taking into account the weakening of the male subject, who has the right and the duty to limit the female word. It means understanding that the centrality of the single logos, of the *phallic axis*, is a cultural need that cannot be refused, and that keeping its absolute singularity means reaffirming the ancient *maîtrise* over what is different, considering it nonetheless *minus habens*.

For Guru-ji, all Muslims should be wiped out from India; for Islamic fundamentalists, the influence of the West should be eliminated from the Arab world; America and Europe try to impose their democracy with the force of arms. *Nihil novi sub sole*, given that history tells us of alternating empires: even though they may last for a millennium and appear eternal, they die, just as languages do, just as every living organism does, allowing other languages and other forms of life to develop.

What is new, however, is that the vast majority of human beings are able to observe in real time the simultaneous actions of different peoples and cultures, all equally convinced of their right and duty to dominate. Are we obliged to hope that one of them prevails, so that the logocentric and phallocentric *axis mundi* may be restored?

Or may we consider the possibility, once reserved to mystics and the wise, of contemplating the great game of life? If our control turns out to be illusory, if we see in front of our eyes the ruin caused by affirming a unique superior principle, then why should we be obliged to choose sides and to affirm that our way out of life's labyrinth is straighter and better than all the others? And how can we believe that this gives us the right and duty to impose it with force?

Contemplating the foot of the friend whom he has killed, Ganesh Gaitonde wakes up from his dream of power, which has turned a nightmare. The truth that he utters before he shoots himself is the same as that which we can find in the *Mahabharata*. When Dharma asks his son for an example of victory, Yudhishtira replies to his divine father: *defeat*.

> 'Sartaj, you called me yaar. So I'll tell you something. Build it big or small, there is no house that is safe. To win is to

lose everything, and the game always wins.' (Chandra, *Sacred Games* 42)

The sacred game of life wins over every attempt to control it and to seize once and for all its meaning.

The fatal bodily struggle between Gaitonde and Jojo, like that between Don José and Carmen, is the sacred game through which, not stopping at the limits ascribed *by* a patriarchal culture to a man and woman *in* a patriarchal culture, they find their deaths. In pathological terms, it is the fatal meaning between the hysteric and the obsessive. But this diagnosis does not take into account the fascination exercised by the countless stories that show it in action, and the meeting is not necessarily tragic: we need only recall that it was hysterical patients who led Sigmund Freud, who was certainly obsessive, to discover psychoanalysis.

There is something so vital in these stories that death itself seems to stop and listen, fascinated by the rhythm of the story like the god Yama, who in *Red Earth and Pouring Rain* sits on his throne of darkness to listen to the stories told by the ape who had been a Brahmin. What Gaitonde and Jojo find, in each other, for each other, against each other, is their story, which we love to listen to, because in the moment in which we identify ourselves with them and transcend the limits of our everyday experience we are returned to a time common with theirs that remembers them in one of the soul's tiny yet immense spaces.

Patriarchy always expels what it cannot dominate or control, but the richness of chaos is no less important because of the life of its miraculously regular processes. When a woman is not considered an emanation of man and reclaims limitless freedom, she meets man who cannot resist the desire to love her in order to become her civilizing hero; the vital and terrifying chaos expelled by patriarchal culture returns from unknown lands, from islands where the only people who put to shore are those who have lost their course.

Gaitonde understands the meaning of being near to Jojo in the same moment in which he gives up trying to dominate reality: he opens himself to the great game that makes all of us meet our own destiny, in an encounter that becomes more tragic the more one deceives oneself that one is able to flee it. Even the attempt to flee one's destiny is still a destiny.

> Maybe Jojo was waiting for me on the other side. Maybe she would curse me and hit me, but finally she would understand. I would talk her and she would understand, as she always had. It was just a matter of talking, and time. And I would curse her for betraying me, for lying to me. But finally I would forgive her. We would forgive each other. (Chandra, *Sacred Games* 816)

A force greater than him, Don José said, made him believe Carmen, even though he knew that she was lying. Perhaps the same force leads Gaitonde to understand what connected him to Jojo to the point of killing her but only to die a little after her, as if their fatal bodily struggle were an encounter leading to a new understanding, the capacity to be together, forgiving each other.

Two sisters, Jojo and Mary Mascarenas, two protagonists meet the Sikh inspector and the famous gangster. A city threatened with total destruction, a difficult path to salvation, only one couple is saved at the end. These are the ingredients of many stories, many fairy tales, but the protagonist does not resemble a hero, even though he has defeated the enemy Guru-ji, and fought against the old king, the powerful corrupt deputy commissioner of police, Parulkar. At the end of the novel, before the blank page—

> Sartaj got off the bike. He put his shoes up on the pedal, one by one, and buffed them with spare handkerchief until they shone. Then he ran a finger around his waistline, along the belt. He patted his cheeks, and ran a forefinger and thumb over his moustache. He was sure it was magnificent. He was ready. He went in and began another day. (Chandra, *Sacred Games* 900)[12]

No hero ends his story polishing his shoes and adjusting his moustache.

A few pages earlier we read of another act that is in no way heroic, like that with which a mother or father cares for a child or a healthy person someone ill. Mary and Sartaj have made love and are now in bed, and she takes out a relaxing facial mask.

> Mary wanted to put mud on Sartaj's face. 'It's not mud,' she said indignantly, but that's exactly what it looked like, mud in a small pink pot.
>
> "Yes, it is,' Sartaj said. 'You went downstairs and got it from under one of the plants.' (Chandra, *Sacred Games* 897)

The narrative voice shares Sartaj's viewpoint, who has had Mary at his house for the first time, and the saviour of Mumbai.

> ...had spent the afternoon tidying up and cleaning away the dust that had accumulated during his Amritsar trip. (Chandra, *Sacred Games* 897)

Having explained how expensive this treatment is in the beauty salon where she works, Mary Mascarenas sets to work.

> 'Arre, don't move, baba.' She dipped two fingers in the pot, and painted the stuff over his forehead. It felt cool going on, cool and smooth. 'Pull your hair back.'
>
> She worked carefully and slowly, her tongue between her teeth.
>
> [...]
>
> When she had finished, and nodded with satisfaction, he took the pot from her and scooped up a dab and smoothed it along the line of her cheekbone. The stuff was red and softer than ordinary mud, very even and fine-grained, and it went on easily. (Chandra, *Sacred Games* 898)

This is a reciprocal act of caring, neither humiliating his virility nor making her feel less ready to accept him. Many pages earlier, the Sikh inspector had confessed to her his uncertainties about his job, telling her that much of it depended on luck.

> 'You sit around, and something drops into your lap. Then you pretend that you knew what you were doing all along.'
>
> [...]

> 'You have to be listening, but sometimes the trouble is that you don't know what you're listening for. Like there's a song, but you don't know what the tune is. So you just have to wander around, looking and listening. It can make you feel like a fool.'
>
> She was very direct now, her eyes locked on to his. 'You are not a fool,' she said.
>
> It was a declaration, and Sartaj didn't hesitate now. (Chandra, *Sacred Games* 592-93)

Although the hierarchy is dissolved along with the *phallic axis*, an exclusively male possession, this does not mean that men and women stop desiring one another. A myth, even if, like an empire, it lasts for millennia, may be a season of human life, just one stage in the sacred game.

Salman Rushdie's novels, mentioned earlier, and more innovatively and richly, those of Vikram Chandra, offer the possibility of sharing a viewpoint that enriches our understanding of the western patriarchal culture, which seems to pervade all the cultures of the planet in the very moment that it is showing signs of decline.

A different perception of I and the self, both difficult and a daily event for those who, like the current author, practise psychoanalysis, finds a profound and luxuriant expression in *Sacred Games*. An Indian author, with a culture of incomparable antiquity and richness behind him, after its long struggle with English culture, tells the story of our time and of the male subject in a new way. The choice of the English language allows translation, in the sense of the Latin *transducere*, *to traduce*, an awareness of time and space that allows the subject to renarrate itself beyond the fall of the male *phallic axis*.

A different way of experiencing time, of including in one's consciousness the perception of death rather than struggling against death: is this not the meaning we may grasp in the sadhus who create vast mandalas of coloured sand only to destroy them? Sartaj sees them by chance during his investigation, whilst they are creating a peace mandala.

> It was restful to watch the fall of the sand from the sadhu's hands, their sure and graceful movements. After a while, the general structure of the mandala emerged for Sartaj in dim white outline. Inside the final circle there were going to be several independent regions, ovals, each with its own scene or figures, human and animal and godly. Between these ovals, at the very centre of the entire wheel, there was a shape, Sartaj couldn't make out what it was. Outside these ovals there was the inner wall of the square, and outside the square there was another wheel, and more figures, and then a rim with its own patterns, all of it hypnotically complex and somehow pleasing. Sartaj was content to be lost in it.
>
> 'When they are finished, saab, they wipe it all up.'
>
> 'After all this work?' Sartaj said. 'Why?'
>
> Ganga shrugged. 'I suppose it's like our women's rangoli. If it's made of sand, it won't last long anyway.'
>
> Still, Sartaj thought, it was cruel to create this entire whirling world, and then destroy it abruptly. But the sadhu looked quite happy. One of them, an older man with greying hair, caught Sartaj's eye and smiled. (Chandra, *Sacred Games* 221-22)

It is cruel to make a figure that will be destroyed, as long as one is trying to gain mastery over life. But we may begin asking ourselves whether the mandala of coloured sand is not in fact truly useful for peace. Reading *Sacred Games*, we may think that it is worthwhile telling and retelling its meaning, like that of the rangoli and of the thousands of humble everyday tasks of men and women whose words do not reach us.[13]

Notes

1. I will tell you a story that will grow like a lotus vine, that will twist in on itself and expand ceaselessly, till all of you are a part of it, and the gods come to listen, till we are all talking in a musical hubbub that contains the past, every moment of the present, and all the future. (Vikram Chandra, *Red Earth and Pouring Rain* [London: Faber & Faber, 1995] 617). For the meaning of this image, which twines around the title on the cover of the edition of the novel quoted, see

also S. Albertazzi and A. Gasparini, *Il romanzo new-global. Storie di intolleranza, fiabe di comunità* [Pisa: ETS, 2003]; A. Gasparini, "Farewell, Father Œdipus. Freedom and Uncertainty in Vikram Chandra's *Sacred Games*," to be published in the anthology *Exploring Hidden Connections: Critical Insights into Vikram Chandra's Fiction*, ed. Sheobhushan Shukla, Anu Shukla, Christopher Rollason (New Delhi: Sarup & Sons).

2. Rasquita: *Carmen, take my advice, you'd better not stay here.*
   Carmen: *And why not, may I ask?*
   [...]
   Carmen: *I am not the sort to be frightened by him, I have stayed, since I have something to say.*
   [...]
   Mercedes: *Carmen, believe me, be careful!*
   Carmen: *I'm not afraid!*
   Frasquita: *Be careful!* (Ib.)

3. Carmen: *What you ask can never happen!*
   Carmen never yet has lied!
   Her mind is made up completely,
   For her and you ... it's the end.
   To you I've never lied!
   For us both it's the end.
   To you I've never lied!
   For both us it's the end.
   Don José: *Carmen, you have your life before you,*
   O my Carmen, oh let me save you,
   Save you, for I adore you,
   Then you will have saved me too! (Ib., Sc. II)

4. Carmen: *No use your saying: "I adore you!"*
   You will get no more from me.
   You waste your time,
   I'll give in no more,
   Not to you! (Ib.)

5. She has to be lovely / She has to be silent / She has to stay at home.

6. But morning overtook Shahrazad, and she lapsed into silence, leaving King Shahrayar burning with curiosity to hear the rest of the story. [...] The king thought to himself, "I will spare her until I hear the rest of the story; then I will have her put to death the next day." When morning broke, the day dawned, and the sun

rose; the king left to attend to the affairs of the kingdom... (*The Arabian Nights* 18).

7. A beautiful example of the power of the name is in the tradition of *The Thousand and One Nights*: when a demon, a djinn, refuses to convert to Islam, Solomon condemns him to enter a brass pot, which he then seals up with his ring, on which the secret name of God is impressed. Then, the enchanted demon is thrown into the sea, where it would be still lying, had a fisherman not found it by chance.
8. Carmen (trying to get past):—*Let me pass, let me pass!*
Don José: *On my soul,*
I'll ever let you pass, Carmen,
I'll make you follow me!
Carmen: *Let me pass, Don José, I'll never go with you.*
[...]
Don José: *No, by the saints, you'll not do that,*
Carmen, for you're coming with me.
Carmen: *No! No! Never!*
Don José: *I am tired of using threats!*
Carmen (furiously): *All right, kill me at once, or let me go inside.* (Ib.)
9. Don José (out of his mind): *Now for the last time, you fiend,*
Will you come with me?
Carmen: *No! no!*
(half-voice, with rage) *You remember this ring—the ring that once upon you gave me...*
Take it!
(throws it at him)
Don José (drawing his knife, moves in on Carmen): *Well then! Be damned!*
(Carmen retreats... Don José pursues her... Fanfares and shouts in the arena)
Chorus: *Toreador, on guard now!*
Do not forget that when you draw your sword,
Two dark eyes look down,
And love is your reward.
(José has stabbed Carmen.... She falls dead. José kneels beside her.... The curtain to the arena opens. The crowd comes out of the bullring)
Don José (rising): *You can take me away.... I am the one who killed her.*
Ah! Carmen! My Carmen ... I adore you! (Ib.)

10. She was lying then, sir, as she has always lied. I don't know that that girl ever spoke a word of truth in her life, but when she did speak, I believed her—I couldn't help myself. (Trans. Lady Mary Loyd; 2003-2008 Project Gutenberg Literary Archive Foundation). http://www.gutenberg.org/catalog/world/readfile?fk_files=226779&pageno=18
11. I thought: we are blessed. And how strange it is that we can learn to hate even this, that we forsake these gifts and seek release; the sheets are cool and smooth below me, and this I am grateful for, I can feel the breath slide in and out of me, and this I am grateful for; surely, this must be enough, to feel these things and know that all this exists together, the earth and its seas, the sky and its suns. (Vikram Chandra, *Red Earth and Pouring Rain* 20). Sanjay, who in another life has committed suicide, has now the body of an ape and has to die again. He is contemplating the common beauty of the world the night before telling his story. This deep feeling of beauty is connected with the presence of death, as well as of Eros with Thanatos. It seems to me that Vikram Chandra's narrative springs from this deep connection. Regarding suicide and love for reality; see also A. Gasparini, "Farewell, Father Œdipus," 2008.
12. Sartaj, who is the only Sikh police inspector in Mumbai, has a beard, a magnificent moustache and very long hair. Like every Sikh man he has the name Singh, just as every Sikh woman has the name Kaur. These common names are meant to reduce the gap between the castes. It is charming that the main character of *Sacred Games* belongs to a culture that started its dream and its quest of a juster community assuming a collective legitimation of children and foreseeing long hair and beards for men.
13. Whilst I finish this essay, 7 May 2008, midnight, a speaker on the television says that a peace mandala is to be created tomorrow in Vicenza, Italy.

Works Cited

Albertazzi, Silvia and Adalinda Gasparini, *Il romanzo new-global. Storie di intolleranza, fiabe di comunità*. Pisa: ETS, 2003.

Arabian Nights, The. Tran. Husain Haddawy. Based on the text of the Fourteenth-century Syrian Manuscript edited by Muhsin Mahdi. New York, London: W.W. Norton, 1990.

Carmen (1875). par Henri Meilhac et Ludovic Halévy. Musique de Georges Bizet. Columbia Center for New Media Teaching and Learning, 2002; http://www.columbia.edu/itc/music/reserves/cd2283/text/act04.html

Chandra, Vikram. *Red Earth and Pouring Rain*. London: Faber & Faber, 1995.

_____. *Sacred Games*. London: Faber & Faber, 2006.

Freud, Sigmund (1927). *The Future of an Illusion. The Standard Edition of the Complete Psychological Works of Sigmund Freud*. Vol. 21. Trans. James Strachey. London: Hogarth Press, 1968.

Gasparini, Adalinda. *Farewell, Father Œdipus. Freedom and Uncertainty in Vikram Chandra's Sacred Games;* to be published in the anthology *Exploring Hidden Connections: Critical Insights into Vikram Chandra's Fiction*. Ed. Sheobhushan Shukla, Anu Shukla, Christopher Rollason. Delhi: Sarup & Sons.

Mérimée, Prosper (1875). *Carmen*. Paris: Éditions Garnier Frères, 1960.

Rushdie, Salman. *The Moor's Last Sigh*. London: Vintage, 1995.

____. *Midnight's Children*. London: Vintage, 1981.

(Translated from the Italian by Luke Seaber)

4

Reconsidering Gender-Power Hierarchy in a Post/Colonial Society: Masculinities in Amitav Ghosh's *The Hungry Tide*

Susmita Roye

Abstract

'Masculinity' is the term that touches most the raw nerve of a colonised people, and it becomes even more charged when the people concerned have succeeded in shearing off the hyper-masculine control of imperialism. The supposed effeminacy of the colonised male (coupled with his barbarity) in/famously forms the cornerstone of the colonialist ideology. And, it is by celebrating this (shameful) femininity of native men that Gandhi paved the way to India's independence, thereby not simply destabilising but finally derailing the imperialist's male chauvinism. However, it is only glaringly obvious that even in the post-independent era, India is a prey to the neo-imperialist gender/power hierarchy where the power-wielding (hence hyper-masculine) indigenous elite can keep the masses in an iron grip. In *The Hungry Tide* (taken up as a case study here), Amitav Ghosh dramatises this neo-imperialist definition/representation of (native) masculinity through the overly stern governmental treatment of the Dalit 'offenders' in the Morichjhãpi incident. Especially through the four leading male figures in the novel—Nirmal, Kanai, Horen and Fokir—the divergent versions of and the steep gradation in this 'modern' masculinity in an independent India are subtly presented. This article aims at exploring both the significance as well as the signification of such plural masculinities floating in a postcolonial society.

I

Gaining independence from colonial rule is more than "the soul of a nation, long suppressed, find[ing] utterance" (Nehru) or a nascent nation etching its map on the world atlas. It is more than a glorious journey from the 'darkness of captivity' to the 'light of freedom.' Beneath the careful cover, it is an entire people's emerging from prostrate effeminacy to upright masculinity. The supposed effeminacy of the colonised male (coupled with his barbarity) in/famously forms the cornerstone of the colonialist ideology. Since the non-masculine native male is devoid of sufficient courage, a challenging attitude or an iron zeal, and is thus incapable of upholding values like achievements, competition, control, sportsmanship, efficacy and service, he is deemed incapable of controlling others or protecting his own possessions. Consequently, he needs to be ruled over and guided by the masculine white man, who of course additionally brings 'civilisation' with him. However, in the process of consolidating the white Self against the coloured Other, the white man has to assume an almost stifling hyper-masculinity, which reverts back to his own society and culture with a force not always beneficial. "It de-emphasize[s] speculation, intellection and '*caritas*' as feminine, and justifie[s] a limited cultural role for women—and femininity—by holding that the softer side of human nature [is] irrelevant to the public sphere" (Nandy 32). Nevertheless, this side-effect can easily be and indeed is often ignored as this loss is generally considered immaterial compared to the immense material gains generated by colonialist enterprises. Moreover, this ensures for the white man an elevated position in the world where, as Frantz Fanon asserts in *Black Skin, White Masks* (1952), he never feels himself inferior in any respect to the coloured man. His whiteness certifies his (hyper-)masculinity which in turn authorises his world-wide rule. The myth of the 'dependency complex of the colonized peoples' is more firmly established; the emblematic emasculation of the colonised man is more thoroughly accomplished while his ruler's complacent self-confidence is further inflated. Hence, no wonder that, at the height of its dominance and success, the British Empire should be "a global sprawl of *hubris*" (Boehmer, 13, emphasis mine) and this 'hubris' undoubtedly at the same time derives from and further reinforces the white man's hyper-masculinity. On the other hand, an assault is deliberately mounted on this very hubris when, discarding its so-called 'dependency complex' and questioning its effeminate image, a colonised people clamours for sovereignty. If having remained shackled in an imperialist rule confirms their effeminacy, then tearing away from that bondage to heal their wounded self-respect after putting up a brave fight against a hyper-masculine power surely proclaims their ascent to masculinity. If being controlled is being effeminate, then gaining control is certainly re-gaining not just lost liberty but also lost masculinity.

In India's case, the path to re-gain masculinity was paved by an unhesitant embrace and encouragement of femininity. Ashis Nandy emphasises the fact that Mahatma Gandhi opposed the idea of competing British hyper-masculinity by imitating it on a grander scale. What instead he proposed was admitting their femininity (which was their label as a colonised people) without being ashamed of it and using it as a tool against the rulers. Thus, to use Nandy's helpful terms, Gandhi rejected 'antithesis' for 'synthesis' with colonial forces. However, we must simultaneously keep in mind what Mrinalini Sinha rightly reminds us of. It is that "...colonial masculinity points towards the multiple axes along which power was exercised in colonial India: *among or within* the colonisers and the colonised as well as *between* colonisers and colonised" (Sinha 1, emphasis mine). Obviously, neither the colonisers nor the colonised were 'homogeneous groups.' Nonetheless, the historical constructs carefully fitted them into categories not to be violated and in such a scenario, the heterogeneity *within* the categories/groups is little noticed or noticeable. In fact, attempts were consciously made to crystallise the 'group' into a 'category,' and only the *inter*-category (instead of *intra*-category) differences were deliberately made visible. Consequently, the colonisers appeared homogeneously masculine and the colonised unvaryingly effeminate. Gandhi accepted without much ado this strategy of collective representation and ingeniously shaped it into a weapon for himself.

Therefore, 'Masculinity' is the term that touches most the raw nerve of a colonised people, and it becomes even more charged when the people concerned have succeeded in shearing off the hyper-masculine control of imperialism. If indeed the "empire was, at least in part, a textual exercise" (14), as Elleke Boehmer suggests, then certainly this phenomenon of moving from effeminacy to masculinity, so intrinsically related to the making and breaking of an empire, is reflected in literary works as well. Colonial literature of Anglo-India presents innumerable 'feminine' native men who dress elaborately, use kohl, personify cowardice and lack a moral backbone. It is often assumed that the Indian male, being dominated outside home, expresses his manliness more brutally over his women at home. Contradicting this view, the picture of an Indian man who is unable to control the women of his own household is often found in Raj literature. At times, when an educated native man wants to introduce new ideas and do away with older superstitions, he more often than not fails in the face of a stern opposition from his womenfolk. His emasculation is confirmed beyond doubt when even the zenana-bound purdah women are firmer of character than he is and hold a greater sway over him. Christine Weston's *Indigo* (1943) depicts just such a pitiful condition. However, the British conviction that the native warrior groups like Rajputs, Sikhs, Pathans or Gurkhas are more masculine than the Bengali babu or Marathi businessman or Tamil pundit is also reflected in many of their writings. Maud Diver openly declares that a greater kinship of the British with the Pathans or Rajputs is traceable in their comparable love for danger.

If at all native masculinity is discussed, a distorted version of it emerges. The native soldiers in Flora Annie Steel's *On the Face of the Waters* (1896) are taunted by foul-mouthed courtesans and only then do they recklessly wage a meaningless 'war' against a benevolent rule; of course, they are finally routed by the superior British army, their so-called masculinity aroused at the heat of the moment being exposed as mere sham. Some of Rudyard Kipling's characters prove their manliness by being good hunters and by serving well their white masters when they go out hunting. E.M. Forster's Dr. Aziz does not do credit to his manhood by being over-servile to the compassionate Mrs. Moore and the friendly Adela Quested. The grave risk of his manly appeal to a white woman is only inversely reflected in the hallucination of an attempted rape engendered by Adela's feverish imagination. In fact, rape and unnecessary violence are largely the only expressions of the native male's perverted masculinity in colonial literature. Even in the postcolonial period, writing about the Raj days, Paul Scott brings to life the fears of rape that haunted white women through what Daphne Manners has to undergo.

On the other end of the balancing scales hangs the backlash by Indian authors. Especially in the *post*colonial period, writers like Manohar Malgonkar attacks instead the so-called British masculinity so firmly entrenched in colonial imagination. Using the widely popular Kiplingesque *shikar* motif that so enhanced the idea of British hyper-masculinity, Malgonkar masterfully subverts the same. In *Combat of Shadows* (1962), he shows how the Englishman Henry Winton flees a rogue elephant he has been trying to hunt and slay, and in the process, leaves his native hunter-servant Kistulal to die. Afterwards, the blame of incompetence and effeminacy falls on the dead menial while the master maneuvers to hide his *unmanly* cowardice and maintain the white man's reputation. *So Many Hungers* (1947) shows Bhabani Bhattacharya challenging the image of a benevolent foreign rule by hinting at the white man's ignoble involvement (along with that of avaricious and corrupt native rice-hoarders) in the largely man-made famine which killed millions in Bengal. And of course, such exploitative greed, lack of righteousness and failure to properly handle difficult situations cannot be associated with the 'positive' masculinity that the colonialist ideology paints and endorses.

At the same time, Indian authors do not fail to see slippages of the 'masculinity' they have earned through independence. If Gandhi's celebration of femininity has led Indians to freedom, then their urge to shed dishonorable effeminacy of ages and publicise their new-found masculinity has only taken a wrong twist to exhibit itself through the Partition bloodbath. Paying no attention to a wee voice of reason in Khushwant Singh's *Train to Pakistan* (1956) that asks what bravery lay in killing unarmed innocents, the young Sikh leader stirs vengeful sentiments, appealing to his listeners' manliness and advocating a tit-for-tat policy. The narrator of Malgonkar's *A Bend in the Ganges* (1964) wonders whether fighting the British head-on through terrorist activities were not more 'honest and manly' than sabotaging their violent masculine intent in a mist of non-violence during Gandhian nationalism. Attia Hosain and Bapsi Sidhwa too, among others, launch a merciless onslaught on the 'negative' masculinity that surfaced during India's transition to sovereignty. Such self-examination is both rigorous and painful. Independence raised Indians from emasculation to masculinity; the concurrent Partition carnage put that masculinity to shame.

By the time Salman Rushdie and Amitav Ghosh enter the stage, this masculinity of a post-independence India is thoroughly put to test. These writers challenge, subvert and dismiss any misleading perception of an all-aglow masculinity in postcolonial society. Rushdie's *Midnight's Children* (1981) presents Saleem Sinai whose fate is not merely inextricably chained with but is, to a considerable extent, a personification of the destiny of his 'twin-sister' India. Pounded upon by disastrous accidents just as India is battered by social upheavals and political cataclysms, on Saleem's body are inscribed his nation's wounds. Snot-nosed, blotch-faced, mutilated-bodied, he is a man of bizarre powers and of equally strange failings. His life maps unbelievable ups and downs: deterioration to an animalistic level, abortion and restoration of memory, and even forced castration. One should bear in mind that silent suffering glorifies Mother India's feminine fortitude, but the uncouth manner in which the *male* Saleem handles his sorrows only arouses contempt. It is, moreover, rather intriguing to see that the author should choose an emasculate man to represent the femininity of India. Alu of Ghosh's *The Circle of Reason* (1986) is an odd fellow with a disproportionately large head, 'bulging all over with knots and bumps.' No less 'unmanly' than Saleem, he flees across lands after being mistakenly blacklisted as a terrorist; no less peculiar than Saleem, he fantastically survives the crash of a building on his potato-shaped head. In short, Rushdie's Saleem is only a castrated male and Ghosh's Alu is a caricature of all that maleness stands for. India's sagacious assessment of 'masculinity' has indeed come a long way since independence.

II

Ghosh's *The Hungry Tide* (2004) shall now be taken up as a case study to probe into the divergent versions of and the steep gradation in the 'modern' masculinity of an independent India. And in doing so, this article aims at exploring both the significance as well as the signification of such plural masculinities floating in a postcolonial society.

The evocative power of Ghosh's imagination and word-play in *The Hungry Tide* breathes life into a wilting public memory and forcibly reminds us of the Morichjhãpi massacre of 1978-79. Let us take a quick look at its historical roots. Ever since the Partition in 1947, refugees have flooded into the tiny state of West Bengal, easily trickling in through the porous borders, and the Bangladesh war of 1971 triggered an even greater migration. The Dalit refugees, being penniless and backward, threatened to be a bigger burden on Bengal's meager resources, and were, therefore, dealt with severity. They are said to have been stopped at the frontiers and sent off to Dandakaranya. The Dandakaranya Development Authority (DDA) initially kept them in the (rather infamous) Mana transit camp, near Raipur. The conditions were far from congenial and the refugees chiefly suffered from shortage of drinking water and food, which led to large-scale deaths from epidemics and starvation. The unknown language and culture of local people amid dense forests, along with mounting pressures and threats from unsympathetic DDA officials only added to their misery and sense of alienation. "Another factor which seriously hampered the refugees' move to [and stay in] Dandakaranya was the persistent campaign by the Communists, who urged them...to demand resettlement within Bengal" (Tan and Kudaisya 152). The representative leaders of the refugees are said to have been promised some land in Sundarbans for the rehabilitation of East Bengali refugees when the Communists acquired people's mandate in upcoming elections.

So, when the Communists did come to power in West Bengal in 1977, these marooned refugees saw a ray of hope. Deserting Dandakaranya project, breaking the barricades of DDA officials, they started moving in large numbers towards West Bengal. Their slogan was "Chalo Kolkata, Chalo Sundarban" (Mandal 49)—Let's go to Calcutta; let's go to Sundarbans. Now the Leftist government was alarmed at this. Not a single stone was kept unturned by the government in trying to disperse the arriving refugees or in forcing them to retrieve their steps. Despite this, some thirty thousand refugees found their way to Morichjhãpi, one of the northernmost forested islands of Sundarbans. There they settled down, put in every bit of effort, worked tirelessly to reconstruct their world of their own accord. However, this adamant self-sufficiency was not to be borne quietly by the fuming authorities. Threats, warnings and orders did not work. The government declared that they had violated the Forest Acts and had occupied a territory reserved for Royal Bengal tigers, thereby disturbing the habitat of that species and endangering the ecological balance of the region. On 20 August 1978, thirty police launches came to take these refugees back to Dandakaranya, and when they confronted opposition, opened fire, leading to deaths, and ran over their boats loaded with food grains, timber and firewood, causing irreparable loss to these poor people. In January the following year, the government imposed Section 144 of the Indian Penal Code, brought in more forces, surrounded the island, and prevented movement to and from that place. An economic blockade was declared on 24 January 1979, barring the entry of necessary commodities, including food grains and drinking water, from surrounding villages.

Men, women and children suffered alike, eating the inedible and drinking the undrinkable. Epidemics and starvation claimed hundreds of lives, and, on top of that, they were teargassed or shot at. In May 1979, a reinforced 'Morichjhãpi operation' began. Many were arrested, many more beaten up and dragged to police launches to be taken back to Dandak. Police firing led to deaths and casualties. Huts were razed to ground, fisheries destroyed, schools burnt down, boats scuttled over, women reportedly ravished, corpses thrown into the river. Superior force demolished smoothly the world of the 'inferiors.' In this way, the island was finally 'reclaimed' from the grasp of squatters and 'saved' for the more important Royal Bengal tiger (which is, after all, the national animal of India).

In *The Hungry Tide*, Ghosh weaves his story around this forgotten incident of suppression of unimportant people. He brings three persons from totally different spheres to one place, the Sundarbans. The three characters are Kanai, a translator by profession from Delhi, Piya, a cetologist from Seattle, and Fokir, a local fisherman. The novel follows the trajectory of breathtaking interest that such an extraordinary meeting is bound to result in. The other thread entwined with this main story-line is the anecdote of an older generation comprising of Nirmal, Nilima, Horen and Kusum. It is through Kusum's involvement in the refugee movement and her tragic death that the Morichjhãpi massacre is unveiled to us.

There are four prominent male figures in the novel—Nirmal, Kanai, Horen and Fokir. Nirmal is the headmaster of a school on a Sundarbans island and finally retires from that post during the course of the story. Kanai is Nirmal's nephew who runs a small thriving business in Delhi. He comes to Sundarbans only twice and that too under pressure: the first time, he was rusticated from school and sent to this remote location; and the second time, he reacts to his aunt's urgent request. Horen is mainly a boatman ferrying people across the innumerable water channels that dissect this deltaic region. Fokir is a fisherman in Sundarbans. Horen and Fokir, of course, have their emotional roots deep in the 'tide-country' mud. Although Nirmal admits that he has felt very little kinship with things around him, the fact remains that he has lived in and watched the tide-country from close quarters for years. Kanai, on the other hand, is the only proper 'outsider' in Sundarbans.

To me, however, these four characters signify more than four persons coming from different spheres of life and society. More significantly, these four men obliquely represent the gender idiom of power hierarchy that neo-imperialism surreptitiously borrows from its predecessor and imperceptively keeps alive. Colonialism once announced and eventually established the (nearly) incontrovertible theory of the effeminacy of a people who accept subjugation. Conquest, control and rule are masculine; by the same clue then, being conquered, controlled and ruled is inevitably feminine. The (near) incontrovertibility and imperishability of this theory are confirmed when one realises how it continues till date, albeit with its perimeters shifted to a more 'internal' space. Though no longer explicitly expressed in terms of conquest and rule, the indigenous elite proudly exhibit its masculinity through dominance over the other classes in their society. If by shearing away foreign rule, the once-effeminised Indian people have earned a 'masculine' status, then the honour of that has surely not been evenly distributed throughout the society, thereby creating pockets of power within the country to control and dominate over this largest democracy in the world. It is only glaringly obvious that even in the post-independence era, India is a prey to the neo-imperialist gender/power hierarchy where the power-wielding (hence hyper-masculine) indigenous elite can keep the (effeminised, *not* effeminate) masses in an iron grip. The Morichjhãpi incident, which is at the core of Ghosh's story-telling in this novel, serves to make even more conspicuous the continued strategy of effeminising the dominated to magnify the masculinity of the dominator.

In the novel, Nirmal and Kanai belong to a higher stratum in the society, and hence must be more masculine. As the headmaster of a school, Nirmal is somewhat in a position of control and power (albeit on a smaller scale), using which he can admit Horen's son in his school with ease. He is, moreover, treated with utmost respect by illiterate islanders around him and is universally addressed as 'Saar' in the tide-country. Loosely applying here the Foucauldian argument of interdependence of power and knowledge on rather an insignificant level (which, however, Foucault himself would not have ignored or excluded), we see that the knowledge of an educated schoolmaster as much raises him to a position of power amid illiterates as his position of power authenticates his knowledge in their eyes. In contrast, Horen's thorough acquaintance with the 'Bon-Bibi' legend or with the rhythm of tides and Fokir's skills of catching crabs or sighting dolphins are not the kinds of knowledge for which they may be endowed with a special power that the world will acknowledge. If such attributes of authority, respectability and 'power-knowledge' are linked with masculinity in any small measure, then Nirmal certainly has a strong claim on its honour.

The obviousness of Kanai's 'masculinity' (in addition to his biological 'maleness') is honed by his wealth, status, power and success in the world. The traits of acquisitiveness, competitiveness, ambition, intellect, pride and domineering have been positively associated with masculinity from colonial times onwards. Having all these qualities in him, Kanai proves himself to be masculine even more in his individualism, egotism and possessiveness. Coming from an affluent background, he has never missed an opportunity to raise himself in life. His thirst for success has driven him around the world and made him pick up foreign languages. This *knowledge* of foreign languages has not merely helped him set up a prosperous business which earns him lots of money but has also provided him with a rare *power*—the power of being easily able to communicate with more people than an average unilingual person can do. (For instance, both Piya and Fokir, being unilingual, cannot communicate with each other *with words,* and hence, Kanai steps in that vacuum as their translator.) He already belongs to an influential family, and his profession brings him in touch with more important diplomats, which indirectly adds to his power. And of course, his personal life star-studded with affairs with many women blatantly expresses his masculinity. His confidence in the appeal of his maleness is so high that he wallows in no doubt of his ability to soon start a short-term affair with the American Piya, especially with the loose sex-morals she is supposed to have picked up in the West.

Horen and Fokir, on the other hand, must be effeminate, coming as they do from the dominated class. As already mentioned, their type of knowledge cannot earn them power in the world. On the contrary, their ignorance and poverty make them objects of others' paternalism or exploitation. Horen can only hold his tongue when Nirmal angrily denounces his faith in the 'Bon-Bibi' legend as mere superstition. Fokir can only cower when the furious forest guard tries to penalise him for fishing off-limits. Both are keenly aware of the condescending attitude that Kanai adopts in talking to them. Their insignificance is all the more entrenched by their servility. Despite being inextricably involved in the parallel plots of the novel, these two men faintly glimmer on the fringes of our visibility. Their silence simultaneously signifies their effeminacy (in their *refusal* to raise their voice against injustice) and their subalterneity (in their *inability* to speak of injustice).

Yet, the suggestive richness of Ghosh's artistry will be lost upon us if we fail to perceive that this novel aims at conveying more than the masculinity of the elite/dominating and the effeminacy of the subaltern/dominated males. The simple directness of that equation is fiercely challenged (and effectively thwarted) as the author bends upon problematising this entire issue. Nirmal apparently holds sway over others, earlier as a promising Calcutta intellectual at the heart of a buzzing city and later as a school teacher on a remote island. Nevertheless, the bubble of illusion is easily pricked when one realises how helpless he is in the event of the failure of all his cherished dreams. Once, he aspired to become a renowned writer but is left with frustration and regrets. Later, he wants to see the refugee movement at Morichjhãpi—"an experiment, imagined not by those with learning and power, but by those without!" (Ghosh 141)—crowned with success but instead witnesses its brutal suppression. After the shock of leaving Calcutta under duress, he is unable to be creative as a writer for many years; after the second shock of witnessing the downfall of Morichjhãpi and all that it signified for him, he is unable to remain in his senses and finally dies of heartbreak. Once, he was forsaken by his Communist comrades because they found him too weak to shoulder heavy burdens. Later, the peasant leader at Morichjhãpi loses interest in him the moment he finds out that, in spite of being a respectable 'bhadralok,' Nirmal has no important connections in the upper-most layer of society with which he may be able to help out their cause. Once, he gave fiery speeches at college and political meetings but failed to spit that fire when confronted with a serious challenge and instead suffered a nervous breakdown. Later, when he tries to espouse the cause of the Morichjhãpi islanders, one of his former Calcutta friends almost condescendingly warns him against getting involved in this dangerous project. Hence, Nirmal has miserably failed at various crucial junctures and these have increasingly exposed his weakness. Nilima sadly summarises his life-long achievements in one word: 'nothing.' Failure and weakness are far from worthy masculinity. Therefore, one raises eyebrows at the suggestion of deeming the pitiable Nirmal immaculately masculine.

On the other hand, Horen, despite belonging to the lowest social class, often springs to vibrant masculinity through deeds not adequately appreciated. Not the least among these is his daring to build and regularly visit the shrine of Bon-Bibi amid thick wilderness of a desolate island, disregarding the dangers of man-eating tigers stalking him. He once survived a deadly cyclone with the help of his skills to wrestle with nature's fury, and afterward talks of it in a matter-of-fact tone, taking for granted this remarkable feat of his courage. When the notorious women-trafficker Dilip Choudhury plans to sell Kusum to brothel-keepers as he did with her mother before, Horen swiftly comes to the rescue of the girl he loves. In fact, that night when Kusum fled to safety, she was sitting with Kanai (who was a boy then), and that is the only time, Horen, snatching Kusum away from danger, warns the 'little *babu*' not to mention anything to anyone, otherwise "...you won't be safe either. Do you understand?" (Ghosh 92). One might argue that he could dare so only because Kanai was a boy then and has never spoken with such authority to the adult Kanai on meeting him again. To me, however, this signifies more than the desperation of a lover upon whom is incumbent his beloved's security. The ferocity with which he flings his warning at the dumbfounded boy, especially coupled with the mock-respect in addressing him, is a momentary breach of his otherwise composed deportment through which his wrath against the exploiting class explodes (for, after all, Dilip the landowner too belongs to an upper social layer). During the Morichjhãpi turmoil, he undertakes grave risks to visit Kusum with help. When the police finally crack down upon the defiant settlers with a heavy hand and Kusum is killed in the encounter, he does not lose his mind like Nirmal but instead keeps his calm and shelters her son. For all the lowliness of his class, he demonstrates rare courage, protectiveness and level-headedness, which unmistakably indicate his masculinity. No wonder then that Kusum should love this man rather than the effeminate Nirmal.

Kanai's elitist masculinity seems infallible. He is smart, intelligent, successful and duly snobbish in front of people below his social rank. Nonetheless, just one incident in the novel suffices to blow away that misleading idea. He is masculine but is not infallibly so. If fear and weakness are to be snubbed as feminine, then there are palpable traces of that in this proua man too (and this is only natural). On one occasion, irritated with Kanai's condescension, Fokir challenges him to come ashore on an island where he insists he can see fresh footprints of a tiger. He simply admits that his own fear can make him sense the presence of the carnivore. But to the educated Kanai, such an explanation for a wild guess is flimsy, and though he does not declare himself to be a man of immense courage, he believes that "fear [is] not—contrary to what [is] often said—an instinct. It [is] something learned, something that accumulate[s] in the mind through knowledge, experience and upbringing" (Ghosh 266). Since his 'knowledge, experience and upbringing' are different from an illiterate fisherman's, he refuses to indulge the superstitious fears of the latter. Accepting Fokir's challenge when he goes ashore, he angrily asks Fokir why he is trying to 'frighten' him, which indirectly acknowledges the creeping in of fear into his heart. After he falls down on the mud, he abuses Fokir who comes forward to help him because his elitist pride has been wounded in finding himself under the protective care of a social subaltern. Ghosh describes that with unforgettable words: "the master's suspicion of the menial; the pride of caste; the townsman's mistrust of the rustic; the city's antagonism toward the village" (269). For all his vanity and superiority complex, he realises with shock that on this island, facing a fatal threat, he has come down from his lofty social position in Fokir's eyes and reached the same floor as him because Fokir is now familiarly addressing him, instead of showing the respect he otherwise does. Left alone on that island, Kanai faints of the same fear his masculine pride so ferociously rebuffed.

Conversely, Fokir admits his fear with a childlike simplicity. And yet, it is he who goes out for fishing for days, making light of the grave risks to his life posed by deadly snakes, crocodiles and tigers. When Piya falls into the muddy water of deltaic Ganges, he plunges into the water after her to rescue her. In spite of his superstitious fears, he displays extraordinary bravery and presence of mind in fighting with and killing the crocodile which tried to rock their boat. In the very end of the novel, when Piya and Fokir are caught in a furious hurricane, Fokir utilises all his tactics for survival in such a dire situation, and though he himself dies in the process, he once again saves Piya's life. Surely, this repeated gallantry and show of courage are worthy of the honour of true masculinity. In this case again, the woman is drawn to the soft but more masculine male and not to the self-deluding less masculine one: Piya chooses Fokir over Kanai.

Still, Ghosh's loaded allusiveness is not exhausted. One must not overlook yet another kind of masculinity that he projects—*the masculinity of the female*. Kusum, Nilima, Moyna and Piya are the major female characters of the novel and from each, a certain amount of masculine vigour oozes out. Kusum trifles risks and holds her head high. She not only earns the bread for her family but participates in a risky venture against an offended government and is ultimately killed. Nirmal may give fiery speeches about great revolutions to change the world, but it is the illiterate and underprivileged Kusum who actually dares to be a part of a real revolutionary movement and in turn, inspires Nirmal. Nilima practically is the power-head in her family, and even Nirmal, more often than not, has to meekly obey her orders. With 'manly' dynamism, she has also opened a hospital and runs a charity trust for the welfare of the poor islanders around her. Moyna is ambitious and wants more of life than her social status can offer. Fokir is shown to be in awe of his wife, who controls the entire household. And, Piya is perhaps the most 'masculine' of them all in the lifestyle, dress and profession that she has chosen for herself. Wearing jeans and t-shirts, forsaking homeliness for the adventure of open waters and dismissing security of wedlock for a demanding profession, she is unique and most successfully suppresses the feminine in her. All these women rise above the narrow/-minded constrictions their times and society present, and violate the prescribed code of femininity to a great extent to be able to take control of their lives. And, not to ignore the subterranean implication of all this, the *constructive* masculinity of these females may effortlessly put to shame the inflated false masculine pride of elitist males.

As mentioned earlier, 'masculinity' is a word to which a people with a colonial history react most sensitively. Writers through ages have appropriated, understood and explained this term as per the social and political demands of their times. Ghosh too has made good use of his privilege. His novel subtly shows the (generalised) realignment of gender-power hierarchy from the coloniser-colonised binary of the colonial times to the indigenous elite-subaltern one in a postcolonial society. He dramatises this neo-imperialist definition/representation of (native) masculinity most effectively through the overly stern governmental treatment of the Dalit 'offenders' in the Morichjhãpi incident. However, this notional monopoly of the elite on manliness is merely at the surface of his novel. Deep beneath, it goes on to question and challenge the 'taken-for-granted' element of such a straightforward equation. Most importantly, it explodes the myth of a single tenable kind of 'masculinity' to reveal the diversity as well as the pluralities of the same. In permitting the tides of masculinity and femininity to freely intermingle in both a male and a female, the author forces us to perceive what otherwise our chauvinism refuses to admit: that every man has a bit of the woman in him just as every woman has a bit of the man in her. Water-tight compartmentalisation is unnatural and therefore unhealthy. *Multiple masculinities* are as much a fact as *masculine multiplicities* are.

Works Cited

Boehmer, Elleke. *Colonial and Postcolonial Literature: Migrant Metaphors*. 2nd ed. Oxford: Oxford UP, 2005.

Ghosh, Amitav. *The Hungry Tide*. Boston and New York: Houghton Mifflin, 2005.

Mandal, Jagadis Chandra. *Marichjhapi: Naishabder Antarale* (*Marichjhapi Beyond Silence*). Kolkata: People's Book Society, 2002.

Nandy, Ashis. *The Intimate Enemy: Loss and Recovery of Self under Colonialism*. New Delhi: Oxford UP, 1983.

Nehru, Jawaharlal. Speech on the Granting of Indian Independence, August 14, 1947. The Partition of India. <http://www.indhistory.com/partition-independence.html>.

Sinha, Mrinalini. *Colonial Masculinity: The 'Manly Englishman' and the 'Effeminate Bengali' in the Late Nineteenth Century*. Manchester and New York: Manchester UP, 1995.

Yong Tan, Tai and Gyanesh Kudaisya. *The Aftermath of Partition in South Asia*. London and New York: Routledge, 2000.

5

Kiran Nagarkar and the Discontents of Masculinity

Aysha Viswamohan

Abstract

Masculinity is often explained as something which is traditionally considered to be characteristic of a male. At one level, it is a form of identity that shapes personal attitudes and behaviours; and at another level, it can be seen as a form of ideology, where it presents a set of cultural ideals that establish fixed and appropriate roles, values and expectations for and of men. Postcolonial literature in English from India has dealt with gender issues in different ways, but few writers have addressed the idea of masculinity in such a robust way as Kiran Nagarkar. In this paper, I have attempted to analyse this aspect of the writer's works with particular reference to his novel *Ravan and Eddie*.

> "As with all hard men...there is always someone harder around the corner." (Ward, 2002: 105)

When we consider the issues of masculinity, Norman Mailer's *Tough Guys Don't Dance* (1984) is a work which comes immediately to mind. One of the seminal novels of this genre, it illustrates popular attitudes and moral positioning with regard to aggression, sex, obscenity, violence, and other forms of deviant behaviour. In many respects, *Tough Guys Don't Dance* serves as an extremely revealing cultural barometer, which has the capacity for providing a narrative index to a significant transformation of popular taste and morality. In attaining a balance between the male and the female components of his psyche, Timothy Madden, the hero of *Tough Guys Don't Dance*, is an example of Mailer's dyadic psychology. (When his wife had an affair with a black man, Madden says, "The size put them out of my physical reach—I think it delighted her contempt for me that I was not man enough under such circumstances to load my pistol and do a down-home chase off" [26]). Mailer's work reflects that socio-cultural environments influence the formation of gender identity just as much as the forces of heredity.

Among the postcolonial writers in English from India, few writers can claim to have portrayed the psyche of Indian male as effectively as Kiran Nagarkar.[1] In this paper, I have tried to analyse the construct of 'maleness,' which is a consequence of post-independence society, in Nagarkar's robust novel, *Ravan and Eddie*. The novel provides a fertile ground to many of the discussions about postcolonial masculinity, viz., men's role as a breadwinner of his family, men's sense of diminishing importance at home, and the role of female sexuality in defining 'maleness.'

Ravan and Eddie traces the lives of two boys, Ravan rao Pawar, a Marathi Hindu, and Eddie Coutinho, a Goan Christian, in the CWD (Central Works Department) chawls of Bombay, where their "lives ran parallel. And there's no greater distance on earth than that which separates parallel lines, even if they almost touch each other. One city, one chawl, two floors, two cultures, two languages, two religions and the enmity of two women separated them" (195). The novel subscribes to the belief that "If there are children in books written for an adult readership in the twentieth century, they are depicted with a lack of illusions" (Thody, 1996: 48). True enough, the grim world of CWD chawls is viewed through the young eyes of the two protagonists, who go about their business, devoid of expectations and without the fear of any dejection and disappointment.

The universe of CWD chawls is populated with diverse people, who confront their destinies everyday, and who offer us a slice of lower middle-class Bombay, or Mumbai. At certain level, one can see the underlying theme of the clash of cultures but the book steers clear of a pedantic view and instead delves deeply into the daily lives of the two diverse characters, Ravan rao and Eddie Coutinho, who are at all times farcical, bawdy and over the top. To add to the fun and frolic, there is a vast army of dysfunctional families and crazy characters lining the chawl, yet, Nagarkar observes, "nobody on the fifth floor ever mentioned the Hindus in the other four storeys" (114). Mixed in identity, nationality, race, and language, these characters signify the hybrid, cosmopolitan culture of one of the greatest metros in the world.

At one level, what Nagarkar seems to drive at is that "this world is also joined by shared stories which are not the special property of any particular group. The chawl, with its different floors given to different communities and different stories, is itself an ironic but not pessimistic restatement of the persistence of Nehru's vision of the nation as a mansion with many rooms. In Nagarkar's Bombay the assertion of difference is constantly being thwarted by strange cultural continuities" (Mehrotra, 2003: 324). Thus, the writer provides us with asides and meditations on the role of English in India, on the place of the moving image and cinema, the dilemma of the acute shortage of water for the poor, history of Afghan Snow cream, the plight of the rural dispossessed in a metropolis, and cultural differences between the Hindus and Christians.

While talking about the genesis of his story, Nagarkar, in an online interview with Arnab Chakladar, recalls a lady who lived in a chawl in Mazagaon, Mumbai.

> She was a Roman Catholic and it was a complex of chawls, and in all the chawls the 5th storey was occupied by Catholics and the other five floors by Hindus. This must have registered somewhere in my mind because it did give a very solid anchor to my book: the fact that these two different communities might as well be living on two different planets. In a sense, without my even realizing it, it also became a study of the tepid coldness with which the Catholics and the Hindus dealt with each other in those days. Perhaps they still do. In between there was some hostility as well...the RSS was giving the Christian community a hard time. My Catholics were from that time and since I was trying to do a post-independence take on

> the two communities in chawls, it was very germane to my book, this opposition within the same building, and without being aware that you did not wish to have anything in common. The book deals with the childhood of Ravan and Eddie. (online interview)

The novel begins as we find Victor Coutinho—husband of Violet, father of a daughter, and soon going to be the father of Eddie—gazing salaciously at his neighbour, Mrs. Parvati Pawar. In a bizarre turn of events, thirteen-month-old Ravan tries to jump off a floor as Victor Coutinho ogles at Parvati. As Victor tries to rescue the child, he has a massive stroke and dies on the spot, eyes wide open. Perhaps it is Nagarkar's way of punishing for violating the tenth commandment, "Thou shall not covet your neighbour's wife," however, for the pregnant Violet, it is not her husband who has brought his death upon himself, but Parvati's innocent child, Ram, who is identified as the cause of this tragedy. From that moment onwards, Ram had to bear the stigma of being "Cain. Murderer" (10), for the people of Central Works Department Chawl No. 17. It is a title he has to learn to live with, forcing Parvati to change his name from Ram to Ravan to ward off the evil eyes. "Wait till he grows up and tries to abduct every Sita in town," cautions Ravan's father, Shankar-rao. The fond mother retorts, "Mark my words. Every Sita will be chasing my Ravan" (11). It is this inversion and intersection of mythologies and religious legends, which form the crux of the novel. History for Nagarkar becomes "clairvoyance and fantasy, a commingling of dream and fact" (Sampat-Patel, 2003: 178).

Masculinity in our society often refers to "the power of the state.... Masculinity seems to extend outward into patriarchy and inward into the family; masculinity represents the power of inheritance, the consequence of the traffic in women, and the promise of social privilege" (Halberstam, 2004: 936). It is interpreted differently by different characters, and everyone has his own take on what it takes 'to be a man.' Here are a few musings on 'maleness' as understood by the key players in the novel: "Be a man" (2) says Victor Coutinho, Eddie's deceased father, to himself as he musters sufficient courage to approach

Parvati, Ravan's breathtakingly beautiful mother, towards whom he has been attracted for years; "Every man I know works" (21) says Parvati to her unemployed husband, "I would if you were a man and earned a living like one" (21) Parvati to Shankar, as she denies sex to him; on Shankar Pawar's reading habits, "While his father read about a man who lured women to his home, kept them chained for months and raped them repeatedly, Ravan did his homework on the floor" (46); Mr. Sarang (a neighbour) to Ravan, "Your father looks like a man in good health and you are living proof that he's a capable man. Then how is it that you don't have any more siblings?"; "Mr. Tamhane was a man of infinite faith in the depravity and crookedness of his fellow man" (100); Violet Coutinho's mother urging her to remarry, "He'll earn money as the man of the house should" (154); Eddie's thoughts on his mother's potential husband, "Where was the Man going to sleep? In his mother's bed? Perish the thought" (157); (on comparison between Hindu and Catholic men) "The word for mutton and fish among many of the Hindus was, bazaar. While women did all other household shopping, bazaar was macho and the prerogative of men" (175), and the supreme Nagarkarian assertion, "Men are heroic inside the vagina, in wet dreams, quickies or in love" (310).

Masculinity therefore is a multi-dimensional and many-hued entity, perceived differently by different people. At one point, Shankar-rao Pawar rejoices in a mood of self-congratulations, "Parvati wore the pants in the family but who had gifted the pants anyway? In return, he got three meals daily, tea, snacks, clothes, betel nut to chew, pocket money for the evening paper, two movies a month and, most important of all, peace. Sex was a grey area" (36). Clearly, the reversal of role does not matter much as long as he received his meals and pocket money from his wife. Through his son's eyes, Shankar-rao knew only two postures, "the foetal position and a prostrate one" (45).

In Nagarkar's work, men have various roles to play. Consequently, we have the patriarchs Shankar Pawar and Victor Coutinho, fathers of the two protagonists;

Chandrakant Dixit, freedom-fighter and a die-hard Gandhian; Mr. Tamhane, the mean-spirited neighbour; Mr. Sarang, a bus-conductor and highly-strung father of nine unmarried daughters; Paul Monteiro, "freedom fighter, Gandhi's non-violent disciple, indefatigable copulator, enlightened Roman Catholic from Goa and ceaseless aspirant to fatherhood" (200); Mr. Furtado, a suitor for Eddie's widow mother, but turns out to be an edgy, spineless creature; and Prakash, Ravan's classmate who forces his younger classmates to have oral sex with him, and later ends up marrying his step-mother. Nagarkar delights in delineating his male characters warts and all, and with every conceivable flaw and weakness—obsession with breasts, preoccupation with the size of their penis, masturbation, impotence, pornography, etc. This becomes all the more noteworthy when he pits his men against women of steel, such as Violet Coutinho, Granna (Violet's formidable mother), Parvati, and Shobhan Sarang.

Ravan's interaction with the club-footed Shobhan Sarang and her many sisters borders on the poignant and the farcical. It is a relationship where two negatives are brought together—while Shobhan does not have friends because of her handicap, Ravan bears the cross of 'murdering' Eddie's father, and is therefore ostracised by other children of the CWD chawls. It is in the Sarang household, where the young Ravan, surrounded by girls and their objects of vanity, that Ravan comes in touch with the feminine inside of him. At one point, after being taunted by Mr. Tamhane, Ravan even has vivid dreams of marrying all the Narang sisters and siring children.

According to David Savran, "Despite masculinity's status as an illusion without ontological foundation, a sequence of postures, it has a profoundly real—and, many would say, devastating—impact on the world." (Savran, 1992: 16). *Ravan and Eddie* tackles the serious issue of violence against women. In CWD chawls, violence against women is permissible, encouraged even, through society's imposition of gender roles. The relationship between gender roles and violence is manifest in the way that gender roles are constructed by those cultural institutions that continue to bolster misogynistic and communal attitudes that create a social setting that encourages the commission and often sanctions violence against women. Mr. Sarang's constant bickering bears testimony to such prejudices, "See Suman there, she's thirty-three. Who's going to marry her? Savitri's thirty-one, maybe thirty-two. A few more years and her menopause will start. All of them darkies, who's going to look at them?" (90). When his youngest daughter Tara gets pregnant by her lover, Sarang kicks her belly till she aborts, only because "Who will marry them [his other daughters] once they discover that we have a Mahar, an untouchable...among us?" (113). It thus becomes the prerogative of a patriarch to vent his anger against a daughter who dares to cross the boundaries of caste and community.

In Nagarkar's novel, therefore, it is easy to identify some standard sources of conflict between men and women that lead to men's violent attacks on the women, namely, men's possessiveness and jealousy, men's expectations concerning women's domestic work, the patriarch's sense of the right to punish women for perceived sins, and the importance to men of maintaining or exercising their position in the hierarchy. Conceptualizing these motives as patriarchal techniques of constraining female autonomy, the author illuminates both the real physical threats that women face and the ideological discourse of masculinity that authorises that violence.

Nagarkar satirises a number of traditionally sanctified beliefs, and paternity is one of them. Commenting on Eddie's neighbour, Paul Monteiro's inability to have a child for several years after marriage (Yolanda, his wife, miscarries each time she gets pregnant), Nagarkar says, "Men, as women well know but will wisely not admit, are at best sprinters. When it comes to that marathon called life, it's the members of the weaker sex who have staying power. Paul Monteiro's wife Yolanda didn't throw up her hands because the odds were against her, she merely tried a little harder" (200). The Monteiro's predicament leads to flurry of concern among the inhabitants of the chawl. "Keeping that woman pregnant is a round-the-clock, round-the-year job," said one group. "What do you expect, a Qutab Minar after all these years? He's worn it out till it's disappeared." The other group was equally vehement, "It's she who should be exhausted. All he does is clamber on to her. She is the one who has to do the bearing and the losing" (202). Nagarkar nudges the conventional idea on virility in its ribs when he describes the moment when, while working in his factory, a nearly impotent Paul Monteiro is bitten by an ant, and realises that "his shy, withdrawn and almost non-existent prick had grown into the mother of all hard-ons" (203). Nagarkar demolishes the myth of machismo as he narrates Monteiro's hurried journey from Byculla to Mazgaon chawls because he "knew the depth of his despair at that moment. It occurred to him that the manhood he had preserved and protected for forty-five minutes could vanish with the same celerity with which it had appeared" (204). The fact that the writer dwells on Monteiro's temporary impotence for almost six pages, yet again reflects his preoccupation with crises and discontents of masculinity.

In the patriarchal set-up, domestic violence, both of mental and physical variety, bears the distinction of targeting women, the means of subordinating and castigating them for crossing male-defined borders. Thus, the hard-working Parvati is saddled with her husband's mistress, Lalee, and Parvati and her son are relegated to the kitchen of their one-roomed house. These turns of events at home make Ravan reflect on the nature of relationships: "What was the bond between a son and his father?" he thinks. "He was as attached to the chair or fan in his house as he was to his father. That back which he had turned upon the world and Ravan many, many years ago did not give any purchase to Ravan" (223). His mother's precarious position in his father's life becomes another cause for concern for the young boy. "There were no rewards in life for doing a good job.... Were the roles of husband and wife spelt out when two people got married? When two parties came together was it mandatory that one was subordinate to the other?" (223).

Ravan's interaction with the coquettish Lalee becomes his first brush with sexuality. He is fascinated with her painted lips, her seductive walk, and her exquisite flesh, which is displayed unabashedly for everyone to see. She does her best to win Ravan over with her charm (she calls him "Lalee's lal" (227) and gift of a red shirt, which reminds the boy of his favourite song from a Shammi Kapoor-starrer, "red as, lal lal gal. Red as cheeks" (231). Nagarkar goes deep into an adolescent boy's psyche as he describes Ravan's reaction that when Lalee sucks his bloody finger, the teenager "squirmed with an embarrassment that was mixed with a strange undercurrent of pleasure" (226).

For Robert Bly, poet and the father of expressive men's movement, there are certain things that only a male mentor can do that the mother, no matter how great she is, won't be able to do" (online interview). *Ravan and Eddie* gives us an array of male mentors: priests, leaders, teachers, and film heroes. Among them is Father Agnello D'Souza, almost a surrogate father to Eddie. One aspect that has been explored is the role of self-control in defining masculinity, and that's certainly a key aspect in the imposition of clerical celibacy. Father Agnello D'Souza is the father Eddie never had, an almost benign presence in the boy's life. When Eddie is caught selling film tickets in black, the constable brings the erring lad to Father D'Souza with, "Take charge of your son. Call yourself a priest and yet fathering children all over the place. Like father, like son" (308). It must be observed that we are told very little or nothing about the relationship between Father D'Souza and Pieta Coutinho, Eddie's elder sister. He had officiated at Victor Coutinho's funeral, and had accompanied Violet Coutinho in the van which carried Victor's dead body. He was present when Violet went into labour pains and, gave birth to little Eddie. He takes upon himself the mantle of Eddie's moral and spiritual guide, however, it is by another quirk of fate that Eddie gets drawn to Lele Guruji, and resists the teachings of Father D'Souza. In portraying the love-hate relationship between the two men, Nagarkar again explores an important feature of masculine relations—surrogate fatherhood and its crises.

Lele *guruji*, the head of Mazgaon Sabha, represents militant patriotism and Hindutva. However, it is Eddie (and not Ravan), who joins the organization, and receives the illustrated *Stories from the Mahabharata and Shri Krishna's Life* along with a Wilson fountain pen. Soon Eddie becomes Guruji's favourite student, and the former refers to him as "the prodigal son" who would "bring honour to the Sabha" (33).

Ravan, on the other hand, forges an unlikely bond with Mr. Billimoria, the tae-kwon-do teacher at St. Theresa's School, where he learns the martial art, value of discipline, along with a smattering of English. The relationship begins along the mythological lines, with Ravan observing Mr. Billimoria and his pupils from a safe distance, and then being caught. Soon he endears himself to the teacher, and becomes "the master's younger version and therefore unable to suffer clumsiness" (222). This guru-sishya relationship, in a way, encompasses Nagarkar's vision of crossing man-made boundaries, and reaching out to the 'other' for higher attainment.

Ravan's encounters with Prakash, his wayward and much older classmate, are a source of revelation for the younger boy. Through Prakash's character, the writer investigates a scenario in which a young boy's desire for his (step) mother's body coincides with the wish to kill his father. Further, the anxieties aroused by this double transgression are displaced into male homosexual desire and the impulse to punish the mother who initiated the forbidden desire. As a revealing study of men and masculinity, *Ravan and Eddie* displays an unabashed fixation on the male body. If females are subjects of male gaze, then Nagarkar does not spare his male characters either. Moreover, the reader's look is direct at men, whereas our access to Parvati/Violet is mediated through the men in their lives. (It may be recalled that Kiran Nagarkar's sole film appearance was in an English language film by Dev Benegal titled *Split Wide Open* in 1999. Interestingly Nagarkar played the role of a homosexual priest, Father Bono, who contracts AIDS and dies).

Ravan and Eddie comprises some of the most interesting digressions on postcolonial India, and one such discussion is on the world of commercial Hindi cinema. We are told that the turning point in Ravan's life comes when he watches a Shammi Kapoor starrer *Dil Deke Dekho*. Nagarkar delights in sketching Shammi Kapoor, the ultimate rebel star, who had made a lasting impression on an entire generation. The writer applauds Kapoor of single-handedly changing the face of romantic comedies in India. It might have marked a shift in perception about masculinity when Nagarkar observes, "The romantic heroes of Hindi films before him were soft, shy, tentative or intense. They were gentle and appealed to genteel. Shammi Kapoor...the exact opposite. One of his films was called *Junglee*. That's what he was, wild and uncouth" (187).

It is interesting to note that Ravan's ideal 'male' is the 'unformed,' 'uncouth' and unpredictable, still more masculine Shammi, rather than his romantic, tragic-comic brother, Raj Kapoor, the foremost showman of the Hindi cinema. *Ravan and Eddie* thus celebrates the working-class, rebellious hero, who rebels against "middle-class society and against particular forms of domestication" (Halberstam, 2004: 938). Similarly, it is at a film theatre that Eddie Coutinho learns to "forget to breathe...forget the very name of God" (208). It was while watching Bill Haley's *Rock Around the Clock*[2] at the Strand Cinema that Eddie discovers the joys of dancing with abandon, tastes the pleasure of a female body, and decides what he wants to be—"Bill Haley now and forever" (210). Nagarkar thus highlights how young men develop a fascination for heroes, who become their role models. It is on the basis of this form of masculinity, this way of being masculine—acting, performing or doing masculinity—that these young men gain recognition from their peers. And it is this preoccupation with their heroes which helps the two boys to choose their respective vocations—Eddie follows in the footsteps of popular rock stars, while Ravan decides to become a nightclub singer and drummer.

Constructing the object of analysis thus, it can be argued that Nagarkar's young protagonists have a shortage of recognition from the surrounding social world, which is simultaneously related to class, gender, religion, age, the social geography of the cities and sexuality. This shared condition of life in the shape of a shortage of recognition, prestige, status or affirmation from the surroundings can be a key issue in understanding Ravan and Eddie. The concept of subculture carries many meanings and connotations and can be used in a number of ways. But as a strictly sociological concept it implies that people in relatively underprivileged social positions create subculture as an attempt to collectively solve, handle, cope with, answer or comment upon the problems they share. In a subculture one can find a community with others with roughly the same problems as oneself and in such community lays an opportunity for gaining the mutual social acceptance and recognition one is otherwise excluded from. A subculture can be interpreted as a collective attempt at solving or just coping with shared problems, which might be an overall problem of recognition/symbolic capital. In other words, when these young men experience being denied recognition from the surrounding society, because they do not have the possibility of living up to those criteria which are rewarded with recognition by that very society, they have the possibility of forming groups where they can earn recognition on criteria which they actually can live up to.

In her work, "Female Masculinity," Judith Halberstam asserts, "Far from being an imitation of maleness, female masculinity actually affords us a glimpse of how masculinity is constructed as masculinity" (Halberstam, 2004: 935). The 'masculine' female is represented by the two matriarchs: Parvati Bai and Violet Coutinho.

It is believed, "To 'catch' a husband is an art; to 'hold' him is a job—and one in which great competence is called for" (Beauvoir, 1997: 486). And Parvati learns this art, although rather late in the day. Parvati is too pragmatic to murder Shankar-rao and his mistress, and divorce is an idea that does not even cross her mind. She uses her best weapon, her sexuality to beat Shankar-rao at his own game. Thus, one night after initiating sex with her husband, in the middle of their love-making, she puts a knife on his throat, "You may have sex with me, once or twice a week," she comes straight to the point. But, "if your sister ever shows up here, I'll kill you. If you ever sell any of the goods in our house, I'll kill you" (305), she promises her husband, as he begs for mercy. Nagarkar, yet again turns the construct of 'malehood' on its head when he describes Shankar-rao (we are told he enjoys love-making accompanied with the war cries of "Har Har Mahadev. Kill, kill, kill" (217), the "hungry tiger" (289) and "the Lord of Destruction" (304) succumbing to his more powerful mate, and almost becoming "lifeless" (306) with fear, as he stares in the eye of death.

If Parvati personifies *stree-shakti* (woman power) then for Eddie, the trinity is not "the Father, the Son and the Holy Ghost but his mother, Granna and Pieta" (170), who resemble Brahma, Vishnu and Shiva. Again, it is Violet Coutinho who spurns her weakling of a suitor, Mr. Furtado, who threatens to whip the 'viper' Eddie because the boy paints his mother as a vixen and woman of loose morals, in order to prevent her second marriage. Violet, however, firmly stands by her son: "My son never lies, Mr. Furtado. It does not reflect well upon the listener that he stood and listened for a full thirty minutes to all manner of lies and stories" (171). It is his mother's steadfastness that tortures Eddie for the rest of his life. It is his mother's strength of character for which he could never forgive her.

Both families, resultantly, emerge as an unconventional family unit, with traditional role attributes distributed in an unorthodox manner among its members. If conventional masculinity is commonly perceived as aggression, procreation, violence, and avoidance of emotional display; then it would be worthwhile to consider those works of postcolonial literature in which these traditional notions of maleness come under attack. For example, Mahesh Dattani's *Dance Like a Man*, a play which explores the lives of a dancer couple, Jairaj Parekh and his wife, Ratna. Among the many concerns, the play also discusses the general inhibitions to a man taking dance as a career and that too a dance which is usually and traditionally performed by women. Masculinity is problematised as we learn how Ratna never forgives her husband for being a "failure" and remaining just an "average" person. She blames him for their misfortunes: "You stopped being a man for me the day you came back to this house" (132). Jairaj had been a failure from his father's point of view too. As Jairaj recalls, for his wealthy businessman father, his son's profession was "The craft of a prostitute to show off her wares—what business did a man have learning such a craft? Of what use could it be to him? So no man would want to learn such a craft. Hence anyone who learnt such a craft could not be a man" (136).

Girish Karnad, in his play, *Bali: The Sacrifice*, investigates the construct of masculinity (or rather the lack of it) for a non-violent man. The King, a converted Jain, is tormented by his wife's infidelity, as the Mahout (the man with whom the Queen had slept) taunts the King over his position as a cuckold. We are told that the Mahout is "ugly" and has "beaten women black and blue" (76), while the King, in the Queen's words, is "affectionate, gentle, trusting" (79). But for the Mahout, the King is "a Jain. You can't indulge in violence. You aren't permitted to shed blood. How could you draw the sword?" (88). The Queen Mother is unsparing too: "How can you stand here like this? I should cut her to pieces...feed her to wolves and vultures. Do it, son, now! She has betrayed you. All this nonsense about non-violence. It had to go" (107). When the King refuses to abide by his mother's wishes, she harangues, "What kind of a man are you? You have lost your manhood. You, you impotent..." (108). In *Bali*, thus, Karnad mulls over the traditional expectations of manhood, sexual freedom and gender equations, and it becomes clear that there are no simplistic answers for these questions.

Masculinity and its crises are further explored in Kiran Nagarkar's *Cuckold*, for which he received the Sahitya Akademi Award in 2000. Set in the sixteenth century India, when Mewar was ruled by Rajputs, and was at the peak of its powers. However, the kingdom of Mewar has an intricately built relationship with its neighbours—Islamic rulers in Gujarat, and a weakening Sultan Lodi in the North. Additionally, there is the looming effect of Babur and his advances into Hindustan. Amidst the chaos, the prince,

Maharaj Kumar, heir apparent to Chittor, sets across to tell his story and his life.

The Princess whom he marries too declares on the first night that she is betrothed to someone else, and that someone else is the blue god. He is her husband, lover and she is entirely his; He is the supreme one, Lord Krishna; and she is his beloved, Meera. A dejected and rejected Maharaj, after a failed attempt to rape his wife, yells, "We are man and wife, man and wife" (46). He tries to find peace and love elsewhere, and so begins his journey where he contemplates not just his life, but the existence of god himself and the core of human nature.

In conclusion we can assume, "Genders can be neither true or false, neither real nor apparent, neither original nor derived. As credible bearers of those attributes, however, genders can also be rendered thoroughly and radically incredible" (Butler, 382). Nagarkar's works explore this dimension of identity, besides underscoring the need to cross borders and risking the turbulence that enforces them. *Ravan and Eddie* ends with the two sons of two warring mothers engaged in a martial dance "in perfect harmony, intersecting each other's orbits in a Pythagorean paradise. It was a duet. Two volatile martial arts in a state of continuous equilibrium" (330). Crossing the threshold is dangerous but remains the means by which one can arrive at their home space and escape control and violence. Instead of accepting borders as a means of territorial control, Nagarkar broadens the sense and power of barrier crossing to create a space for men and women free of economic, physical, sexual, and psychological violence. Though Nagarkar's work puts masculinity in crisis, it does not offer a critique of either masculinity or violence. The cultural/sexual/social confusion at the heart of *Ravan and Eddie*, I think, interrogates the discontents of masculinity, eliciting the question of what it takes to be a man, and what might be the alternative to traditional understanding of male sexuality, and maleness. In identifying energy with male camaraderie and bonding, and in continuing to locate feminine sexuality in its traditional place within the family (as mostly maternal), *Ravan and Eddie* may seem to be far from progressive to some. But it does raise the question of desire, of masculine politics and of mobilisation of aggression. Literature today considers "the diversity of ways in which masculinity has been constructed, enacted or even embodied" (Alderson, 2006: 201), and Nagarkar's theses are a respectable—though provocative—addition to the growing corpus of masculinity studies.

Notes

1. Nagarkar writes in English as well as in Marathi. His novel *Saat Sakkam Trechalis* has been translated into English as *Seven Sixes are Forty-Three*. He published a play, *Bedtime Stories*, in Marathi and English.
2. *The Ground Beneath Her Feet* illustrates Salman Rushdie's take on rock 'n' roll in India, where he mentions, "Jack Haley's Meteors and sundry other quaffed and finger-snapping Yanks" (96).

Works Cited

Alderson, David. "Masculinity and Cultural Studies." *Modern North American Criticism and Theory*. Ed. Julian Wolfreys. Edinburgh: Edinburgh UP, 2006.

Beauvoir, Simon de. *The Second Sex*. London: Vintage, 1997.

Bly, Robert. Interview. 25 April 2008. <http://www.pbs.org/kued/nosafeplace/interv/bly.html>.

Butler, Judith. "Subversive Bodily Acts." *The Cultural Studies Reader*. Ed. Simon During. 3rd ed. London & New York: Routledge, 1993.

Dattani, Mahesh. *Final Solutions and Other Plays*. New Delhi: Manas, 1994.

Halberstam, Judith. "F2M: The Making of Female Masculinity." *Literary Theory: An Anthology*. Ed. Julie Rivkin and Michael Ryan. Malden, MA: Blackwell Publishers, 2004.

Karnad, Girish. *Bali: The Sacrifice*. New Delhi: Oxford UP, 2004.

Mailer, Norman. *Tough Guys Don't Dance*. London: Abacus, 1984.

Mehrotra, Arvind Krishna, ed. *An Illustrated History of Indian Literature in English*. Delhi: Permanent Black, 2003.

Nagarkar, Kiran. *Cuckold*. New Delhi: Harper Collins, 1997.

____. Interview. 26 April 2008. <http://www.anothersubcontinent.com/kn3.html>.

____. *Ravan and Eddie*. New Delhi: Viking, 1995.

Rushdie, Salman. *The Ground Beneath Her Feet*. London: Jonathan Cape, 1999.

Sampat-Patel, Niti. "Kiran Nagarkar." *South Asian Novelists in English*. Ed. Jaina C. Sanga. Connecticut: Greenwood Press, 2003.

Savran, David. *Communists, Cowboys, and Queers*. Minneapolis: U of Minnesota P, 1992.

Thody, Philip. *Twentieth-Century Literature*. London: MacMillan, 1996.

Ward, Geoff. *The Writing of America*. Cambridge: Polity, 2002.

6

Mapping Masculinities in Mumbai: A Reading of Shobha Dé's Fiction

Tripti Karekatti

Abstract

The thesis that the elevated status of the "kshatriya" version of Indian masculinity was a result of the hyper-masculinist British imperial ideology is a contested one. The present paper seeks to analyze the ideological structures that underpin the representation of postcolonial Indian masculinities in the novels written mainly for popular consumption by a woman novelist, Shobha Dé. Starting with the assumption that masculinities reflect the characteristics of the spaces in which they are constructed, the paper finds that masculinity mapped by Dé in 'her' Mumbai is but hegemonic masculinity anchored in subordination, heterosexuality and homophobia. Dé's use of twin strategies of cultural non-specificity and conflation of distinct versions of Indian masculinity is necessitated by her typical mapping of Mumbai as "the ultimate whore."

My aim in the present paper is to discuss the representation of masculinities in the immensely popular fiction of Shobha Dé[1] in relation to its cultural and ideological context. I have purposely selected Shobha Dé's texts as they belong to and have remained within the realm of popular consumption and have generated relatively little critical interest. Secondly, produced for mass entertainment, the ideological structures that underpin the ways in which gender is represented are visible just below the surface in these texts. Recent feminist research shows that woman's abject status in patriarchal society conditions her writing about men and masculinity. Her difficulties at "exerting authorial power over men" result in a dialectical image of men: on the one hand critiquing masculinity, and on the other, expressing pleasure in the male and projecting a utopian "New man." Hence, it will be interesting to study how Shobha Dé, being a woman and writing fiction for mass consumption approaches masculinities in her work.

Masculinity and its other equivalents (like 'manhood' or 'the male role') refer to three clusters of phenomena: cultural beliefs about and representations of men which influence the way men live; characteristics that differentiate men from women and the strategy for maintaining men's power. That is, like 'femininity,' masculinity too politically operates on two levels—as a form of identity and as a form of ideology. Unlike the biological state of maleness, masculinity is a gender identity constructed socially, historically and politically. The second wave of masculinity studies has shown that masculinity has multiple meanings which vary over time and across cultures. "Being a man" means different things in different times, different cultures and among different ethnic groups. Naturally, there are multiple masculinities—some dominant and others subordinate/marginalized. Using Gramsci's concept of hegemony, R.W. Connell defines hegemonic masculinity as—

> ...the configuration of gender practices which embodies the currently accepted answer to the problem of the legitimacy of patriarchy, which guarantees (or is taken to guarantee) the dominant position of men and the subordination of women. (1995: 77)

However, Messner (1993: 724) points out that masculinity is defined not only in relation to femininity but also to the other forms of masculinity which may be subordinated to the hegemonic masculinity.

The multiple meanings of masculinity vary not only over time, across cultures, races, ethnicities, castes, classes but also with spaces. Masculinities reflect the characteristics of the spaces in which they are constructed (Philips, 1995, 1997; Sparke, 1996). As such, authors—whether elite serious writers or popular storytellers—are mapmakers charting "masculinist geographies" or spaces in which masculinities are mapped.

Shobha Dé's fiction can be characterized as adventure narrative—albeit sexual—set invariably in one city: Mumbai. Dé is essentially a novelist of Mumbai. In the first paragraph of her first novel the narrator says,

> "Bombay, it is Bombay which shaped me into what I am now and it's the story of Bombay I want to tell." (*Socialite Evenings* 9)

She sticks to this in most of her later novels too. Mumbai being a multicultural city, with people from all over India irrespective of region, religion, caste, class, language, sex, etc., thronging to it, one can expect in Shobha Dé's fiction a variety of Indian masculinities being represented. The present paper is an attempt to explore how Dé maps masculinities in Mumbai.

One of Dé's characters Iqbal, a successful and rich painter, characterizes Bombay as—

> ...the Ultimate Whore, drawing hundreds of customers to her hungry bosom daily, exploiting them and getting exploited in turn. (*Sultry Days* 189)

Once Mumbai is charted as the Ultimate Whore, it is natural that this Mumbai is peopled by the whores, their customers and pimps. The Mumbai mapped by Dé is composed of billionaire industrialists, businessmen, media magnates, film stars, models, journalists, rich and highly sophisticated upper class call girls, pseudo-artists and Kamathipura whores. It is a world of power and exploitation steeped into astonishing scales of wealth and deceit. However, the slum dwellers, lower classes, working classes (and often middle classes too) can rarely make even to the backdrop of these novels. In a sense, it is society with just one class—the upper class. Quite predictably then, the "real men" in this space have to be customers with great sexual prowess and enough wealth to procure the services of the whore.

It is quite interesting to scrutinize who makes up to this category of "real men." Dé's men appear to fall neatly into three slots just as one of her characters, Deb (alias God) pigeonholes them: "can-dos," "no-can-dos" and "gandus (homos)" (*Sultry Days* 45). Just as very few men are able to make it to the category of "can-dos," very few succeed to Dé's notion of "real men."

Being the capital of Maharashtra and Dé herself being a Maharashtrian Saraswat Brahmin (which is much stressed by the publisher as well as by the narrator-protagonist of the first novel), one may naturally expect Maharashtrian community to figure to a large extent both in her work and in the "can-do" category. However, curiously enough, there is no major Maharashtrian male character in any of the novel investigated here. In the novel *Sultry Days* there is a very minor Maharashtrian male character (almost on the fringes of the narrative) who is dubbed "Kawla" (the crow) making it impossible to figure out which religion and caste he belongs to. The female narrator-protagonist (a 'Verma') and others in the ad agency joke about the Maharashtrians' "*phunny*" accent and pronunciation. The narrator even usefully summarizes Maharashtrians for us as those who "suffer from low self-worth." Similarly, there is no major south Indian male character in any of her works. Her typical style is to casually drop judgmental opinions characterising a whole community through single words, phrases or sometimes sentences put into the mouth of some minor character. For example, a Goan is called a "bloody pansy," an Anglo-Indian is a "lad" trying to "pass off as an Irish woman who'd been accidentally born in the wrong country with wrong sex" (*Sultry Days* 95). The South-Indians are "impo *yaar*. They look pretty limp" (*Starry Nights* 46). All intellectuals and really talented men in Dé's fiction are most often Bengalis. But they too cannot make to the coveted category of "real men" as they either cannot "perform" in bed or are not interested in it. For example, Suhas, the Art-film director of *Starry Nights* and Basu the talented painter of *Sultry Days* are both rejected by the female protagonists and humiliated for lack of sexual appetite.[2] An extremely co-operative husband of a careerist woman is laughed at by other women and labelled a "nerd." A person who is sympathetic towards women or one who even listens with interest to his girl-friend or one who shows slightest interest in "non-macho" activities like cooking, sewing is immediately dubbed "sissy."

Then are there no "real men" in these texts? Yes, there are some and they make it to this position, it seems, only on the basis of their capacity to violence (especially towards women), voracious sexual appetite (necessarily heterosexual), their extreme callousness in achieving success and money (which often appear to be synonymous in Dé's work) and their ability to make women go mad for them in spite of (or because of?) their violence to them. Some examples of such "real men" are the reigning Hindi film actor Akshay Arora of *Starry Nights*, businessman Billy Malhotra of *Sisters*, and the highly successful photographer Pebbles Prabhu in *Sultry Days*. Pebbles "the most irresistible photographer in business, with "wild reputations" is said to chew up half-a-dozen models a day and still have the energy to sample some more. The female narrator-protagonist describes him further as—

> ...Pebbles exuded a raw rough-edged sexuality that most models in the city found impossible to resist. He was linked up with the best of the lot and in the ad circles it was rumoured that he changed girlfriends as often as he changed bedsheets. (*Sultry Days* 95)

This makes this thick-set, bull-like fellow with mumbling incoherent speech a "can-do."

Billy Malhotra is so "maddeningly attractive" that his proposal to marry Mikki (provided she relinquishes all her rights in her father's business and signs off to Billy her every single penny) is gleefully accepted. The millionaire protagonist Mikki Hiralal is ready to lick his shoes regardless of her physical, economic and sexual exploitation. In spite of his arrogance, brutality, infidelity and deception, she loves him.

Akshay Arora, a married film star, completely ignores his wife who gave up her career as a successful singer after marriage. He has "flings" with all his heroines (including the protagonist Asha Rani) and exploits all the starlets. He watches sado-masochistic Swedish blue films and often masturbates. By making his wife Malini to wonder if he is "some kind of insatiable monster" Dé actually glamourizes

Akshay's monstrosity and ends up laughing at Malini's failure to understand "can-do" men. The mystery of the magic spell Akshay has cast over the Hindi film audience is suddenly revealed to his brother-agent Ajay while he is studying a pile of Akshay's photos taken from a low angle.

> Ajay sat back. The mystery of Akshay's magic finally unraveled in his mind. Akshay had symbolically fucked his way to the top. Every woman in the audience believed he was doing it to her and her alone. While every man thought he was Akshay—screwing the women of the world. (*Starry Nights* 37-38)

These real men, the "can-dos," stand out against both the other—lesser ("no-can-do") men and the homosexuals ("gandus"). There is no dearth of the latter in Dé's Mumbai with its media-people, artists, film stars, models and business class. Lesbian relationship between a female model/heroine and a female journalist/thug surfaces in at least three of her novels. In *Strange Obsession* it is the central subject. The so-called 'male' in the lesbian pair is made into an extremely cruel, almost insane being going to any length to achieve her woman. Minx of *Strange Obsession* physically tortures her woman—Amrita Aggarwal—a model from Delhi. She throws acid on Amrita's rival's face and mutilates her genitals. She even tries to kill Amrita's boyfriends and husband. Thus she ends up materializing as yet another malicious villain from cheap films. She goes mad before meeting her cruel end. Linda of *Starry Nights* does not use physical violence but uses her lesbian relationship and her gossip column to ruin Asha Rani's life and to boost her own career. Only Feroze of *Sultry Days* is spared such negative portrayal and this is mainly because only the beginning of her relationship with the heroine Kiki figures in the novel.

On the other hand, the gays are portrayed as either villains of the highest degree or as sheer cowards. The very bad men in Dé's fiction—ones who can give shivers to both the brave and talented main characters of her novels—are revealed to be either gays or bisexuals. For example, Varun (*Socialite Evenings*) might have been spared if he was just the ruthless social climber, manipulator and blackmailer that he is. But being interested in men, he becomes the arch villain, deserving nothing but the author's disdain. He is feared and hated by all. One critic tells how Varun drove a talented filmmaker to suicide by hounding him until he was broke both in spirit and economically. But what is worse is:

> Varun is actually a homo. Forget all that wife-shife front. He prefers young *chikna* boys. Just notice how many pretty boys he has successfully launched. All these aspiring heroes have a price to pay—but they don't mind. They know that if they please the boss they are made.... A few who fall out with him talk of his sadistic kinks—but who will believe them? (*Socialite Evenings* 283)

The other gays are "effeminate" cowards and selfish people who cannot be expected to do anything more than deserting their close ones in the time of need. Anjali's second husband Kumar Bhandari (half Punjabi, half Coorg) in *Socialite Evenings* is treated with real contempt because he is gay. Dé takes every opportunity to crack jokes at the expense of the gays. For example, when Kumar's wife Anjali tells her friend Karuna (protagonist-narrator) about how she has been deceived and how she had hoped for a proper marriage, a proper husband and a proper house, Karuna says things like:

> "Maybe he will be proper every which way but bed." (*Socialite Evenings* 126)
>
> "Why don't you relax and make a buddy out of Kumar. Gays do make excellent friends. Go on, try and do that. Imagine, you could have so much fun together. Maybe you could swap lipsticks and eyeshadows." (*Socialite Evenings* 126)

The gay music director in *Socialite Evenings* is teased by someone in the unit.

> "Well, baby, you've got on sufficient makeup for all of us, by the way, isn't purple mascara a bit too much even for a *phoren* paper?" (*Socialite Evenings* 297)

If she creates a homosexual man with power, he invariably has a sadistic element; he exploits others. Dé seems not to notice that her "heroes" also exploit others, but still are "heroes," "can-do" men, because of their heterosexuality. On the other hand, if her homos are men without power, they are "effeminate" homosexuals, that is, with "feminine" aspects such as emotional and physical passivity and weakness. Homophobia is crucial to the definition of masculinity, as it rules out men as potential objects of emotional or sexual attachment. That is why, the sight of Murthi applying balm to the forehead of a completely frightened and flustered Kumar is able to arouse only disgust and contempt in the mind of Karuna. Thus the possibility of a bond between two men, nursing and caring for each other, is marked as illegitimate. Homophobia operates to reinforce oppressive heterosexual themes, such as, male competition for the legitimate sex objects (women). If a man declines to compete in this contest, he is immediately derided as a "sissy" but if a woman contends for the same sexual object (woman) she has to be punished accordingly—with insanity and death—as is Minx in *Strange Obsessions*.

A curious case in this regard is Deb or God who is made Dé's mouth-piece to voice her three categories of men. He starts as an unusual guy with a devil-may-care attitude and a 'rugged masculinity' with significant debts to the "strong and silent" type of *film noir* and westerns. Initially he is a disgusting, dirty guy who neither pursues upward mobility nor accepts upper-class values. He is always smoking beedis, sitting in the college canteen, continuously scratching all his body vigorously. He farts in public without any embarrassment. He is found by the girls revolting and attractive at the same time—"sort of an anti-hero." Girls, in turn, are for him to be used and left. But his "bad boy" masculinity is repeatedly marked as a mask or performance. There are many other things about him which mark him off as different: his sensitivity which he tries to hide, his interest in arts, literature, nature, cooking, sewing, etc. He has musical talent and well-manicured nails. He talks to his bike. For the father of the female protagonist (Nisha Verma), God has no future, no looks, no money, nothing. God's contempt for work is exactly what Nisha likes in him. She feels he is a genius (her father counter-asks "Genius at what? Living off other people?"):

> "And unlike other boys, he didn't *want* to work. I thought that was terrific. He actually rejected work. He had contempt for it. I told my father that with a lot of pride, during an argument. He nearly fell off his easy chair in anger." (*Sultry Days* 14)

God, a working class boy, is actually trying to reject the masculinist role forced on him by the patriarchal society. He is rejecting the "breadwinner" role thrust on him. Being from a working class family, it's not going to be too easy to perform this role satisfactorily. (It must be noted here that even gays in Dé's fiction fulfill the "breadwinner" role efficiently.) The qualities Nisha sees in God are worth quoting in full:

> "God could quote from the Upanishads. He had read Don Quixote in the original Spanish. He knew how to pronounce and eat escargots. He could tell you all sorts of interesting things about insects. Or rain forests. He knew all the Beatles songs by heart. And was on first name terms with several painters and poets. He could cook and sew. And he knew how to fix the world's best fluffy omelettes. Dogs, cats and other animals were instinctively drawn to him. He could tie a tiny bandage around a house sparrow's injured leg. Or repair a torn wing with cello tape. I'd watched him bottle-feed nine hungry boxer puppies when their mother had died delivering them. He was fantastic with electronic gadgets. He enjoyed the opera as much as Bade Ghulam Ali. And he had seen *Citizen Kane* fourteen times.... He'd stitched me a blouse once, using bandhni scarves and mirror-work pieces. While walking down a dirty road, he'd spot a gulmohur tree in the distance and stop to admire it. He created hair-ornaments for me using fresh green leaves, marigolds and twigs...." (*Sultry Days* 14-15)

The "bad boy masculinity" mask he sports often threatens to slip off. And he is embarrassed when he feels it slipping. He is clearly embarrassed about those qualities in him which have something to do even remotely with "femininity"—creating, nurturing, being sensitive, emotional, etc. He derides the men in whom he sees some of the "feminine" qualities by calling them "queer." For example, when Nisha calls Lucio sensitive as he notices her shampooed hair, pre-menstrual pimples, her make-up, etc., God laughs derisively and says,

> "Sensitive, my ass. Moony—that's what, stupid bugger. Must be a queer—lipstick, pimples, saris ... ha!" (*Sultry Days* 67)

The traditional view tends to equate masculinity with domination and power (Kaufman, 1994). His real fear then seems to be "not fear of women but of being ashamed or humiliated in front of other men, or being dominated by stronger men" (Leverenz, 1986: 451). As Leverenz points out, homophobia is a central organizing principle of our cultural definition of manhood. God seems to be haunted by this fear: the fear that other men will unmask him, emasculate him, reveal to him and the world that he does not measure up, that he is not real man. And that is why he wears the mask of 'rugged masculinity.'

As the novel progresses, he starts changing. Most alarmingly, he starts pursuing upward mobility and starts conforming more and more with the upper-class values that he scorned so much earlier. He gives up cooking, sewing, playing the flute, even talking to his bike. God is the only major male character in Dé's fiction who is neither born in the richy-rich class nor is able to make it to it. He is the elder son of a communist who lives in a *chawl*.[3] The narrator seems almost apologetic when she says,

> And although he poured scorn on the Commies, he did believe in the philosophy which was understandable given his background. (*Sultry Days* 14)

And in spite of all his later "wheeling and dealing," God ends up dying "like a dog," "defiant and alone" in a hospital, "gone off in a puff of foul-smelling smoke without saying goodbye to anyone." From the very start we know that he is doomed as he neither belongs to the upper classes and nor is "the rugged bad boy" he tries to appear. Hence, he can't make it to the "can-dos" category.

Incidentally, majority of the "can-dos" happen to be Mehras, Aroras, Mehrotras, Agarwals, etc.[4] However, it must be mentioned that even in the case of the "can-do" Punjabi, Haryani and Marwari communities, Dé does not bother to create/represent their typical culture with any depth and serious specificity. Not going beyond the descriptions of branded clothes and accessories and the superficial references to "parhatas soaked in ghee" and oily "pakoras," she prefers a general cultural vagueness and non-specificity. A typical technique she uses is of avoiding the surnames of the people as far as possible. For example,

> "Have to go to the Lala's house to see his cars and paintings."
>
> "Which Lala? You mean the guy who lives in that absurd-looking bungalow and behaves like an eighteenth century feudal lord?" (*Sultry Days* 98)

In the absence of the surnames, it becomes impossible to make any inferences about the region from which the person hails or the caste to which he belongs. An even better technique Dé uses (and to a greater extent) is that of avoiding even the first name! For example,

> "'His next project is with that sexy child from France. What's her name? That Muslim female who smokes Ganja all the time and is hooked up with some German'" (*Sultry Days* 121)

The man who presides over the poetry reading sessions of the 'Anglo-Indian Poets Association' and who is the founder-editor of the first Indian literary quarterly—*Plume*—(in *Sultry Days*), is just called D.O.M. (the Dirty Old Man). God's father is just a 'comrade.'

This non-specificity is not accidental. It is a carefully wrought strategy Dé shares with numerous other mass culture products, for example, popular Hindi films. Cultural non-specificity is deliberately aimed at so as to allow reader's/audience's easy identification with the leading male character. Dé consequently tries to reap the benefits of thus created pseudo pan-Indian culture which seems to make possible a single unproblematic pan-Indian masculinity and pan-Indian femininity. That is, bypassing problematic issues of caste, class, religion, race, community and language differences, a single, homogenous, 'Indian culture' is made to seem exist which automatically renders the possibility of masculinit*ies* and femininit*ies* unimaginable.

Thus the Masculinity mapped by Dé in her Mumbai is nothing other than hegemonic masculinity resting on subordination, heterosexuality and homophobia. It is used by one section of the men to savor and retain their superior status and to subordinate women and other men. Über physicality, heterosexuality, exaggerated sexual prowess, violence, overconfidence, fearlessness, impassive nature, high socio-economic status are the intrinsic characteristics of this hegemonic masculinity. Connell (1995: 156) states that hegemonic masculinity has social authority and is not easy to challenge openly. Dé does not bother to challenge it. As James D. Reimer puts it, "it is not sufficient to know the limitations and negative effects of our present ideals manhood. There also must be a recognition and reinforcement of positive alternatives to traditional masculine ideals and behaviours." (Reimer, 1987: 98). Some women writers like Toni Morrison, Leslie Silko, Louise Erdrich have started doing this. However, the mass entertainer in Dé seems to have overpowered the female writer and she ends up endorsing 'the normative and normalizing function' of hegemonic masculinity (Donaldson, 1993).

Another important phenomenon observed in Dé is the conflation of distinct versions of Indian masculinity. Meanings of masculinity vary across cultures and communities and they "admit to cultural borrowings" (Cornwell and Lindisfarne, 1994:12). So it is possible to "conflate" masculinities imported from elsewhere with that of a particular community to produce new configurations. Dé grafts the qualities and the ideology of the "*kshatriya*" model of Indian masculinity[5] onto the "*vaishya*" community in Mumbai hailing mainly from Gujarat, Punjab, Haryana and Marwar, thus making these men physically very strong, attractive, powerful, prone to violence, and womanizers with exaggerated sexual prowess. They still retain some of the qualities associated with the "vaishya" men: shrewdness, money-mindedness, expertise in calculations, excellent managerial capabilities, keen eye for profit and opportunities and so on. But gone are other qualities like physical frailty and the tendency to give more importance to money than to even women and sex.[6]

This grafting of "*kshatriya*" model of Indian masculinity onto the "*vaishya*" community is necessitated because the power to purchase (economic status) and to enjoy (sexual prowess) become the only important qualities in a space (Mumbai) mapped as "the Ultimate Whore."

Notes

1. Shobha Dé (b. 7 January 1948) is an Indian columnist and novelist. She was a successful model, had a career in journalism and founded and edited three magazines—*Stardust*, *Society*, and *Celebrity*. At present, she is a freelance writer and columnist for several newspapers and magazines. Her other works include *Superstar India*, *Snapshots*, *Spouse: The Truth About Marriage*, *Speedpost, Surviving Men, Selective Memory*, *Second Thoughts*, *Small Betrayals*, *Shooting from the Hip* and *Uncertain Liaisons*.
2. For the sake of variety, some foreigners are also thrown in; for example, the Australian husband of Asha Rani in *Starry Nights* and a 'Black' (just called 'Stash') in *Sultry Days*. When Asha Rani is returning to her Australian husband, she has sex with an elderly Indian in the plane, thus symbolically rejecting the white heterosexual male and foreshadowing the actual rejection. In case of Stash one socialite says, "Every woman must have a black experience—at least once in her life. And Stash is mine."
3. Regarding his caste, we are left clueless. Except that his name is "Deb or Dev" (does that mean he is a Bengali?) there is no other information given.
4. Peculiarly, the "males" in the lesbian pairs of Dé are never from Punjabi-Haryani-Gujarati-Marwari Hindu communities. Feroze (a Parsee) and Linda are both non-Hindus and Minx is an Iyyengar, that is a South-Indian Hindu.
5. See Nandy (1983) for an account of the impact of the British rule on the restructuring of masculinities in India and Sinha (1995) and O'Hanlon (1997) for a challenge to his thesis.

6. As seen by other Indian communities, including Maharashtrians. This version appears only once: Marwari lady Bindiya's husband in *Sultry Days* is described as a "stupid person" who "joined the family business without even finishing school. Now he is good at only one thing—making money." He does not have even the slightest suspicion of his wife's affair as "he was so busy setting up his factory. He used to be away from morning till late at night" (*Sultry Days*, 125-26).

Works Cited

Connell, R.W. *Masculinities*. Cambridge, UK: Polity Press, 1995.

Cornwall, A. and L. Nancy. *Dislocating Masculinity: Comparative Ethnographies*. New York: Routledge, 1994. As quoted in Petersen, Alan. "Theorizing Masculinities: 'Men's Studies' and the Politics of Knowledge." *Men and Masculinities* 5.3 (2003): 54-69.

Dé, Shobha. *Socialite Evenings*. New Delhi: Penguin Books India, 1989.

____. *Starry Nights*. New Delhi: Penguin Books India, 1991.

____. *Strange Obsession*. New Delhi: Penguin Books India, 1992.

____. *Sultry Days*. New Delhi: Penguin Books India, 1994.

Donaldson, M. "What Is Hegemonic Masculinity?" *Theory and Society*. Special Issue: Masculinities 22.5 (1993): 643-57.

Kaufman, M. "Men, Feminism and Men's Contradicting Experiences of Power." *Theorizing Masculinities*. Ed. H. Brod and M. Kaufman. Thousand Oaks, CA: Sage Publications, 1994. 145-46.

Leverenz, D. "Manhood, Humiliation and Public Life: Some Stories." *Southwest Review* 71 (1986).

Messner, M. "'Changing Men' and Feminist Politics in the United States." *Theory and Society*. Special Issue: Masculinities 5 (1993): 723-37.

Nandy, Ashis. *The Intimate Enemy: Loss and Recovery of Self under Colonialism*. Delhi: Oxford UP, 1983.

O'Hanlon, R. "Issues of Masculinity in North Indian History: The Bangash Nawabs of Farrukhabad." *Indian Journal of Gender Studies* 4.1 (1997): 1-19.

Phillips, R.S. "Spaces of Adventure and Cultural Politics of Masculinity: R.M. Ballantyne and *The Young Fur Traders*." *Environment and Planning*. D: Society and Space 13.5 (1995): 591-608.

_____. *Mapping Men and Empire: A Geography of Adventure.* London: Routledge, 1997.

Sinha, Mrinalini. *Colonial Masculinity: The 'Manly Englishman' and the 'Effeminate Bengali' in the Late Nineteenth Century.* Manchester: Manchester UP, 1995. Rpt. New Delhi: Kali Press, 1997.

Sparke, Matthew. "Displacing the Field in Fieldwork: Masculinity, Metaphor and Space." *Body Space: Destabilizing Geographies of Gender and Sexuality.* Ed. N. Duncan. New York and London: Routledge, 1996. 212-33.

7

"Tridib's Gastric": The Contradictory Sexual Politics of *The Shadow Lines*

Stephen da Silva

Abstract

Postcolonial theory challenges the pieties of Indian nationalism and the fetishizing of national borders, concerns that are resonant with the representation of perverse masculinity in *The Shadow Lines*. In his novel, Amitav Ghosh uses a scatological idiom and an associated perverse narrative logic to undermine the temporal and spatial certainties that sustain both the fictions of colonialism and nationalism, as well as those of compulsory heterosexuality. This subversion, however, coexists with a conventional male homosocial plot in which the historical and personal pain of male subjects is healed through the figure of a mediating, regenerative woman. The contradictory sexual politics of this text call into question any necessary connection between subversions of the heterosexual norm and modernist/postmodernist deformations of realist narratives and teleological models of history.

Amitav Ghosh's *The Shadow Lines* uses a scatological idiom and an associated perverse narrative logic to undermine the temporal and spatial certainties that sustain both the fictions of colonialism and nationalism, as well as those of compulsory heterosexuality. This subversion, however, coexists with a conventional male homosocial plot in which the historical and personal pain of male subjects is healed through the figure of a mediating, regenerative woman.[1] The contradictory sexual politics of this novel call into question any necessary connection between subversions of the norm and modernist and postmodernist deformations of realist narratives and teleological models of history.

In both sexological and psychoanalytic developmental narratives, the perverse pleasures of the immature child are sacrificed to attain the goal of heterosexual maturity.[2] In particular, adult anal pleasure is proscribed as a mode of regression. Drawing on the language of evolution, late-nineteenth-century sexologists viewed sodomy as a form of atavism. Sherwood Williams describes the sexologist Wilhelm Bolsche's characteristic view of sodomy's atavistic position in phylogenetic evolution:

> In the bestseller *Das Liebsleben in Der Natur.* (1893-1903; *Love-Life in Nature*), Wilhelm Bolsche argued...that the desire for anal sex implied a regression to an earlier evolutionary period. According to Bolsche, mankind's first ancestors were hermaphrodite; after them on the evolutionary cycle, however, from a salamander on up, cloacal love continued to play a decisive role for a long time.... The crocodile was finally able to move beyond this primitive means of conception by creating a protopenis.... Thus, when modern men experience an urge to penetrate the anus, they are reverting to a precrocodillian form of desire. (727)

Williams's discussion focuses on the "penetrat[ive]" "urge," but presumably by Bolsche's logic, the desire to be penetrated anally is even more archaic than the desire to penetrate anally since the latter appetite's satisfaction does not require a crocodillian appendage.

While Sigmund Freud with some courage pointed out that the disgust provoked by anal pleasure was purely conventional, he too represented anal desire as developmental phase that must be sacrificed on the way to genital maturity. In *Three Essays on the Theory of Sexuality*, after linking "disgust" to the "purely conventional" one page before, Freud goes on to associate the condemnation of sodomy with conventional disgust: "Where the anus is concerned.... It is disgust which stamps that sexual aim as a perversion" (152). Unhappily, in that same text, Freud maintains, "in inverted types a predominance of archaic constitutions and primitive psychic mechanisms is regularly to be found" as demonstrated by "the retention of the erotic significance of the anal zone" (146). Again, he associates anal desire with archaic, even bestial sexual practices in his case history on the Wolf Man: "copulation from behind—*more ferarum* [in the manner of the beasts] may, after all, be regarded phylogenetically as the older form [of intercourse]" (41). In *Civilization and Its Discontents*, Freud explains that this supposedly older form of eroticism is supposed to succumb to the "organic repression of civilization" (100). Both the evolutionary and the psychoanalytic narratives, then, use a spatial (i)logic to reinforce their temporal paradigms: in both accounts, a rigid boundary is drawn between the "front" associated with genital maturity and the "back" associated with the utilitarian task of evacuation and the renounced pleasures of pre-socialized childhood.

Colonial and nationalist models of history are as teleological as these psychosexual paradigms. Uday Singh Mehta has pointed out how salient to British imperial discourse in India was the idea that "India is a child for which the empire offers 'tutelage'" (32).[3]

Teaching his childlike charges to move forward to civilized modernity legitimates the colonialist sacrificing the traditions of indigenous peoples. While the nationalist is often deeply nostalgic, like the colonialist, she values the future because it promises the recuperation of an imaginary national unity that existed prior to foreign infiltration. The nationalist fetishizes borders because she sees them as physically liberalizing the truths of history.

The narrator's grandmother in *The Shadow Lines* exemplifies nationalist attitudes towards time and space. She passionately values the idea of a national tradition. Hence, she disapproves of Ila's living in England: she tells the narrator, "Ila has no right to live there. She doesn't belong there. It took those people a long time to build that country; hundreds of years" (76).[4]

Linked to this history teacher's idealization of tradition is her naïve faith in national borders. Not realizing that borders in maps are conventional constructions, she wonders when she flies back to her home in East Pakistan whether she will be able to see some tangible dividing line between India and East Pakistan like "the long black line with green on one side and scarlet on the other...in a school atlas" (148).[5]

In the nationalist narrative, local interests must be sacrificed to achieve that fetishized national unity. To quote further from the narrator's grandmother's description of why Ila does not belong in England,

> Everyone who lives there has earned his right to be there with blood; with their brother's blood and their father's blood and their son's blood. They know they're a nation because they've drawn their borders with blood.... Once that happens people forget that they were born this or that, Muslim or Hindu, Bengali or Punjabi; they become a family born of the same pool of blood.... (76)

It is apt that the narrator's grandmother should visualize the unified nation as a family[6] because just as familial ideology wilfully forgets the perverse pleasures of the child, so he can move forward to being a patriarch (while the grandmother vaguely refers several times to "they," her opening sentence, "everyone who lives there has earned *his*," etc. reveals that the real subject of the nationalist narrative is male), so too the local interests of Muslim, Hindu, Bengali, or Punjabi must be willfully forgotten to achieve India's national unity.[7]

As has been mentioned above, men are salient to the nationalist grandmother's narrative—brothers, fathers, and sons shed their blood to form those mystified borders—bearing out Suvir Kaul's contention that "the weight of sexual and cultural definition is borne unequally by men and women, with men as the putative agents of socio-cultural transition and women as its more or less traumatized subjects" (143).[8] The primal image that haunts the grandmother's memory embodies the homosocial phallocentrism of nationalist mythologies: in the grandmother's imagination, the figure who incarnates

India's lost national promise is her terrorist classmate whom she had seen arrested by the British in Dhaka:

> the shy bearded boy was standing now, his face impassive, his back erect, his gaze fixed on the policeman, clear direct and challenging. He seemed absolutely unmoved.... Neither then nor later when they handcuffed him and led him from the room, did he betray his fear or allow his gaze to drop from the officer's face. (37)

Note, the phallic rectitude of the nationalist, his lack of feminizing emotion. Mark also how the English officer and the Indian male nationalist lock gazes in this tableau, while the Indian woman looks on, not truly an actor in this drama, only able vicariously to participate through her identification with the male nationalist. This nationalist tableau uncannily replicates an imperial fantasy, for as Revathi Krishnaswamy points out in her reading of Kipling, in the colonial homosocial imaginary, the hope of bridging the gulf between East and West rests uneasily upon the fantasy of Englishman and colonialist subject, "two strong men," "standing face to face though they come from the ends of the earth" (Krishnaswamy 15).[9] While the two men are locked in a kind of intimacy, they are separate phallic entities, as opposed to a dangerous anal fluidity that I will argue becomes associated with the figure of Tridib.

If women cannot be active agents in this nationalist drama, they do have a role to play in the domestic realm. The narrator's grandmother, who is a headmistress, attempts her own version of nation building within her school by mandating that "every girl who opted for home science ought to be taught how to cook at least one dish that was the speciality of some other country than her own" (114). It is entirely appropriate that Ghosh should use food to signify the nationalist grandmother's desire to erase local differences since he will use the figure of excrement to subvert nationalist pretensions to achieve a transcendent unity.[10]

The narrator's grandmother hopes that her grandson might recuperate the lost nationalist promise represented by her terrorist classmate: she tells the narrator, "[National unity] is what you have to achieve for India" (76). Specifically, she exhorts her grandson to acquire a virile physique because "you can't build a strong country...without building a strong body" (8). If, as Partha Chatterjee has convincingly argued, one strain of Indian male nationalism affiliated itself with a stereotype of idealized pure, asexual Indian femininity, as opposed to the worldly masculinity represented by colonialism (147-48), another strain of Indian nationalism challenged the colonial stereotype of the effeminate Bengali babu by valorizing an exaggerated physical virility (Roy Indian 107-10). The way to overcome the humiliation of colonial feminization would be to aspire to a strong male body.

In order to achieve his historic goal, the narrator must use his time productively. "Wasted time," the narrator's grandmother sternly tells him "begins to stink" (11). Again, through the figure of the toothbrush, Ghosh returns to an oral-alimentary idiom to figure the grandmother's conservative attitude toward time: "For [my grandmother], time was like a toothbrush: it went mouldy if it wasn't used" (4). The nationalist grandmother's desire to transmute stinky wasted time into an idealized product, a unified nation, is isomorphic with the logic of capitalism in which, as Dominique Laporte has argued, stinky matter/shit is transmuted into deodorized money (76-95), a logic that has been satirized by Ghosh in his first novel *The Circle of Reason*.[11]

For the grandmother, Tridib, who is supposedly "working on a Ph.D. in archaeology" but prefers not to engage in productive labour and spends most of his time with "the young men...at the street-corner addas and tea-stalls" embodies the seductive dangers of that temporal stink. So, it is no wonder that she should jealously try to guard the narrator from his friendship.[12] Unlike the phallic, self-contained nationalist, Tridib is associated with a fluid, uncontrolled anality: he regularly "drops in" to the narrator's house to "shit" "the rivers of hard-boiled tea he had drunk at roadside stalls all over south Calcutta," "a condition known to us as Tridib's Gastric" (6-7).

Juxtaposing Tridib's fluid excrement with the mystified blood that the grandmother invokes in her celebration of national tradition is instructive. Blood, according to the grandmother, is something that binds the national family together. By contrast, while Tridib "drops in" on the family to expel his waste, that liquid waste comes from outside the family.[13] Further, while the nationalist heroes of the grandmother's allegory; heroically choose to shed their blood, Tridib's gastric masters and dispossesses him: Although the possessive or genitive phrase "Tridib's gastric" might suggest that Tridib owns his gastric, the following passage makes clear that it is "Tridib's bowels" that are the real agent; he is merely the object of the sentence, neither in control of his body nor the verb in the sentence, "Every once in a while a rumble in [Tridib's] bowels would catch him unawares on the streets" (4). Inasmuch as, being mastered or dispossessed is culturally coded as feminine, Tridib's gastric also feminizes him.

It is true that Tridib dies in a riot, his "throat" "cut from ear to ear," shedding his blood in the conventionally heroic, masculine mode that the narrator's grandmother celebrates. However, May will explain to the narrator that Tridib's death in the forgotten riot was pointless. He dies to prevent May from being attacked by the mob, but she believes that "the mob wouldn't have touched me, an English memsahib" (246). In the grandmother's nationalist myth, the blood of heroic men is productively recycled into the nationalist family, but like Tridib's shit, even the blood that he sheds is excessive and wasteful, an exuberant expenditure that cannot be productively recuperated in nationalist terms.[14]

The link between Tridib's anal excess and male homoeroticism is suggested by the fact that the rivers of tea he is shitting were consumed in the company of young men at tea stalls and street corner addas all over Calcutta. Indeed, we learn from Dipesh Chakrabarty that there was a whole discourse associating addas with misogyny and an evasion of domestic responsibility: "Nripendrakrisha Chattopadhyay... asserted 'the biggest natural enemy of adda are [sic] women' (qtd. in Chakrabarty 207); in a similar vein, Nirad Chaudhri declared, "The strong herd instincts of the natives of Calcutta has virtually killed family life. There is no custom among them of a man sitting with his wife and children in the evening" (qtd. in Chakrabarty 185). It is precisely Tridib and his male friends' neglect of "their mothers and wives" that provokes the narrator's grandmother's contempt. Specifically, she evokes the image of "the dung heap" to describe the fate of these young men's mothers: "All fail cases, she would sniff; think of their poor mothers, flung out on dung heaps" (5). Mired in unproductive male homoerotic pleasure, traditionally associated with sodomy and "dung," idle Tridib and his male friends consign their mothers and by implication the idealized, feminized nation, Mother India, to the dung heap. Finally, spatial metaphors evocative of sodomy underline the connection between Tridib and a suspect male homoeroticism: for instance, we are told that the narrator "doubles back through back lanes" to avoid his grandmother's surveillance and meet Tridib (8).[15]

Tridib's gastric may originate in idle, wasteful, homoerotic pleasure at the addas, but even his professional, scholarly activity does not meet the disciplinary requirements for conventional masculinity. Tridib has a passion for archaeology, but the nationalist grandmother refuses to take that passion seriously. Perhaps part of her contempt springs from archaeology's intimate attention to the materiality of history, a quite literal grubbing among the debris and shit of history, one might say, rather than an allegiance to some idealized national historical narrative.[16] For the grandmother, the emblem of male intellectual success is "a marble bust in the corridors of Calcutta University or the National Library" (7), for such a bust has no real body, no lower appetites. Not only does Tridib deal with the shitty materiality of history, his epistemological stance might be described as feminine or feminizing: Tridib tells the narrator "that one could never know anything except through desire," "a longing for everything that was not in oneself, a torment of the flesh" (29). If in a Cartesian epistemological model, the observing subject disinterestedly observes the object, and if in one version of nationalist epistemology, historical knowledge is material that is appropriated for the national good, in Tridib's model, the observing subject is unmanned by his desire for the otherness of knowledge.[17]

Tridib's fluid excess[18] is explicitly contrasted with the nationalist grandmother's dry, contained, dare one say constipated worldview: we are told that the omelette that the grandmother offers him after his visit to her lavatory is "a leathery little squiggle...which would lie balefully on its plate challenging Gastric to battle" (5). The "leathery little squiggle" appropriately represents the grandmother's philosophy because it has solid defined boundaries, and, as we have already seen, boundaries or borders are important to the grandmother "because" "she liked things to be neat and in place" (145).

The narrator's phrase "things to be in place" is particularly resonant if we consider it as a sort of unconscious echo of Mary Douglas's crucial definition of dirt as "matter out of place" (Douglas 35).[19] Laporte reminds us of the importance of regulating dirt to the civilizing mission of imperialism: "the barbarian craps where he pleases; the conqueror emblazons his phrase with the primordial prohibition, 'No shitting allowed' (57) and goes on to cite the passage in James Joyce's Ulysses where Professor McHugh observes that—

> ...the Roman like the Englishman who follows in his footsteps brought to every new shore on which he set his foot...only his cloacal obsession. He gazed about him in his toga and he said, "It is meet to be here. Let us construct a water closet." (Joyce qtd. in Laporte 57)

Ghosh also satirizes the imperial obsession with regulating and disciplining waste: when May, an English woman, visits his house the narrator's grandmother's uncle asks nervously, "What if she wants to shit? My father always said that the first thing to remember if a foreigner comes to your house is to buy toilet paper. He knew: he read books" (209). That a westernized literate Indian should recognize the importance of having toilet paper is not surprising since nationalist elites necessarily internalized and replicated imperial values.[20]

Joyce's and Ghosh's satire aptly captures the salience of sanitation to the British imperial civilizing mission, as well as to the unifying mission of nationalism. Subaltern matter must be disciplined and regulated: clear cut boundaries must be established to exclude abjected waste, dirt, matter out of place.[21] In that sense, the nationalist grandmother's fetishizing of borders is analogous (anal-ogous) to the British imperial drive to regulate waste.

The analogy between policing borders and regulating shit is amplified in the grotesque bifurcation of the grandmother's house in Dhaka. In the course of a quarrel, the grandmother's father and uncle choose to divide the family house. The absurd division "partition[s] a lavatory, bisecting an old commode" (121). As Meenakshi Mukherjee has pointed out, "houses have a synecdochal relation to countries in this novel" (262), so the verb "partition" implicitly evokes the 1947 partition of India and Pakistan. Just as borders between the two newly founded nations arbitrarily ran through the middle of villages resulting in horrendous bloodshed, so too the grotesque boundary between the two halves of the house is an irrational construction. Ironically, one of the same old men responsible for fragmenting the family house insightfully deconstructs the arbitrary nature of all borders: he declares, "I don't believe in India Shindia. It's all very well you're going away now, but suppose when you get there, they decide to draw another line somewhere?" (211). Indeed, "another line" was drawn not on the Indian but on the Pakistani side of the border: the novel consistently refers to the grandmother's birth place as "East Pakistan," the appropriate name for that region during the time period over which the action of the novel takes place; but at the time of the novel's writing and publication, a line had long since been drawn between East and West Pakistan, creating the state of Bangla Desh.

Rather than monumentalizing borders, as nationalists do, Ghosh suggests through the narrator's voice that "a place does not merely exist...it has to be invented in one's imagination" (21). These "inventions" are invariably informed by subjective desires and interests. Thus, the narrator associates "Cairo" with "the pointed arch in the mosque of Ibn Tulun...and the Great Pyramid of Cheops," associates Cairo, in other words, with the seductive lessons learned from the would be archaeologist Tridib. On the other hand, Ila, who has spent all her life traveling around the world with her diplomat father associates "Cairo" with an airport where "the Ladies is way on the other side of the departure lounge" (20). To state the obvious, once again a bathroom is being invoked to call into question the positivist spatial certainties of nationalism. Places are constructions that are informed by one's subjective desires.[22]

In addition to disrupting nationalist spatial models, Tridib's gastric also calls into question a nationalist model of history. As Anjali Roy points out, national histories are singular, and they subordinate or exclude "local" "microhistories" which do not neatly fit the main story line (42).[23] Consider, for instance, how difficult it is for the narrator to find about the Calcutta riots of 1964 from turning to history books. The library devotes "whole shelves of books," "political analyses, memoirs, tracts" to India's wars with China and Pakistan in 1962 and 1965 respectively, but he can find nothing on the riots (217). So, he has to turn to the contemporary newspapers to try and find out what provoked those riots. However, even the newspapers are dominated by stories of national, rather than local interest. Thus, the newspaper for January 10, 1964 in which the narrator finally finds information about the Calcutta riots focuses on India's test match with England and Kamraj's speech at the 68th session of the Congress Party in Bhubaneshwar. The story of the riots is relegated to a "short report at the bottom of the page" (218). Benedict Anderson has suggested that the ritual of reading the daily newspapers binds together the members of the national imagined community (33-34). Given the affective investment that former British colonies invest in cricket matches, particularly a cricket match against their erstwhile imperial master, it is not surprising that the story of the test match should displace the story of a local riot, though this displacement reflects an epistemic nationalist violence in some ways more insidious than the literal violence of the riots.

That Ghosh should choose to use Kamraj's speech to the Congress Party session in Bhubaneswar as an emblem for the imagined national community's narrative is also significant: While Jawaharlal Nehru, India's first prime minister, was alive in January 1964, he would die later that year, and Kamraj would play a key role in choosing his successor. When Nehru's successor, Lal Bahadur Shastri, died in 1966, Kamraj would again play a key role in propelling Indira Gandhi to the premiership. His pivotal role at the party convention in 1964 played no small part in allowing him to become a king maker in Indian national politics. Here is the historical narrative that Kamraj presents in his speech:

> Even during the days of the freedom struggle, the Congress organization had broadly indicated that the society which it envisaged after achieving independence was...a progressive one based on the modern concepts of social, political, and economic equality and justice.... When the masses realised that the Indian National Congress stood for the betterment of their economic condition and their social progress, they joined the organization in large numbers.
>
> (www.indiannationalcongress.com/history/presidents/k_kamaraj.html)

In this story, a monolithic organization offers the masses of India the promises of modernity, and the masses enthusiastically respond creating a national community. It's a story that conveniently forgets the immense heterogeneity of the Congress Party. As Ashwini Kumar, a journalist writing two years before Kamraj made his historic speech, rightly pointed out the "Congress Party...is no party in a real sense but only a collection of diverse interests and loyalties" (35). Further Kamraj's story of the masses waking to modernity willfully forgets local and regional differences. This is particularly ironic because among the North Indian dominated national leadership, Kamraj stood out as a Tamilian who linguistically and racially was different from the Congress

Party elite. He was a politician, moreover, who had played a key role in South Indian regional politics as the chief minister of Madras state (modern Tamil Nadu). Kamraj famously was one of the few Congress Party leaders who did not speak English at a time when English acted as the national language to a far greater extent than Hindi did. Despite personally embodying local difference, Kamraj tells a familiar story of a unified nation, a story that has to forget minor regional stories like the riots that are so salient to the narrator's life. And Kamraj's story predictably dominates the archival record.

For Ghosh, Marxist internationalism is just as blind to regional difference as democratic nationalism. Malik, a Marxist, accompanies the narrator to the library. When the narrator cannot find a record of the riots, Malik contemptuously dismisses their importance, "it [the riot] must have been a local thing.... Malik was bored now. He stole a look at his watch" (216-17). I read that watch as a signifier for a Marxist model of history. In a revolutionary emancipatory narrative, local contingencies are a waste of time.[24] Ila says something similar to Malik when she and the narrator are in London: after infuriating the narrator by declaring that "nothing really important ever happens" in India, she goes on, "Well, of course, there are famines, riots, and disasters.... But these are local things, after all—not like revolutions or anti-fascist wars, nothing that sets a political example to the world, nothing that's really remembered" (102). According to Ila's arrogant totalizing view of history, not to be remembered is to be unimportant, so the local is unimportant. Both the grand narratives of nationalism and Marxism, then, have no space to narrate the riots which are so central to the narrator's memories. Highly suggestively, given my emphasis, Mukherjee frames "the narrator's desperate search...to recover lost events" "as a resistance to being swallowed up by narratives made up by others" (264). If we swallow Mukherjee's reading, we might think of the narrator and Tridib's personal histories as an obstinately unassimilable excremental supplement that will not be seamlessly digested by the national or Marxist narrative.

In contrast to the monologic narratives represented by the papers and the history books, Tridib offers us multiple stories that are invariably informed by subjective interests, and these stories are figuratively linked to his fluid anal excess. "Everyone," Tridib contends "lives in a story...my [the narrator's] grandmother, my father, his father, Lenin, Einstein...they all lived in stories because stories are all there is to live in" (179).[25]

Indeed, the clause "everyone lives in a story" does not adequately capture the multiple narratives within which we are inscribed. In particular, Tridib has the propensity to revise his life story continually and this is precisely what makes him so both so exasperating and seductive to his friends. Ghosh metaphorically links the plural narratives, "disconcerting streams of talk...that come gushing out of" Tridib to his perverse gastric (9).[26]

But *The Shadow Lines* does more than describe Tridib's perverse historical model, it dramatizes it. As readers, we are faced with multiple, overlapping stories that we constantly have to evaluate. For instance, with the narrator, we hear from Ila how she was rescued by Nick Price from being bullied at school. Yet May's version of the story is very different: in her story, Nick "didn't stop to help Ila.... He didn't want to be seen with Ila" (75).

Even more disturbing for the reader of traditional realist fiction than the multiple versions of stories is the wide gap between the "fibula...the order of events referred to by the narrative" and "the sjuzet" "the order of events presented in narrative discourse" (Brooks 12). Events are presented radically out of chronological sequence so that as readers we have to negotiate several different temporal moments within the course of a page or two. Take the opening of the novel, for instance, "In 1939, thirteen years before I was born, my aunt Mayadebi, went to England with her son and Tridib." Although the opening prepositional phrase, "in 1939" might seem to suggest a comfortable, defined temporal moment, the very next clause throws us thirteen years forward to the narrator's birth. The second paragraph begins, "It startles me now to discover how readily the name comes off my pen as 'Mayadebi.' As readers, we are unclear as to the exact meaning of the shifter "now," and how exactly it relates to 1939 or the year of the narrator's birth. The following paragraph complicates matters even further, "Mayadebi was twenty-nine when they left and Tridib was eight. Over the years...I have come to believe that I was eight too when Tridib first talked to me about that journey. I remember very hard trying to imagine him back to my age." Here we have yet another chronological zone: a moment when the narrator was perhaps eight years old. But even within this scene, the verb "remember" reminds us of the "now" from which the narrator is now reconstructing that moment (3).

Or, take the narrator's meeting with May. It is after this meeting that the narrator will learn how Tridib died, so it effectively is the conclusion of the fabula. However, it appears on page 13 of a 246-page novel. In that meeting, May refers back to the time when she met the narrator in Calcutta. But she also refers back to 1959 when she first began to correspond with Tridib at his written request. Note the vertiginous number of chronological shifts that appear within the span of a short paragraph:

> *Later*, when we were eating our dinner, I discovered that in 1959, when he *was twenty-seven and she nineteen*, they had begun a long correspondence. Tridib had written first.... He had always sent Mrs. Price cards at Christmas, *ever since they left in London in 1940*. But *that year* [if other readers have similar reactions to mine, it takes a moment to figure out that "that year" refers to 1959] he had inscribed a little note in her card saying that he remembered her very well, thought she could not possibly remember him...and he hoped that *some day she would find time* to write to him. She was both touched and intrigued; she *had already heard* a great deal about him. (17, my emphasis)

When Kaul says that Tridib "teaches the narrator the contemporanaeity of the past" (277), "to be able to see historical memory as vital to any understanding of the present" (277), he domesticates the temporal wildness of the novel. I would argue that with its frequent shifts among time zones, the novel makes it extremely difficult to keep past and present apart; memory rather than serving to help in understanding the present merges complicatedly with present experience, so it is impossible to separate them into discrete entities. If, as critics like Lee Edelman have pointed out, the sodomite has been culturally condemned as one who preposterously confuses back and front, past and present, the pleasures of childhood with the proper genital pleasures of adulthood, then by analogy, *The Shadow Lines* might appropriately be described as a sodomitic narrative because it makes it impossible for readers to draw distinct boundaries between past and present, before and after (183), the kind of boundaries that so comfortingly inform teleological nationalist histories.[27]

And yet, even though *The Shadow Lines* so radically disrupts the spatial and temporal underpinnings of compulsory heterosexuality, its sexual politics at another level faithfully reflect that paradigm's trajectory. After all, however much the text may playfully trouble the concepts of "going" and "coming," it is divided into two sections entitled "Going Away" and "Coming Home." The novel begins with the narrator losing his beloved Tridib and it ends with his lying in May's arms learning the details of Tridib's death. I will concede that the emphasis on May's androgyny slightly problematizes describing her as maternal, "I saw her, picking her way through the last stragglers, her shoulders rolling, like a boxer's.... Her voice had a deep, gravelly, almost masculine texture" (15). However, the name "May" both partially echoes the name of Tridib's mother, Mayadebi, and recalls the first sentence of the novel, "In 1939, thirteen years before I was born.... Mayadebi went to England with her son Tridib," and it also evokes a Romantic thematics of regeneration associated with maternal nature and the month of May. At one level, then, May's arms represent the maternal home supposedly located outside history.[28] Further, through sleeping with May, who has slept with Tridib, the narrator vicariously recovers the lost male object of his desire, or "redeems" his pointless death to use May's theological idiom. Indeed there are several interlocking homosocial triangles sustaining the narrator and May's erotic encounter:[29] May can be said to mediate between Tridib and his English mentor Snipe, for he makes his first epistolary overture to her after hearing the story of Tristan and Isolde from Snipe. Of course, the story of Tristan and Isolde involves an erotic triangle among Tristan, Mark, and the mediating Isolde. To represent woman as the comforting maternal space outside history and to affirm male homosocial pathos are part of an all too familiar reactionary script, one that might seem to run counter to the values embodied by Tridib's gastric.

When the narrator first hears of "Tridib's Gastric," he imagines that it "was the name of an organ peculiar to Tridib—a kind of aching tooth that grew out of his belly button" (5). The tooth growing out of the belly button is a curiously phallic image, and in that sense, what the narrator considers a childish misunderstanding is actually a useful way of thinking of Tridib's gastric. Tridib's passive, fluid anality might seem to be anti-phallic, but one of its possible effects is precisely to consolidate and sustain the power of that phallic tooth and its masculinist conventions. The phallic tooth and the fluid gastric, it turns out, can quite comfortably coexist.

It is tempting to assume that modernist and post-modernist deformations of realist conventions necessarily have subversive effects. But I would argue that while it is productive to draw analogies between heterofamilial psychosexual narratives and the ideologies of colonialism and nationalism, one cannot assume that formally subverting those conventions necessarily results in progressive political effects. The effect of such gestures, as Colleen Lamos has pointed out in her discussion of postmodern irony, is "multivalent" and "contingent" (103). I have read Tridib's fluid gastric as a figure that challenges monologic nationalist history and rigid national borders. Less comfortingly, but not inconsistently, one might also read it as a figure for the multiple, sometimes contradictory, and never entirely predictable effects produced by narrative perversity.

Notes

1. Eve Kosofsky Sedgwick theorizes male homosociality in *Between Men: English Literature and Male Homosocial Desire*.
2. I feel justified in invoking Western discourses of sexology and psychoanalysis in reading a text set in India because there is textual evidence that these discourses are familiar to and often partially inform the assumptions of the middle-class Westernized characters in Ghosh's novels. For instance, in *The Shadow Lines* Ila both invokes and mocks psychonalysis when she accuses the narrator of suffering from "vagina envy" (19). In his first novel *The Circle of Reason*, Ghosh satirizes the scientistic pretensions of phrenology that was linked to sexology in its biologism and vulgar use of evolutionary logic. Further evidence of the importance of psychoanalysis and sexology for Westernized Indians of a certain class can be found in Ghosh's essay "The March of the Novel through History" where Ghosh points out that among the few non-literary works on his grandfather's bookshelf were "a few works of anthropology and psychology; books that had in some way filtered into the literary consciousness of the time.... *The Collected Works of Sigmund Freud*...Havelock Ellis and Malinowski on sexual behavior and so on" (www.amitavghosh.com/bookcase.html).
3. There is a growing body of persuasive scholarship exploring psychoanalysis' eurocentrism and complicity with colonialism—see, for instance, *Vishnu on Freud's Desk*, Hartnack, and Kovel. However, any attempt to insulate India from Western discourses like psychoanalysis, in the name of some kind of misguided cultural purity, would be to insist precisely on the clarity of those national borders which the novel most corrosively calls into question.
4. Amitav Ghosh discusses his impressions of Mehta's book, *Liberalism and Empire* and his correspondence with the historian in "Correspondence with Professor Dipesh Chakrabarty on *Provincializing Europe*" which can be found on Ghosh's website www.amitavghosh.com.

   In *In an Antique Land*, Ghosh also demonstrates that cultural miscomprehension often leads to one culture infantilizing another: The author and the Egyptian teenager Jabir have a conversation filled with cultural miscomprehension. Later, an astonished Jabir, speaking to his friends, patronizingly dismisses Ghosh: "he doesn't know a thing...not religion, not politics, not sex, just like a child" (63). Jabir's misprison of Ghosh's intellectual capacity is reminiscent of psychoanalytic accounts of fetishism: the male child gazing at the female genitalia does not visually register those genitalia. All he sees is the penis that is not there—she has nothing. Similarly, Jabir can only see the Egyptian values that Ghosh does not have; he cannot register Ghosh's values, "he doesn't know a thing."

Significantly, Jabir is only willing to respect Ghosh when he discovers that India is capable of producing technology, namely a water pump, "I stayed up a long time that night, marveling at the respect the water-pump had earned me; I tried to imagine where I would have stood in Jabir's eyes if mine had been a country that exported machines that were even bigger, better, and more impressive" (74). If in psychosexual developmental narratives, heterogenous desires must be subordinated to the telos of heterosexual union, Ghosh seems to suggest that transnationally cultural differences get subordinated to the telos of Western technological modernity. So, the Egyptian who reads the Indian as having "nothing" suddenly sees him with new respect when he registers that India has modern technology.

4. While Ghosh is critical of the grandmother's nationalist fetishizing of the past, he is equally critical of Ila's pathologically self-enclosed presentism: "For Ila the current was the real; it was as though she lived in the present which was like an airlock in a canal, shut away from the past and future by steel floodgates" (30). Fittingly, Ila is given a gift of an "automatic watch" "for her eighth birthday" since she denies history's significance and sees time as purely mechanical and functional (42).

5. The desire to substitute some literal line or grid in the place of amorphous, shifting borders haunts much postcolonial South Asian diasporic fiction. In Siddartha Deb's recent novel, *The Point of Return*, for instance, when Babu and his father are crossing the border between India and Bangladesh, we are told, "They stepped out to look at Bangladesh. There was nothing particular about the place where they had stopped.... Nothing save the topography distinguishing it, no flags, guns, signposts...not even the splash of fish interfered with the still landscape, the flattened out blank spaces with their soft colors running into each other, waiting for a black grid to impose meaning on the land" (66). The "soft colors" of "the blank spaces" "running into each other" intertextually resonates with

the image of the shadow lines in Ghosh's novels and the desire for a "black grid to impose meaning" could be used to describe the narrator's grandmother's investment in national borders in *The Shadow Lines*.

6. While the grandmother compares the unified nation to a family, Ghosh sets up an opposition between the family and the nation. In his cyber correspondence with Dipesh Chakraborty, Ghosh writes, "Two of my novels (*The Shadow Lines* and my more recent *The Glass Palace*) are centered on families. I know that for myself this is a way of displacing the nation. In other words, I'd like to suggest that writing about families is one way of not writing about the nation." The claim that writing about the family has the potential to displace the nation seems unpersuasive because the private/public binarism that sustains the distinction between the nation and the family is itself arguably a discursive product of the modern nation.
7. The narrator's grandmother shrewdly places strategic forgetting at the heart of the nationalist project supporting Ernest Renan's acute contention that "forgetting...is a crucial factor in the creation of a nation" (11).
8. Partha Chatterjee offers a slightly more nuanced account than Kaul of the gendered inflections of Indian nationalism in a specifically Bengali context. Chatterjee, in a Gramscian or Foucauldian mode, argues that nationalism simultaneously disciplines and empowers women. According to Chatterjee, "the home was not a complementary but rather the original site on which the hegemonic project of nationalism was launched. Women from the new middle classes...thus became active agents in the nationalist project—complicit in subordination under new forms of patriarchy" (147-48). The nationalist binarism between "the spiritual and the inner, on the one hand, and the material and the outer, on the other" and its alignment of the former set of terms with "nationalism's...claim to hegemony" (147), vitally empowered women and the domestic realm, in Chatterjee's account.

   Chatterjee's interpretation of the gendered nature of nationalism is of particular relevance because he was Ghosh's colleague at the Center for Studies in Social Sciences in Calcutta (Ghosh has a Ph.D. in Social Anthropology) and acknowledges Ghosh's influence on his scholarship in *The Nation and Its Fragments*. In *In an Antique Land*, Ghosh too warmly acknowledges Chatterjee's influence on his work.

While it is true that the discourse of domestic morality offers the grandmother in *The Shadow Lines* a certain amount of power (she is able, for instance, to discipline her grandson's sexual appetite, specifically the predilection for prostitutes that she imagines he has), and while it is true that nationalism drew on the same highly moralized domestic discourse, the strategic power that such an idiom offers women seems highly circumscribed.

Far less persuasively than either Kaul or Chatterjee, Anjali Roy argues that through the figure of the grandmother, "Ghosh creates a *matria* history" and "engages with the silences and amnesia of the dominant patriarchal nationalism" (42). The grandmother, I would suggest, embodies the ethos of nationalism rather than challenging it or offering a counter narrative to it. On my first reading of the novel, I was troubled that the figure of a woman should be the text's synecdoche for the most reactionary features of nationalism. Given Chatterjee's convincing genealogical account of the intimate connection between the discourses of nationalism and domestic morality, Ghosh's authorial choice now seems less problematic. For an anthology that explores the vexed links between contemporary Hindutva nationalism and women, see *Women and Right-Wing Movements: Indian Experiences*.

9. In his latest novel *The Glass Palace*, Ghosh rings a variation on this image of two men, one Indian and one English, locked in a gaze of mutual aggression and intimacy: when Arjun Roy, one of the first Indian officers to be commissioned in the British Indian army, tells his commanding officer Buckland that he is going over to the Indian National Army, which supported the Japanese in the Second World War, an enraged Buckland responds, "I'll see you hang, Roy, I will." Arjun, who has felt his masculinity and honor compromised by his complicity with British colonialism and petty anti-Indian racism, replies, "On that day if it comes... *we'll look at each other as honest men....* For that alone, this will have been worthwhile" (388, my emphasis).

10. I do not mean to suggest that the link between food and nationalism only exists in the feminine or domestic realm. In *The Glass Palace*, Ghosh shows the important role that food played in the British-Indian army. Hardy or Hardayal Singh, one of the first Indian officers to be commissioned in the British Indian army, does not like the Anglicized food of the officers' mess. He "started visiting the other ranks' messes" to eat "dal-roti" (244).

The Indian soldiers beneath Hardy begin to despise him because he is not able "to stomach the food that officers eat" (245). Significantly, when the Indian NCOs go to complain about him to the commanding officer, they use his Indian name, "Hardayal Singh," rather than the nickname "Hardy," that the English have given him. By his hankering for Indian food, Hardayal Singh has shown to the NCOs, with their internalized idealization of all things British, that he is not a socialized Englishman; he remains an unregenerate Indian and hence is not officer material. Later in the novel, Arjun Roy's ambivalence about his British masters and his Indian identity is signified by his inability to decide between "canned goods" and "freshly-rolled parathas and chapattis... frying onions and chopped tomatoes" (358). Hardy, by contrast, gets up from the table and deserts the canned food to get himself "chapattis and ande-ka-bhujia" (358). Hardy's unequivocal allegiance to Indian food mirrors the alacrity with which he deserts the British Indian army to join the Indian National Army in the cause of nationalism.

11. In *The Circle of Reason*, Ghosh foregrounds the link between human waste and its deodorized capitalist avatar money. Alu, for instance, promotes a utopian scheme to do away with money, and his slogan is "we will wage war on money; no money, no dirt" (281). A few pages later in the novel, Mr. Lal shows off the video game he has bought for his son to Jyoti Das. The intrinsic worth of the video game is supposedly signified by the amount of money that Lal has spent on it, "two months' savings." However, when Sunil, Lal's son, is asked to display the video game for the edification of his guest, the terrified boy, unable to manage the complicated gadget and fearful of parental wrath, urinates, "a yellow mess was dribbling down his thighs and a stain was spreading across the back of his shorts" (288). Sunil's mess is a malodorous and desublimated form of Lal's savings and the shiny video game on which it was expended. Like Ghosh, postcolonial African writers, like Armah, use scatological imagery to critique rampant capitalism in the developing world. For a reading of excremental imagery in postcolonial African writing, see Esty.

    Critics of capitalism like Gandhi may have seen religion as an alternative to capitalism, but in *The Circle of Reason*, Ghosh suggests that traditional Hinduism is homologous to capitalism in its repudiation or sublimation of the stinky materiality of existence. In the novel, Dr. Mishra with sadistic relish instructs Mrs. Verma on how a corpse has to be purified for a traditional

Hindu burial, "You'll have to reach into the bowels and clean out all the dead faeces. You'll have to scrape the insides of the rectum and the anus to make absolutely sure that they're absolutely clean; that not the faintest trace of mortal shit remains to defile the sacred fire" (410).

For Ghosh, Muslims come off no better than Hindus in regard to squeamishness about excremental materiality: in *In An Antique Land*, Ghosh satirically describes the Muslim cleric Ustaz Mustafa's "ceaseless vigilance...to keep particles of impure matter like goat's droppings and cow dung from touching his jallabeya since he would otherwise be obliged to change his clothes before going to the mosque again. This meant that he had to walk with extreme care in those liberally manured fields, with his hem plucked high above his ankles" (51).

To move from a Marxist and religious idiom to a postructuralist one, Roland Barthes reminds us, "Shit has no odor when it is written" (137). In that sense, as a writer, Ghosh is inescapably complicit with the idealization of matter he critiques. He transmutes shit into odorless words. Further, critical readers like myself have our hands dirty as well as we transform his excremental representation into yet more language with our commentary.

12. In fact, the grandmother tries to guard both the narrator and his father from Tridib's seductive "orbit": "she would not allow herself to take the risk of having him for long in our flat where I or my father might be tempted to move into his orbit" (5). Tridib's gastric is associated with an anti-patriarchal impulse. Not only is he literally at odds with his father, through him Ghosh effects an act of revisionary, filial insurrection against a canonical father, Joseph Conrad. Padmini Mongia and John Thieme point out the intertexual link between Conrad's 1917 novel *The Shadow Line* and Ghosh's *The Shadow Lines* (Mongia, 226; Thieme, 70), although Thieme misnames Conrad's novel as *The Shadow Line*, an error of some interpretive consequence since, as Mongia points out, while Conrad advances a single developmental narrative in this novel, Ghosh insists on the radically subjective, plural nature of truth in his novel, hence "Lines" rather than "Line." Neither Mongia nor Thieme, however, address the thematics of sodomy and anality that inform both novels in very different ways.

While Ghosh perversely affirms Tridib's refusal to mature and his jubilant celebration of anality, Conrad tells a more traditional developmental narrative. In his text, the narrator has to recognize that "one closes behind one the little gate of mere boyishness" (3, my emphasis), "the region of early youth must be left behind" (4, my emphasis), so one can move forward to the shadow line that separates callow youths from worldly, experienced men. To cross that daunting shadow line, the narrator traverses a treacherous tropical landscape whose description is redolent of a miring anality. Here, for instance, is the narrator's first sight of Bangkok: "There it was, spread largely on both banks...an expanse of brown houses of bamboo, of mats, of leaves, of a vegetable-matter style of architecture, sprung out of the brown soil on the banks of the muddy river" (69, my emphasis). At the end of the novel, despite the malevolent paternal shade of the former captain, the narrator has left behind the anal landscape of the tropics and has met the challenge of crossing the shadow line to achieve adult manhood. David Spurr points out that "the principles of exclusion, boundary, and difference which enter into the debasement of the primitive are connected to the fear that the white race could lose itself in the darker ones...the idea of going native" (82). Consonant with Spurr's insight, Conrad's novel is haunted by the fear that the white man will soften and sink into the simultaneously repulsive and seductive fecal materiality of the East, that he may go brown, as it were: Captain Giles, the narrator's good father (as opposed to the malign figure of the dead captain) warns the narrator, "some nice boys go soft mighty quick out here.... Things out East were made easy for white men.... The difficulty was to go on keeping white and some of these white boys did not know how" (14).

13. In his psychoanalytic-Marxist account of homosexuality, Guy Hocquengham suggests that the anus has been "privatized," as opposed to the privileged, public phallus, because "your excrement is yours and yours alone" (96-97). Tridib's excrement potentially messes up or queers the private/public division of heteronormative capitalism. He may shit in a closed room, but the shit originates in a public homoerotic space. Discussing the relationship of Tridib's gastric to capitalism is beyond the scope of this essay which is focused (rather anally?) on the challenges that his gastric poses to nationalism.

14. Ironically, while Tridib might die performing a gesture that might be considered traditionally virile and heroic, even this gesture is implicated spatially with his predilection for that which lies behind: the car carrying Tridib, May, and the grandmother is

moving forward. However, the mob attacks the rickshaw behind them, carrying the narrator's grandmother's uncle. "grandmother wanted the driver of the car to drive away" (245), but May misguidedly jumps out and runs back toward the rioters and the rickshaw. Tridib pursues her backward and dies at the hands of the mob. Significantly, all May can see of Tridib's death is a mass of men's backs:" Then the mob dragged [Tridib] in. He vanished. I could only see their backs" (245).

15. The narrator's intense affective investment in Tridib might be also described as homoerotic. The narrator stresses his identification with, rather than his desire for, Tridib: for instance, he fantasizes that "I was eight...when Tridib first talked to me about [his] journey [to England]," the same age that Tridib was when he left on that journey; similarly, he fantasizes that Tridib "had looked like me" (3). However, as Diana Fuss, among others, points out, it is impossible strictly to quarantine desire from identification (Fuss 4), so the narrator's intense identification with Tridib is imbricated with homoerotic desire.
16. I am indebted to Padmaja Challakere for this insight.
17. I should add that I am reading Tridib's (and perhaps Ghosh's?) epistemological model, not endorsing it. For my money, the formulation is mystificatory and anti-intellectual in the extreme. Note too the recuperative dialectic involved in this desire. One is supposedly racked and feminized by one's desire for the otherness of history, but that lack pays off in the long run because one ends up with a compensatory profit, one is "carried...beyond the limits of one's mind to other times and other places" (29). Surrendering to the desire for history's otherness turns out to be a ruse that allows one to erase the past's alterity, to move, indeed, beyond mediation altogether "to a place where there was no border between oneself and one's image in the mirror" (29). Kaul offers a more charitable reading of this passage. He concedes that the "desire" Tridib invokes "can... only exist exist prior to historical and geographical calculation, and is manifestly unrealizable," yet he holds that "in its function as critique and as utopian hope," it has a useful role to play (142).
18. I might be straining, interpretively that is, excessively here, but I am tempted to juxtapose intertextually Tridib's gastric with Ghosh's erudite description, in *The Glass Palace*, of the horrific effect of anthrax on elephants: "When anthrax erupts on an elephant's hide, the lesions develop a volcanic energy...he

carbuncles are most numerous around the hindquarters, and as they grow they have the effect of sealing the animal's anus. Elephants consume an enormous amount of fodder and must defecate constantly...their intestines continue to produce dung after the excretory passage has been sealed, the unexpurgated fecal matter pushing explosively against the obstructed anal passage. The pain is so great that a stricken elephant will attack anything in sight" (80). Undoubtedly, undermining national and temporal boundaries is risky and unsettling, but rigidly adhering to boundaries and attempting to contain the messiness of history and transnational hybridity, as the grandmother tries to do results in the blind, painful destructiveness that characterizes the lethally constipated elephants.

19. Also, see Julia Kristeva's theorizing of the abject. For Kristeva, the abject which includes "dung" is that which "disturbs identity, order, system. What does not respect borders" (4).

20. In Siddhartha Deb's recent novel *The Point of Return* this point is brought home by the distance between the Westernized son Babu and his father's attitudes toward toilet arrangements. Babu is shocked when his father "using one of those spades with the blade at right angles to the wooden stock...meticulously dredge[s] the soil and dirt that had collected in the unpaved drain." For, Babu this action "reveal[s] the peasant who had always lived beneath the suits and ties [of his externally Westernized father]" (18). Later in the novel, discussing the house they are building, Babu asks his father, "'What about the toilet? Is it going to be Indian style or will you have a Western commode?'

    Now, he [Babu's father] lost his temper, 'Your forefathers went into the fields for their morning chores. In the cities, people use train tracks. Who do you think you are with your ideas of reading magazines in the toilet? ...Listen, we are not Englishmen, no matter what you might think because of your school'" (67-68). Significantly, Babu's predilection for commodes is linked to his hankering to be English and his internalization of Western reading habits. His forefathers saw shitting as "a chore"; by contrast, like an Englishman, he wants to combine shitting with reading magazines, probably written in English.

21. For an excellent account of how imperial values shape sanitation policy, see Warren Anderson. Anderson's specific focus is American colonialism in the Philippines, rather than British colonialism in India, but his argument remains germane to a

British context. He intriguingly suggests that the colonial desire to situate every native in her proper place might in part be a form of compensation for the colonialists themselves being out of place (643).

Laporte focuses on Joyce's satire of British colonialism. However, Kelley Anspaugh has pointed out that Joyce also uses a scatological idiom to undermine Irish nationalist pieties (22). David Lloyd provocatively suggests that nationalism itself can be seen as a waste product of colonialism, so it is fitting that Irish writers like Joyce and Beckett should draw on a scatological idom to satirize nationalism (41).

Perhaps one of the most prominent postcolonial writers to emulate the ambivalent colonial preoccupation with subaltern shit is V.S. Naipaul. On his website, Ghosh simultaneously acknowledges Naipaul's influence and tries to distance himself from some of the outrageous ideas of his precursor: "Naipaul has really been for me perhaps the most important influence.... [But] I feel I see the world in a completely different way from Naipaul." In *An Area of Darkness*, Naipaul repeatedly, in outraged tones, comments on the Indian propensity to defecate in public: "Indians defecate everywhere. They defecate mostly beside the railway tracks. But they also defecate on the hills; they defecate on the river banks; they defecate on the streets" (74); "The woods [of Chandanwari] were already littered with uncovered excrement; hanks and twists of excrement crowned every accessible boulder of the Lidder River beside which we had camped" (167). But this promiscuous excremental tendency is not confined to Indians; it is found among other colonized peoples as well. Thus, Naipaul comments caustically on the Pyramids' "function as a public latrine [which] no guide book mentions" (14). The image of the "people of Goa" defecating "beside the Mandovi river" is pointedly contrasted with the written injunctions of the former colonial power, Portugal, attempting to keep matter in its proper place: "every hundred yards or so there is a blue and white enameled notice in Portugese threatening punishments for soiling the river" (74). While Naipaul is ostensibly outraged at the proliferation of Indian shit, the excessive space that the topic occupies in his book suggests the author's ambivalent fascination with Indian waste. Shankar has ably traced Naipaul's obsession with Indian excrement, but he reads this fascination in purely negative terms, missing the eroticized ambivalence that informs this recurrent topos in Naipaul's work.

22. Meenakshi Mukherjee points out that the positivist discourse of "cartography" gets called into question by the idiom of subjective imagination (256). There is a tension in the text between an emphasis on spatial specificity—"The spatial movement from a flat in Gole Park to a house in Southern Avenue with...Garhiat Road occupying a central place, charts [the narrator's] Calcutta moorings precisely.... We know not only the names of places where the narrator lived but often their exact addresses also (the Prices lived in 44 Lymington Road in West Hempstead; the old house in Dhaka was 1/31 Jindabahar Lane)" (259)—and the text's insistence that places are subjectively imagined constructs. Poststructuralist accounts of the contradictory grammatical and rhetorical role that deictics play may be pertinent here. Deictics or shifters are signifiers, like "here" or "now," that rhetorically emphasize temporal or spatial specificity. Paradoxically, however, shifters only can be interpreted in terms of a specific context. By the same token "44 Lymington Road" might seem to indicate a very specific space, but that space only gains significance in relation to the particular desiring perspectives of specific characters.
23. Anjali Roy also persuasively argues that Ghosh "finds in the spoken word, which relies on the dynamics of memory, a way of recapturing the foreclosures and absences of written records" (42). As a deconstructive reader, I am suspicious of Ghosh's romanticizing of speech over the written word. Clearly, oral histories have their own foreclosures and absences; they too are mediated texts. For an acute critique of phonocentrism, the persistent privileging of speech over writing, see Derrida's *Of Grammatology*.
24. More broadly, Ghosh often uses the image of a man gazing covertly at his watch to signify a certain cultural arrogance, a disrespect for cultural or temporal otherness. In *In an Antique Land*, for instance, the Egyptian Ustad Mustafa unable to comprehend Hindu philosophy's difference from Islamic values stops "paying any attention to [the narrator who has been compelled to explain those values to him].... 'Well thanks be to Allah,' he said quickly, eying his watch. 'Now that you are here among us you can understand and learn about Islam'" (48).
25. I did not cite the whole of Tridib's speech. The clause after "stories are all there is to live in" reads, "it was just a question of

which one you chose" (217). The humanist voluntarism implied by that last clause is belied by the whole of the novel: the grandmother, for instance, does not get to choose the story by which she makes sense of her life; she is subjectively constituted by that narrative. Ghosh's narrative, I would suggest, is cannier than Tridib's voluntarist formulation.

Incidentally, note that Lenin is one of the historical fathers who is squarely situated within a personal story, as opposed to some objective historicist narrative of class. Several South Asian diasporic texts use Lenin as figure to satirize traditional Marxism's contempt for local differences and the contingent. In Salman Rushdie's *The Moor's Last Sigh*, for instance, Grandfather Camoens scandalizes the Communist Party by leading a troupe of Lenin imitators who have local features and declaim Marxist jargon in local languages. For the party faithful, Camoens is seen as committing "an insult and offence" against father Lenin by allowing local differences to erase the universality of Marxism-Leninism. Similarly, in Arundhati Roy's *The God of Small Things*, the Malayali Marxist leader Comrade Pillai ruthlessly sacrifices members of his community to serve the interests of the grand narrative of Marxism. Pillai's insensitivity to the particular and the contingent is signaled by his naming his son after the father of Soviet Marxism.

26. The narrator absorbs Tridib's habit of constructing stories about the past. Robi, who takes a positivist attitude toward the past, bluntly advises him "not to bullshit" (56). Tridib and the narrator transvalue plural stories of the past; for Robi, on the other hand, there is one true historical account; other accounts are waste, "bullshit."

27. Edelman points out that sodomy has been associated with a scandalous metaleptic inversion of causal logic. In Edelman's terms, Ghosh's earlier novel *The Circle of Reason* might also be aptly described as a sodomitic text because it repeatedly undermines the narrative of cause and effect that sustains the pseudo-science phrenology: for instance, Balaram, the would-be phrenologist believes that "the skin around [Bhudeb Roy's] squamous suture" foundationally affects his personality and makes him "acquisitive and secretive," but his skeptical friend Gopal declares, "he knew for certain that Balaram had begun to talk of Bhudeb Roy's Acquisitive organ on the upper edge of the front half of the squamous suture, only after he discovered that Bhudeb Roy was taking fifty rupees for himself from the parents

of each child he admitted to the school. And as for the Secretiveness, on the posterior part of his squamous suture, he had no doubt that Balaram had noticed that long after he had heard that Bhudeb Roy had another steady trickle of money flowing in from the police station in the next village, in exchange for secret monthly reports on almost everybody in Lalpukur" (21). In other words, the supposedly foundational symptoms that Balaram reads on Bhudeb Roy's skull are in fact projections, mere retrospective effects, of the information that he knows about Bhudeb Roy's actions.

28. A number of feminist scholars have explored the association of women with a timeless space outside history. For two particularly perceptive accounts, see Crosby and Felski.

29. While Kaul in a footnote accurately comments on the "homosocial fellowship" (128) between Nick and the narrator, he is blind to the homoerotic bond between the narrator and Tridib, and thus he is able to make the sweeping and inaccurate claim, "*The Shadow Lines* describes no sexual or romantic relationship between two people who share an identity of nationality, race, or cultural experience" (144). Pace Kaul, Tridib and the narrator share an identity of nationality, race, and cultural experience, and in my reading, they also share a romantic relationship, albeit sublimated. Having said that, one must acknowledge the validity of Kaul's contention that interracial/transnational relationships are symptomatically crucial in the text.

Works Cited

Anderson, Benedict. *Imagined Communities: Reflections on the Origin and Spread of Nationalism*. London: Verso, 1991.

Anderson, Warren. "Excremental Colonialism: Public Health and the Poetics of Pollution." *Critical Inquiry* 21.3 (Spring 1995): 640-99.

Anspaugh, Kelley. "Ulysses upon Ajax?: Joyce, Harrington, and the Question of Cloacal Imperialism." *South Atlantic Review* 60.2 (May 1995): 11-29.

Barthes, Roland. *Sade/Fourier/Loyola*. Trans. Richard Miller. Berkeley: U of California P, 1976.

Brooks, Peter. *Reading for the Plot*. New York: Alfred A. Knopf, 1981.

Chakrabarty, Dipesh. *Provincializing Europe*. Princeton: Princeton UP, 2000.

Chatterjee, Partha. *The Nation and Its Fragments: Colonial and Postcolonial Histories*. Princeton: Princeton UP, 1993.

Conrad, Joseph. *The Shadow Line*. New York and Garden City: Doubleday, Page & Co., 1917.

Crosby, Christine. *The Ends of History: The Victorians and "the Woman Question."* New York and London: Routledge, 1991.

Deb, Siddartha. *The Point of Return*. New York: HarperCollins, 2003.

Derrida, Jacques. *Of Grammatology*. Trans. Gayatri Chakravarty Spivak. Baltimore: Johns Hopkins UP, 1976.

Douglas, Mary. *Purity and Danger: An Analysis of the Concepts of Pollution and Taboo*. London, Boston, and Henley: Routledge & Kegan Paul, 1966.

Edelman, Lee. *Homographesis*. New York and London: Routledge, 1994.

Felski, Rita. *The Gender of Modernity*. Cambridge, Massachusetts and London: Harvard UP, 1994.

Freud, Sigmund. *Civilization and Its Discontents*. Volume 21 of 24. *The Standard Edition of the Complete Psychological Works of Sigmund Freud*. Trans. & Ed. James Strachey. 1930. London: Hogarth Press, 1955. 59-155.

____. "From the History of an Infantile Neurosis." 1918. Volume 17 of 24. *The Standard Edition of the Complete Psychological Works of Sigmund Freud*. Trans. & Ed. James Strachey. London: Hogarth Press, 1955. 7-123.

____. *Three Essays on the Theory of Sexuality*. 1905. Volume 7 of 24. *The Standard Edition of the Complete Psychological Works of Sigmund Freud*. Trans. & Ed. James Strachey. London: Hogarth Press, 1955.

Fuss, Diana. *Identification Papers*. New York and London: Routledge, 1995.

Ghosh, Amitav. *The Circle of Reason*. 1986. New Delhi: Ravi Dayal, 2000.

____. "Correspondence with Dipesh Chakrabarty on *Provincializing Europe*." 23 July 2003 <http:www.amitavghosh.com/html.>.

____. *In an Antique Land*. New York: Vintage, 1994.

____. "The March of the Novel through History: The Testimony of My Grandfather's Bookcase." Originally published in *Kunapipi, A Journal of Postcolonial Writing* 19.3 and *Kenyon Review* 20.2 (Spring 1998). 10 March 2003 <http:www.amitavghosh.com/bookcase.html.>.

____. *The Shadow Lines*. 1988. Viking Penguin, 1990.

Hartnack, Christiane. *Psychoanalysis in Colonial India*. New York: Oxford UP, 2001.

Hocquenghem, Guy. *Homosexual Desire*. Trans. Daniella Dangoor. 1978. Durham: Duke UP, 1993.

Kamaraj, K. 23 July 2003. <http:www.indiannationalcongress.com/history/presidents/k_kamaraj.html.>.

Kaul, Suvir. "Separation Anxiety: Growing Up Inter/National in Amitav Ghosh's *The Shadow Lines*." *Oxford Literary Review* 16.3 (1994): 125-45.

Kovel, J. "On Racism and Psychoanalysis." *Psychoanalysis in Context: Paths between Theory and Modern Culture*. Ed. Anthony Elliot and Stephen Frosh. London: Routledge, 1995. 205-22.

Krishnaswamy, Revathi. *Effeminism: The Economy of Colonial Desire*. Ann Arbour: U of Michigan P, 2001.

Kristeva, Julia. *Powers of Horror*. Trans. Leon S. Roudiez. New York: Columbia UP, 1982.

Kumar, Ashwini. "Nehru's New Centrism." *Reporter* 5 Dec. 1963: 32-35.

Lamos, Colleen. "The Postmodern Lesbian Position: On Our Backs." *The Lesbian Postmodern*. Ed. Laura Doan. New York: Columbia UP. 85-103.

Laporte, Dominique. *History of Shit*. Trans. Nadia Benabid and Rodolphe el-Koury. Cambridge, Massachusetts and London: MIT Press, 2000.

Lloyd, David. *Anomalous States: Irish Writing and the Postcolonial Moment*. Durham and London: Duke UP, 1993.

Mehta, Uday Singh. *Liberalism and Empire*. Chicago and London: U of Chicago P, 1999.

Mongia, Padmini. "Postcolonial Identity and Gender Boundaries in Ghosh's *The Shadow Lines*." *College Literature* 19.20 and 3.1 Double Issue (Oct. 1992 – Feb. 1993). 225-28.

Mukherjee, Meenakshi. "Maps and Mirrors: Co-ordinates of Meaning in *The Shadow Lines*." *The Shadow Lines* Educational Edition. New Delhi: Oxford UP, 1995. 255-67.

Naipaul, V.S. *An Area of Darkness*. London: Andre Deutsch, 1964.

Renan, Ernest. "What is a Nation?" *Nation and Narration*. Trans. Martin Thom. Ed. Homi Bhaba. London: Routledge, 1990. 8-22.

Roy, Anjali. "Microstoria: Indian Nationalism's 'Little Stories' in Amitav Ghosh's *The Shadow Lines*." *The Journal of Commonwealth Literature* 35.2 (Spring 2000): 35-49.

Roy, Arundhati. *The God of Small Things*. New York: HarperPerennial, 1998.

Roy, Parama. *Indian Traffic*. Berkeley: U of California at Berkeley P, 1998.

Rushdie, Salman. *The Moor's Last Sigh*. New York: Vintage International, 1995.

Sarkar, Tanika and Urvashi Butalia. *Women and Right-Wing Movements: Indian Experiences*. London and New Jersey: Zed Books, 1995.

Shankar, S. "V.S. Naipaul, Modernity, and Postcolonial Excrement." *Textual Traffic: Colonialism, Modernity, and the Economy of the Text*. Albany, NY: SUNY Press, 2001. 149-86.

Spurr, David. *The Rhetoric of Empire: Colonial Discourse in Journalism, Travel Writing, and Imperial Administration*. London and Durham: Duke UP, 1993.

Thieme, John. "Passages to England." *Liminal Postmodernisms*. Ed. Theo D'haen and Hans Berten. Amsterdam and Atlanta, GA: Rodopi BV, 1994. 57-78.

Vaidyanathan, T.G. and Jeffrey T. Kripal, eds. *Vishnu on Freud's Desk: A Reader in Psychoanalysis and Hinduism*. Delhi: Oxford UP, 1999.

Williams, Sherwood. "The Rise of a New Degeneration: Decadence and Atavism in *Vandover the Brute*." *ELH* 57.3 (Fall 1990): 709-36.

8

Masculinity vs. Femininity: Perpetuation and Transgression in Arundhati Roy's *The God of Small Things*

Fewzia Bedjaoui

Abstract

British colonization of India has challenged the traditional indigenous culture to the point that some native men/women developed a particular interest in British ideals which brought confusion, frustration or acceptance. Bound to or destroyed by the pressures intrinsic to the conflictual remnants of English colonial and postcolonial India, some men want to fulfil the myth of masculinity vs. femininity whether that desire comes from biological impulses or societal expectations while others are striving to inscribe their own destiny, creating a space for themselves within society, as it is subtly illustrated in Arundhati Roy's *The God of Small Things*.

The myth of masculinity vs. femininity has historically been seen in terms of the difference between men's and women's affective life and this supposed a division of affect and anatomical (sexual) difference. It supports the privileged position enjoyed by men and perpetuates women's oppression within the patriarchal order. While conformity to the myth reinforces men's power and hierarchy, challenges to the myth represent challenges to the organisation of society. How men and women negotiate these changes will vary, depending on their ability to risk changes to the way their lives have been lived.

The articulation of man/woman relationship gives a link to such a serious question and demands critical attention to the various aspects, notably anthropological, philosophical, psychological, social, political and aesthetic. Nevertheless, according to the Hindu tradition, the man/woman relationship is quite complex as the Hindu philosophy transcends all notions of western masculinity and femininity. Since caste and patriarchy have an intrinsic nexus with gender in the lives of men and women, they contribute to a particular degree to men's superiority and women's inequality. Since a man is by nature supposed to be superior, the differences between men and women are thus natural and unavoidable. Patriarchal definitions of masculinity/femininity include woman as a man-made category.

Yet, for better or worse, British colonization of India has challenged the traditional indigenous culture to the point that some native men and women were to develop a particular interest in British ideals which brought confusion, disappointment, frustration or acceptance. They are thus bound to or destroyed by the pressures intrinsic to the conflictual remnants of English colonial and postcolonial India. The consequent process of construction/deconstruction through transgression gives a new vision of Indian man and woman, pleasing to western mind and feelings and yet reflecting part of their Indianness.

In *The God of Small Things*, Arundhati Roy presents a slice of life in a small Indian town where male hegemony as well as androcentric power relations are prevailing. She portrays identities that are rooted in traditional gender definitions, notably Chacko, the son, and Pappachi, the father. On the other hand she describes different types of male and female identity challenging the myths, respectively the young Dalit carpenter, Velutha, and the divorced progressive daughter, Ammu.

Hindu symbolism has a powerful impact on the construction of masculinity and femininity within Indians. As it has been revealed in the novel, Indian men and women who resisted Hindu traditions are accused of transgressing and violating the oppressive patriarchal patterns within Indian family structure and therefore are condemned to ostracism till death.

In *The God of Small Things*, three generations of a Syrian Christian family live together in Kerala. Mammachi, who intensely loves her son Chacko, remains entirely indifferent to Ammu, her daughter. This clear difference, shown in terms of emotional investment is to be transmitted to the grandchildren as the only one who is taken into consideration is the son's daughter.

In a wider social context, this preference is depicted in the literary writing as a standard behaviour. In reality, sexism is sanctioned by law concerning inheritance rights since the son is legally and religiously to inherit the complete family wealth. Such a prejudice against daughters is revealed by Kochu Maria. This very pragmatic domestic help connects affective feelings to inheritance rights, notably when she refers to Sophie, the daughter of the sole male child of the family, i.e. Chacko: "When she grows up, she will be our Kochama, and she'll raise our salaries, and give us nylon saris for Onam" (Roy 27) and claims that the children, even son of a divorced daughter are the husband's family responsibility: "Tell your mother to take you to your father's house.... There you can break as many beds as you like. These aren't your beds. This isn't your House" (Roy 83).

This clear policy of exclusion regarding daughters either married or divorced supports the sons and the progeny as the only active individuals of the following generation. Even more, there is no need to waste money on the education of girls as they are temporarily staying in their parents' home. Thus, Chacko is sent to Oxford, whereas Ammu is simply ignored and left at home to the extreme point that no traditional responsibility of arranging a husband was shared.

> Pappachi insisted that a college education was an unnecessary expense for a girl.... Since her father did not have enough money to raise a suitable dowry, no proposal came Ammu's way. Two years went by. Her eighteenth birthday came and went. Unnoticed, or at least

> unremarked upon by her parents. Ammu grew desperate. All day she dreamed of escaping from the clutches of her ill-tempered father and bitter, long suffering mother. (Roy 38)

But, Ammu's marriage and fast divorce have awful consequences mirroring the socio-cultural stigma attached to divorces in India.

Certainly, the world religions possess their own laws which manage divorces within their own communities as well as different regulations governing divorces in interfaith marriages. There are root causes for which divorces are granted, notably adultery, desertion, cruelty, impotency and chronic disease. But it seems Indian divorcees are more harshly judged than men, as reflected in *The God of Small Things*: "Ammu left her husband and returned, unwelcomed to her parents in Ayemenem. To everything she had left from only a few years ago, except now she had two children. And no more dreams" (Roy 42).

As any other Indian divorcee who often returns to her own family, she is not at all warmly welcomed, for a divorced woman is an economic burden on her family, particularly if she has children. Unavoidably, Ammu would face great difficulties to remarry since her parents would find that they had already discharged their parental obligations to their daughter. Though divorce remains a highly stigmatizing experience, a woman's caste is a fundamental characteristic in her acceptance back into a society, as women from higher caste have an easier time than middle or lower caste divorcees; the latter are given lowly household chores to perform and bad food for survival.

> Divorce is not an option whatever the husband might be; and such an action results from a regarded atypical status in Indian society as it is clearly expressed by Baby Kochamma that she had no position anywhere at all and by Chacko: "die-vorced? His voice rose in such a high register that it cracked on the question mark. He even pronounced the word as though it was a form of death." (Roy 130)

Beside the fact that English remains inevitably a large issue for the family, Chacko is described as being educated at

Oxford and such an education earns him great respect and gives him special prestige in the family unit. Thus, "he was permitted excesses and eccentricities nobody else has" (Roy 38). Mammachi boasts of Chacko's accomplishments at Oxford which irritates and frustrates Ammu into declaring that "going to Oxford didn't necessarily make a person clever" (Roy 56). This last statement is in complete contradiction with the belief that the foreign educated has a new frame of reference for thinking, i.e. a new set of beliefs about the western world and new ideas to be transmitted to be useful to his people. Yet, he fails partly to come out of his self-imposed cocoon and remains bound to his family although he is courted by the idea of freedom, notably to "marry our conquerors" (Roy 56).

The next Anglophilic character is Pappachi. "Even in the stifling Ayemenem heat and every single day, Pappachi wore a well-pressed three-piece suit and his gold pocket watch" (Roy 49). English habits and clothing make him resemble the Gentleman, i.e. a dignified figure though "every night he beat her [his wife Mammachi] with a brass flower vase" (Roy 47). England has "created the Gentleman" (Kazantzakis 171), another mania, the characteristics of which are taste, discipline, helpfulness, rationality.

Indeed, social norms or rules are ways of doing things or patterns that become routine over a certain period of time. These patterns are so socially legitimized that they get reproduced, because of the complex way in which identity and roles are intertwined. There are three fundamental institutions in society which combine their practice and reinforce the ideology of the social construction of gender, notably the state, the community and the family. It is also critical to realize that those social rules and norms impact men and women in different ways depending particularly on their caste. The power of social rules lies in the fact that they appear to be consensual and non-negotiable while in fact they are based on inequality and power equations. Those who are found to be outside the borders of their own culture are stared at, exploited and feared. The apparent transgression of the natural order embodied by deviant characters constitutes a threat to beliefs, values and culture.

As in many male-dominated cultures, taboos and other moral do's and don'ts, erecting barriers and governing sexual relations are particularly aimed at controlling both men and women. The former involve rules for male behaviour and primarily limit and sanction for transgression. Distinctive customs, i.e. ways of controlling sexuality are a factor among others (linguistic, religious) that help any individual within his culture identify each other and distinguish himself from others. Probably, traditional Indian men in *The God of Small Things* do not want to lose the security and stability the old system gives them.

In this context, the Hindu culture fails to recognize the issue of equality, particularly within the private/public spheres. This private/public dichotomy prevailing in patriarchy forges rigid categories in which women are given 'feminine' attributes—irrational, partial and sentimental—while men particularly fit into the public sphere being rational, objective and other-regarding. The Hindu myth of masculinity/femininity exaggerates the difference between men and women since it is caste-constructed. Notably in the Hindu culture, femininity is a very active element. The feminine principle is composed of vulnerability, an appeal of dependence and goodwill that confers on the masculine principle a driving ethos of superiority.

Ammu exemplifies the type of woman who is a victim of the conventional society which does not allow women to hold their own and considers the issue of identity as completely contrary to nature, reason and commonsense. She experiences a fragmented identity, one that creates much confusion in the depth of subjectivity. Yet, "For all women, as for men, the need for self-fulfilment, autonomy, self-realization, independence, self-actualization is as important as the sexual need, with as serious consequences when it is thwarted" (Friedan 9).

Indeed, the woman writer translates her anger at the destructive effects of patriarchal oppression by constructing

Ammu as a character not only moulded by her own experience as a divorced woman, but as the daughter of a caged mother, submissive, oppressed and resigned, and of a violent father—

> As she grew older, Ammu learned to live with this cold calculating cruelty. She developed a lofty sense of injustice and the mulish, reckless streak that develops in Someone Small who has been bullied all their lives by Someone Big. She did exactly nothing to avoid quarrels and confrontations. In fact, it could be argued that she sought them out, perhaps. (Roy 181-82)

—and by her enforcement of patriarchal forms through particularly Baby Kochamma:

> ...ex-nun, and incumbent baby grand aunt.... Baby Kochamma resented Ammu, because she saw her quarrelling with a fate that she, Baby Kochamma herself, felt she has graciously accepted. The fate of the wretched Man-less woman.... She subscribed wholeheartedly to the commonly held view that a married daughter had no position in her parents' home. As for a divorced daughter—according to Baby Kochamma, she had no position anywhere at all. And as for a divorced daughter from a love marriage, well, words could not describe Baby Kochamma's outrage. As for a divorced daughter from an intercommunity love marriage—Baby Kochamma chose to remain quiveringly silent on the subject (Roy 45-46).

The antagonist pattern of free male-female relationships produces solely alienation in an Indian patriarchal society. Patriarchal power conferred the right to romantic and sexual conquest only on men as a mark of their superiority. Roy challenges Indian patriarchal representations of the female body, behaviour and language, i.e. all forms of independence and autonomy that are forbidden for a woman to veil the markers of her feminine identity.

The character of Ammu is shown as introducing alien values which lead to an unresolvable crisis of the family, though the brother's behaviour is not regarded as disturbing or destabilizing the family order: it is perceived as normal.

Yet, the inter-caste erotic love between a Christian high caste woman and a young Dalit carpenter which inevitably challenges the traditional socio-religious behavioural code, is to make her the epitome of ultimate transgression, being perfectly aware both of her own sexuality and emotional needs but capable of acting on this basis as well.

> Occasionally when Ammu listened to songs that she loved on the radio, something stirred inside her. A liquid ache spread under her skin, and she walked out for the world like a witch, to a better, happier place. On days like this, there was something restless and untamed about her. As though she had temporarily set aside the morality of motherhood and divorcehood. Even her walk changed from a safe-mother walk to another wilder sort of walk. She wore flowers in her hair and carried magic secrets in her eyes. She spoke to no-one. She spent hours on the riverbank with her little plastic transistor shaped like a tangerine. She smoked cigarettes and had midnight swims.... On the days that the radio played Ammu's songs, everyone was a little wary of her. They sensed somehow that she lived in the penumbral shadows between two worlds, just beyond the grasp of their power. That a woman that they had already damned, now had little left lost, and could therefore be dangerous. (Roy 44)

Indian women are denied erotic desire as a mode of asserting autonomy and thus female sexuality in India continues to be addressed only within the immoral West vs. authentic Indian paradigm established during colonialism. The Indian woman can never be wholly located in the arena of tradition lest India's image be cast as primitive, nor can she be identified only with the modern, and thus becomes un-Indian. She has to belong to both realms carefully apportioning modern ideas with dollops of tradition.

Everything which is considered objectionable in society is labeled western and antiethical to indigenous culture, specifically polluting the Indian middle-class mind. Thus, the incursion of western values as well as the portrayal of vulgar and obscene women are reminiscent of themes developed during the nationalist struggle against the British colonial rule. During colonialism the binary opposition between tradition and modernity worked to justify western intervention. In colonial discourses modernity was a trope meaning the West, progress, civilization and democracy. Tradition was an exoticized culture bearing the burden of repressive practices. Yet, in *The God of Small Things* tradition is invoked to signify civilization and morality.

Therefore, in colonial and postcolonial contexts the private and public realms took on different shapes in *The God of Small Things*. The Indian culture is affected by the linguistic and racial differences of the English colonial characteristics. Roy sets her tale in post-independence India, in her native state of Kerala which has both a long-standing tradition of militant communism and old Syrian Christian community with a specific assimilation to the Hindu casteist system, the characteristics of which are to be closed, cloistered and xenophobic. Besides, the characters are the children of the caste system, capitalism, western/English education. Hybridity becomes of thematic importance as it allows Roy to break free of phallocentric ideals, constraints and language by reclaiming her mind and body as her own. Through Ammu's deeds, Roy shakes the phallocentric boundaries on the societal expectations concerning gender and sexuality and Velutha's socio-religious casteist boundaries.

To what extent does the ongoing conflict inherent in social stratification at different levels, i.e. English vs. Indian, emotive vs. social, touchable vs. untouchable, man vs. woman create bad people that live life and experience emotion from an inward and good people that conform to dominant gender norms?

At this level, it is worth mentioning Aristotle's understanding that man is by nature a political animal, i.e. a human being with the power of giving a speech. Aristotle defines society as the institution determining the necessities of its members. In every society individuals behave according to socio-religious conventions and the realization of two fundamental desires: differentiation from the others and integration into their own community. They have a fundamental need to make their own lives meaningful through frameworks of meaning regulated by ethical codes, elicited by social cues and expressed in established channels, socially and religiously. All values derive from the individuals constituting a given society and the latter requires taboos, restrictions to limit any individual's life and freedom.

Following this line of thought, it might appear that human beings dictate and interpret the values and importance of limits. Boundaries exist to define the physical world and to define human existence in God's world. Those who fail to follow the definite rules of a particular religion are guilty of spiritual transgression, i.e. they become sinners and crossing God's boundaries brings disharmony and chaos. That probably means that the primary vehicle for action is religion. Foucault's notion of transgression is related to the profane which is itself dependent on its boundaries for its own definition. Foucault on transgression talks of particular sexualities viewed as profanation where the sacred, God and man, is regarded as illegitimate, i.e. the transgressive nature of sexuality is given a transcendent meaning. "Profanation in a world which no longer recognizes any positive meaning in the sacred—is this not more or less what we may call transgression?" (Foucault 30).

Nietzsche's affirmation that God is dead goes beyond its traditional meaning and is closely linked to the death of humanity. Are there any more needs in oneself? Why is one no longer able to be satisfied? The "will to truth" (qtd. in Bose 66) challenges centuries of moral interpretation. Could Nietzsche's statement be understood as the end of transcendent justifications for transgression? Indeed Foucault's "will to resist" and Nietzsche's "will to Truth" (qtd. in Bose 66) are changed with nihilism favouring the eradication of restrictive moral criteria, but they do not suggest transgressions for transgression's sake.

How can one know when to transgress and when not in a world that no longer recognizes any meaning in the sacred? If there is no limit, there is no transgression.

> The play of limits and transgression seems to be regulated by a simple obstinacy: transgression incessantly crosses and recrosses a line which closes up behind it in a wave of extremely short duration, and thus it is made to return once more right to the horizon of the uncrossable. (Foucault 33-34)

What happens is that it is easier to include the transgressive act into a positive vision of human emancipation.

Therefore, the term transgression raises a twin question concerning negation and affirmation. Obviously, transgression is synonymous with violation, infraction, infringement as well as sin, offence. Thus, to transgress is to pass beyond any limit and boundary. The transgression of conventional identity or behaviour constitutes perversion, deviancy or immorality. To what extent a transgressive act stands as a positive vision of human emancipation or at least of human activity? To transgress the status quo could be interpreted as progress or freedom which means release from particular norms. The destruction of standards and restrictive moral principles valorizes transgressions or the will to transgress. Beyond all reason nature has infinity of forms and any individual is to be free, be himself or herself crossing the lines set by limits.

Velutha is to transgress patterns of thinking and behaving that are dominated by emotions, such as love and fear. Ammu and Velutha are ready to break socio-religious laws and to die for desire, for love. They both violate the most fundamental love laws that govern their socio-religious life. The transgressions are the result of conscious decisions by the highly emotional characters.

Probably, it remains not simply bodily needs; it seems that the erotic experience is also the pursuit of a utopia in which ideals fuse, being greater than what a momentary sexual pleasure can offer. Young discusses the development of literary theories that seek to "cross the boundary to the social...by using history or the history and culture of colonialism or sexuality." Theories of sexuality according to this model, necessarily invoke "the notion of transgression, the crossing of the law as a supremely human and therefore political act" (12).

A politics of desire, particularly individual ones, could probably be regarded as viable a politics as any other. Nancy Amstrong and Leonard Tennenhouse on the ideology of sexual conduct in literature and history discuss the political validity of sexual desire: "the terms and dynamics of sexual desire must be a political language. We must see representations of desire, neither as reflections nor as consequences of political power, but as a form of political power in their own right" (1987).

Desire need not be interpreted but remains simply a pleasure, a state of human nature both natural and spontaneous. In *The God of Small Things* this desire is prevalent in an erogenous domain, the erotics, one which is completely cut from the world of any societal or government politics, and which rejects any pseudo truth that would stand above the validity of the erotics as truth. As Bose said: "I made no difference whether they were proletarian or what their ideology was. The problem was the biological nature of these men. The only real conflict seemed to me to be between women and men" (Bose 61).

Ammu and Velutha should not cross the barriers of caste in desiring one another and yet they do cross them. They experience moments of sheer ecstasy in which happiness in its absolute weight makes them realize the dire consequences of their action.

The Elizabethan connotation of dying as a consummation of the sexual act is relevant in the sense that this absolute happiness is synonymous with an unbearable burden: "if he touched her, he could not talk to her, if he loved her, he could not leave, if he spoke, he could not listen, if he fought, he could not win" (Roy 33).

They both die in predictable ways. Ammu lived unallowably and thus also died badly. Death remains a punishment for the transgression of societal and government rules. But, a woman's transgression is universally more easily condemned, particularly by the socio-religious rules that govern love and desire. Ammu's mere womanly eroticism could be conceived as a particular desire as worth dying for.

Besides, Velutha's sexual transgression could be seen as revolutionary and Ammu's an elitist indulgence. Ammu is not only seeking sexual satisfaction but to touch the Untouchable. Velutha is described as being a more fully committed political character because of his participation in the communist uprising in Kerala, possessing obvious leftist Naxalite convictions. Both are raging against the diverse circumstances of their respective lives and it is through this feeling of a shared anger that she finds possible to desire the Untouchable, Velutha, to be connected to him mind and body.

> Suddenly Ammu hoped it had been him that Rahel saw in the march. She hoped it had been him that had raised his flag and knotted arm in anger. She hoped that under his careful cloak of cheerfulness he housed a living; breathing anger against the smug, ordered world that she so raged against. She hoped it had been him. (Roy 175-76)

Velutha was nurturing the anti-caste aspirations in love and desire: "He tried to hate her. She's one of them, he told himself. Just another one of them. He couldn't. She had deep dimples when she smiled. Her eyes were always somewhere else. Madness slunk in through a chink in History. It took only a moment" (Roy 214).

But, it is Ammu who really takes the initiative of destroying the sexual taboo and hence asserts her own biological desire for a man who has to be confined to the impermissible boundaries of untouchability. In doing so, she achieves a subversion of both caste rules and woman domination over man by being the initiator of the sexual act.

Is desire a lack or as Nietzsche calls it "will to power?" (Bose 66). The desire of sexual fulfilment is an end in itself and a process which leads to these acts of transgressions, of rebellions which are particularly linked to cultural histories. The Indian society is a casteist society which perpetuates through generations coded love laws specifying who to love and how much with an entire disconsideration for probable anomalies or abuses: "...that it really began in the days when the Love Laws were made. The Laws that lay down who should be loved and how, and how much" (Roy 32-33).

The God of Small Things delineates a politics of desire into death as the chosen path. Death is thus perceived as a penalty Velutha and Ammu are consciously going to pay for their personal sexual fulfilment. The protagonists are really in charge of their lives and destinies once they become aware of and recognize their authentic self. Yet, a conventional meaning of self includes being fundamentally aware of oneself in relation to determine them. Velutha's and Ammu's transgression is not conducive to beneficial social change and genuine spiritual transformation. It is severely punished and reinforces existing stratification. What remains problematic is to view her and Velutha's punishment as a routine enforcement of prevailing socio-religious codes. Their respective punishments for their specific sexual transgression must be viewed as a model of thorough separation frustrating fundamental commonality.

Indeed, Velutha's death is horrible, carried out from fear and hatred and a deep desire to maintain the status quo. But it is this lack of emotion from the policeman that reveals that Untouchables are not just considered as members of the lowest possible social standing, but as rabid animals. Indeed, Velutha's death gives an awareness of Indian culture beyond the simple constructs of Touchable and Untouchable. He will die brutally for his love, but it is still worth it, which makes the moment poignant. The scene of the love shared between Ammu and Velutha is moving because the poetry overwhelms the content and one perceives the dire consequences Velutha must face, and it stands at the end of the novel to heighten the emotional intensity of the work's final moments. Ammu broke the rules. But what are the Love-Laws? Is Ammu's affair with Velutha a flagrant violation of what Roy calls society's Love-Laws? They have been there from the beginning. Is there some kind of human intuitive perception? Are they an inherent part of the caste system? If one loves the wrong person in the wrong place, one breaks the love-laws and will suffer the dire consequences. Does it say that life is deceitful and is this what happens? Does *The God of Small Things* make value judgements about decisions that are made? One's school-fed knowledge of the Indian culture and the various key concepts is being challenged and that awareness of a culture so different from others' hits one. Yet, the strangeness of the caste issue in India in *The God of Small Things* is that caste is a serious question in a context where all the characters are Christians. Such a faith which prevails since the pre-colonial period would reject caste division and confer a safe haven for the Untouchables. In the novel, Velutha is Christian but remains an untouchable, though Christianity is casteless. Probably the fact that Ammu's family is Syrian Christian gives it a sense of pride and higher status *vis-à-vis* other Christians, notably Velutha who is refused his upward mobility. Hindu caste practices remain deep-rooted in the Indian psyche.

The key question in *The God of Small Things* is Roy's attack of Indian patriarchy, notably the oppressiveness of caste and gender and remains as such on the side of progressive forces against the growth of right wing forces with their narrow sectarianism. She reveals the inherent paradoxes of Hinduism, notably the fundamental divisions of gender and caste in Hindu society and a real antagonism between the pantheist view of Hinduism, including the belief that all things involve the divine and its social organization through the unchanging caste system. While Hinduism urges its believers to help the poor with great care and attention (Velutha receives education; Ammu's father paid for the surgery of Velutha's father), since love is a practice of Hindu dharma, the reality is that the different castes are still openly reinforcing social limits (behaviour of Ammu's parents and the police towards the untouchable Velutha). The caste system is not equalitarian and institutionalizes inequality on the basis of individual's birth (just like racialism).

But, there is no forgiveness in the societal Indian context of *The God of Small Things*, when one knows that forgiveness is valued and supported by some modern western societies as a social and coping skill, for it helps people to stay valued members in an interdependent society. The benign view of the human nature in which people are socialized to be good is shaken in *The God of Small Things*. What about the conciliatory philosophy preached by Mohandas Karamchand Gandhi? He believed that in order to effect social change, individuals must change first. His philosophy of non-violence towards others, which claims that no truth can be held absolutely by anyone and thus any deed of violence is unfounded, for nobody, can impose his own truths upon others. Undoubtedly, Ammu transgresses the zealously held Indian social values. Velutha too transgresses them in his own way. They both violate the expected positive norms and standards and create discomfort and anger for those involved. Yet, the unforgiving resolution from the family and policemen is to prove the negative quality of the lovers' relationship to the unfortunate outcome, i.e. death and not to give full attention to the more positive life arenas.

The colonial and postcolonial period in India witnessed a substantial degree of change, conflict, rejection, accommodation and transformation in lifestyles both among men and women. Indian men/women who are caught in this wind of change react, because while there are comparatively few women who have access to education, they nevertheless begin to question both traditional and modern values. The novel of Roy reflects her concern about an unfair social order, an urge for a fresh look at the social ideology and gender relationships of an unequal stratified Hindu society. Symbols and images of national and cultural identity, purity and dirtiness, the right behaviour and caste, the gender issue and social (political) status, as well as personal experiences are tackled in particular ways. Indeed, the need to improve men's and women's situations through education within traditional value systems is encouraged but there is also the latent fear of what consequences might result should such forces of change be set free. In *The God of Small Things*, gender and sexuality are dimensions where man and woman identity construction is fraught with complex choices. The tensions are sharpened, on the one hand, by the fossilization of Indian traditional culture and, on the other hand, by the flexibility of western cultural practices.

The novel is to be viewed through the lens of history and resistance, the relationships between the emotional and material complexity of living in the cultural borderlands in order to have interpretations that more accurately reflect Indian writer's home experience. Masculine and feminine identities are illusions, made possible through repeated cultural performances in act, speech, body, language and dress. As a result, identities appear as natural categories of existence. The coherence of man/woman is part of the socially instituted and maintained norms of intelligibility, i.e. male-masculine vs. female-feminine. What exists outside this strict construction remains unintelligible, transgressive, and misunderstood. It does probably mean that identity is an illusion or repeated performance of gender, race and sexuality. Yet, it is a common assumption that identity formation is a universal feature of human experience, one's source of meaning and experience. It is true that the construction of meaning via cultural practices is a human universal, but it does not follow that this invariably takes the form of identity construction. It is fair to say that the impact of westernization or globalization on the Indian cultural sphere has sometimes been viewed in a pessimistic light. It is associated with the destruction of cultural identities, victims of the encroachment of homogenized and westernized culture, i.e. with the construction of hybrid identities, neither indigenous nor exogenous.

Indeed, education in general has levelled human being's capacity to produce goods, means of survival to a mere intellectual competence, which obviously would set men and women to equal potential of power. Consequently, the conception of the family drawn by the traditional division of tasks is somewhat disturbed and necessarily affects men more, since they are the ones who have to come to terms with a less authoritarian, and less leading role, leaving room for women's rising social importance. Roy shows that it is probably difficult to understand why in this age of enlightenment, some Indian men still keep old values and attitudes about gender roles and sex as well as casteist differentiation where even Indian men as Velutha are victimised. Even more, the construction of a fluid masculine identity beyond casteist borders raises questions that Dalit men keep expressing on daily basis, but often are of no avail since traditional men remain deaf to what is always felt as the questioning of a right and never perceived as the request for a fair, morally acceptable social status as it has been illustrated by Velutha. Until the myth of masculinity is given up or reshaped to reflect reality, some men seem to want to fulfil this myth whether that desire comes from biological impulses or societal expectations while others are striving to inscribe their own destiny, creating a space for themselves within society.

Works Cited

Armstrong, Nancy and Leonard Tennenhouse. *The Ideology of Conduct: Essays in Literature and the History of Sexuality.* London: Methuen, 1987.

Bose, Brinda. "In Desire and in Death: Eroticism as Politics in Arundhati Roy's *The God of Small Things.*" *ARIEL: A Review of International English Literature*, 29.2 (Apr. 1998): 59-72.

Friedan, Betty. *The Feminine Mystique.* Harmondsworth: Penguin, 1971.

Foucault, Michel. *Language, Counter-Memory, Practice.* Ithaca: Cornell UP, 1977.

Kazantzakis, Nikos. *England.* Trans. Amy Mims. Oxford: Bruno Cassirer, 1971.

Roy, Arundhati. *The God of Small Things.* New Delhi: India Ink, 1997.

Young, Robert J.C. *Torn Halves: Political Conflict in Literary and Cultural Theory.* Manchester: Manchester UP, 1996.

9

The Inheritance of Loss: Mapping Postcolonial Indian Masculinities

Purnendu Chatterjee

Abstract

In terms of critical literary study on fiction, the domain of masculinity has drawn far less attention from scholars than the domain of feminism. However, in reality, masculinity has been no less influenced than feminism by the various cross-currents that affect society. This paper seeks to explore the different shades of Indian masculinities in the postcolonial context. In doing so, the paper highlights the effects of globalization, terrorism and divisive movements and the first world-third world disparities on Indian masculinity as revealed in *The Inheritance of Loss*.

With the onset of Renaissance in England, MAN suddenly came into focus. The glorification of manhood received a fillip when the British naval forces under Sir Francis Drake defeated the so-called invincible Spanish Armada in 1588. The famous 16th century surgeon Ambroise Pare suggested that men were more perfect creation of Nature than women and hence it was impossible to change from a man to woman, though the reverse is acceptable.

> Nature tends always toward what is most perfect and not, on the contrary, to perform in such a way that what is perfect should become imperfect.[1]

The Augustan age ushered in the concept of homo economicus—men, and not women, were at the fountain head of trade and commerce—and the Rousseauvean concept of the Noble Savage was an exaltation of masculinity. The Industrial Revolution of the 18th century led to a meteoric rise in England's capital formation. This sudden increase in capital made it necessary for the English people to set up colonies in order to channelise their capital. Naturally, their colonial quests were underlined by a sense of masculinity. Tales of adventure and heroism were abundantly produced and Robert Baden Powell went so far as to base, as Elleke Boehmer points out,

> ...the ethos of the Scout Movement on the belief that colonial frontier life was guaranteed to train boys to be manly men.[2]

In the colonies the English people upheld their superior position over the natives. Arthur C. Danto aptly points out:

> The superiority of Western civilization was never doubted, and one of the premises of Victorian anthropology was in effect that there is a moral direction in history as there is in evolution, that societies and species evolve toward optimality, and that Western Europe was history's masterpiece just as *Homo sapiens* was [sic] Nature's.[3]

As far as India was concerned, the infamous Macaulay Minute of February 2, 1835, declared the superiority of the colonial education over the native education. The target of colonial education was the males and aimed at creating a kind of inaccurate doubling of the colonized as a reflection of the colonizers. This often resulted in, what Homi Bhaba terms, "metonymy of presence."[4] The "metonymy of presence" refers to the mimicry by the colonized of the colonizers. Bhaba elucidates his concept of the "metonymy of presence":

> Those inappropriate signifiers of colonial discourse—the difference between being English and being Anglicized; the identity between stereotypes which, through repetition, also become different; the discriminatory identities constructed across traditional cultural norms and classification, the Simian Black, the Lying Asiatic—all these are metonymies of presence.[5]

The coloured colonized in their desperate bid to imitate the white colonizers become impoverished specimens of humanity who are almost the same as the colonial masters, but not the same—in Bhaba's words "almost the same but not white."[6] These Mimic men, living within the interfaces of two cultures, develop split identities. They hate to imitate, but cannot help imitating. This flawed mimetic effort obviously results in the creation of frustrated men who cannot come to terms with themselves as well as with the society at large. In this paper, I propose to consider Kiran Desai's treatment of the terrain of postcolonial Indian masculinities in her Man Booker Prize winning novel *The Inheritance of Loss*. I am using the term 'postcolonial' not only in the sense of historical time, but also to mean that Desai's novel subtly and subversively scrutinizes the colonial relationship. This paper shall highlight the various trajectories of gender relationships that Desai presents in the novel. The varying mores of gender relationships will also reveal that in the postcolonial age Indian masculinities are more akin to Bhabha's concept of the Mimic man and Mrinalini Sinha's concept of Effeminate man rather than to Radhika Chopra's concept of Alpha man or to the Kshatriya model of Masculinity. The paper shall also make a passing reference to gender-bending which is, as David Glover and Cora Caplan suggests,

> ...the subversion of a role through parody or the deliberate cultivation of ambiguity: what was once dutifully thought to be fixed becomes chameleon-like, a part to be played with style, a chance to mock and shock.[7]

However, before attempting to study Kiran Desai's treatment of postcolonial Indian masculinities in *The Inheritance of Loss*, I shall briefly highlight the construction of masculinities in India.

I

An early attempt to explore the construction of masculinities in India can be found in the writings of social psychologists like Sudhir Kakar and Ashis Nandy. Kakar has inquired into the unambiguous nature of the normative matrices, family structures and socialisation processes which shape the psyche of Indian men. Social psychologists stress on the process of 'socialisation' which describe how a child learns to become a man or a woman and how social institutions and socio-cultural setting condition a child to grow as a man or woman, under the given set of norms, roles and institutions, from the early childhood. Family is seen as primary socialiser and social institutions like schools and peer groups act as secondary socialisers, in the process of socialization. In the view of cultural constructionists masculinity is often understood and described in various metaphors of roles, performances and scripts. Such conceptions and metaphors are used to get insights that are of use to development practitioners seeking to work with men toward gender equitable society. One insight is to separate men from their masculine roles in order to create a space within which their gendered realities, and the process of their gendering, can become more visible to men themselves. This introspective consciousness would be essential for making men more gender unbiased as it affects their lives as well as those of women, giving a gendered structure to their minds and consequently to there social realities.

Another view is to understand masculinity as discourse(s), especially as power discourse(s). This view takes the concept of masculinity beyond men, manhood and the biological or cultural bases of masculine nature or identity. The development practitioners are generally concerned with exploring men's affiliation to gender equality and to replicate this relationship in the context of relations of power not only between but also within the genders. Viewing masculinity as discourse helps development practitioners to understand this placement by defining the values and practices that create such hierarchies of power. Gender based violence, heterosexuality, misogyny, homophobia, racism and class/status/caste-based discrimination are all the implications of the 'politics of masculinity' that is associated with and deployed by men to claim power over women, and by some men to claim power over other men. Connell appropriately defined it in following words:

> 'Masculinity,' to the extent that the term can be briefly defined at all, is simultaneously a place in gender relations, the practices through which men and women engage that place in gender, and the effects of these practices in bodily experience, personality and culture.[8]

Masculinity is a way to explain and describe the broad spectrum of realities associated with men and their worldview—but there are different ideas codified in different terminology: biological determinism or essentialism, the normative definition, which says masculinity is what, ought to be, cultural or social constructionism as well as masculinity as a power discourse. In the view of biological determinists, masculinity is men's basic nature, and as such helps to explain not only differences but also inequalities between men and women. Men's political, economic and cultural entitlements arise from their being 'masculine,' as variously reflected in genetic predilection to aggression, physical strength and sexual drives in contrast to passivity, weakness and sexual reserve of femininity. Normative views stresses on social norms and study of normative stereotypes or 'normative ideals' which a man or woman ought to be or do. This view can also be implacable in understanding 'Dharma' or 'Jaati dharma' as reflected in expressions like 'kshatriya dharma,' in classical writings on caste and varna system in India.

Different masculinities occupy different places in a power relationship in the public sphere. Thus masculinity can be understood as hegemonic masculinity with its essential hierarchies of power relationships. In the particular context of India, caste masculinities can be understood with the concept of hegemonic masculinity. Lower and upper castes occupy there appropriate places in traditional hierarchical Indian society according to their socio-political status and dominance. Viewing masculinity as power discourse has broadened our understanding of dialectical social structure. Thus different masculinities occupy different places on a power continuum and there is no chance of absolute masculinities. Even women also occupy a place on same power continuum with lesser or greater degree of masculine traits. The definition given by Connell warns us that masculinity is not the property of men, and reminds us to be wary of using the terms 'men,' 'male' and 'masculinity' interchangeably. Discourses of masculinity are available to, used by, and imposed upon both men and women. The sociologist Connell has criticized male sex-role theory, in which men are supposed to take on certain "roles," as reifying expectations and self-descriptions, exaggerating consensus, and bypassing historical alteration. Instead, he has suggested that masculinities are relational: different masculinities are constituted in relation to other masculinities and to femininities through the structure of gender relations and other social structures such as caste, class and colonialism.

Ashish Nandy has provided an elaborate account of the impact of British rule on the restructuring of masculinities in India. He argues that the hyper-masculinist British imperial ideology warped the fluid gender identities which characterised pre-modern Indian society, resulting in the inflation of the Kshatriya model of masculinity, which had earlier occupied a limited social space. However, recent historians like Rosalind O'Hanlon and Mrinalini Sinha has challenged this concept. Mrinalini Sinha has pointed out "effeminate masculinity of Bengalies" and contrasted it with "manly Englishman." Feminist writers pointed towards 'misandry'—a belief that masculinity itself is responsible for most of the world's woes—which sometimes reflected negatively in the women's movement.

To understand the social structure and functional nature of masculinity it becomes important to explore the socio-economic bases of masculinity which is institutionalized and widely expressed as 'patriarchy.' Patriarchy is said to secure the subordination of women and the empowerment of men. Thus, women are considered to be essentially passive and emotional, suited to child-bearing and home-making. Hence they are confined to the private or domestic sphere, resulting in their marginalisation. This marginalisation of women is manifested in domestic violence, gender based violence, sexual violence against women, poor health and lack of education in women and among various other forms, especially in India. On the other hand, men, who are thought to be naturally active and rational, are accorded a major role in the public or political sphere. In both the public and domestic spheres, patriarchy refers to the institutionalization of men's power over women within the economy, the polity, household and heterosexual relations.

Normative stereotype of the male has to play three major roles—as protector, provider and procreator—in both public and private sphere of their life, in patriarchal societies. 'Provider' role, in domestic sphere, is associated with men as 'breadwinner,' earning money or feeding family or providing them a social status through hard work. To sexually satisfy the wife or partner is also linked with men's provider role. The role of 'procreator' is intricately tied with masculine sexuality. As 'procreator,' capacity to father a child is at the centre of manhood as reflected in various studies in India including the ICRW study. 'Sexual prowess' is closely associated with the procreator role. Men's third normative role in patriarchal gendered society is the role of a 'protector.' In the domestic sphere, the protector is seen as a fearless, courageous man who protects the honour of the household by protecting women and children of the family. Inability to do that is seen as 'unmanly' by majority of respondents in various studies carried out in India and across the world. This protection to women and family is linked to men's control on women and family. Like men, women should also fulfil their normative roles as assigned in a patriarchal society and that is primarily to take care of household chores and children and to fulfil the sexual and other needs of men. Women's deviation from their gender role may challenge the masculinity of men and may be manifested in violent behaviour and sexual violence against women, in men. The findings of INCLEN 2000 study, which states that domestic or gender based violence is a pervasive problem in India that it cuts across age, education, social class and religion, can be understood in the light of above-mention phenomenon of 'failed' masculinity. These studies show

how any deviation or failure to fulfil the responsibilities assigned to the normative stereotypes in these societies might be manifested in various forms of gender based violence, reinforcing Moore's writings that gender based violence is intricately linked to the real or perceived fulfilment of masculinities.

In their introduction to Theorizing Masculinities, Harry Brod and Michael Kaufman suggest we are now witnessing the emergence of a "second wave" of critical studies on men and masculinities. While they don't identify exactly what constituted the "first wave," we assume the equivalence with the first-wave of feminist history, and it perhaps indicates a period of relatively homogeneous theorizing and activism in men's studies evolving into a second period in which theory and activism are more attentive to diversity. Brod and Kaufman claim that the second-wave studies of masculinities are committed in theoretical and activist work to critical analysis of power relations and to—

> ...the ever-growing recognition that we cannot study masculinity in the singular.... Rather, we wish to emphasize the plurality and diversity of men's experiences, attitudes, beliefs, situations, practices, and institutions along lines of race, class, sexual orientation, religion, ethnicity, age, region, physical appearance, able-bodiedness, mental ability, and various other categories with which we describe our lives and experiences.[9]

II

Kiran Desai, in her novel *The Inheritance of Loss*,[10] subtly irradiates several shades of postcolonial Indian masculinities. The central male character in the novel, Jemubhai Patel, finds himself languishing on the interface of English and Indian cultures. Educated at Bishop Cotton School and having developed a profound veneration for the portrait of Queen Victoria that stood at the school's entrance, Jemubhai had grown fond of the colonial masters. Such was his proclivity for the English life that he married for the purpose of going to England a woman who brought him dowry, disregarding the possibility of a happy conjugal life at home. Once he boarded the SS Strathnaver, he began hating everything related to the indigenous culture. His father's instruction to throw the coconut overboard as an auspicious prologue to the voyage only gave rise to a sense of pity and shame in his heart.

> Jemubhai looked at his father, a barely educated man venturing where he should not be, and the love in Jemubhai's heart mingled with pity, the pity with shame. (37)

A sense of humiliation gripped him when he felt that the food that his mother had packed for him—the profundity of a mother's love was quite lost on him—did not meet the norms of food that the colonizers consumed. So, in order to avert himself from being belittled by the colonial masters, Jemubhai threw the food packet overboard. Desai brings out, in graphic manner, Jemubhai's desperate attempt to eschew his Indian affiliations.

> Jemu picked up the package, fled to the deck, and threw it overboard. Didn't his mother think of the inappropriateness of her gesture? Undignified love, Indian love, stinking, unaesthetic love—the monsters of the ocean could have what she had so bravely packed getting up in that predawn mush. (38)

The passage is not only a clear indicator to the locus of the author's sympathies, but also a lucid exploration of Jemubhai's psychic myopia. Jemubhai's refusal of his hearth and home is caused by his intense desire to ape the English to perfection. The colonizers' effort to create an image of their own selves among the colonized, as already mentioned, led to a stunted growth of masculinity. His predilection for all that the English life and culture presented to his imagination made him a close kin to Ralph Singh in V.S. Naipaul's *The Mimic Men*:

> We pretended to be real, to be learning, to be preparing ourselves for life, we mimic men of the New World, one unknown corner of it, with all its reminders of the corruption that came so quickly to the new.[11]

Jemubhai too found out the corruptions inherent in the Brave New World that he had imaginatively conceived. He quickly realised that England was not only a "Land of Hope and Glory," but also of "tiny gray houses in gray streets, stuck together and down as if on a glue trap" (38). Much to his disillusionment, he found that England was not a vast panorama of ultimate grandness; it was a land that circumscribed in her folds poor and unaesthetic lives.

Hardly had his disenchantment set in than he felt the brunt of being an alien in the land of his dreams. The attitude of indifference and insult that was cast on him made him eschew society and hide himself in a shell of loneliness.

> He worked twelve hours at a stretch, late into the night, and in thus withdrawing, he failed to make a courageous gesture outward at a crucial moment and found, instead, that his *pusillanimity* and his loneliness had found fertile soil. He retreated into a solitude that grew in weight day by day. The solitude became a habit, the habit became the man, and it crushed him into a shadow. (39) [italics mine]

Jemubhai felt in his heart that he was a mimic man—almost white, but not quite—and he lacked the courage and conviction of the normative masculine characterised by strength, virility and courage to break through his shell. The expression "pusillanimity" shows that under the influence of the colonial culture, Jemubhai had become a specimen of mimic Indian masculinity. Jemubhai's attempt to internalize the culture of the colonizers is not rooted in a transcendental choice-freeze. He had the vast and glorious Indian culture ready at hand. He could easily have used it as frame of reference to exercise his option of proudly carrying abroad his unmasked brown skin. Jemubhai, however, attempted to uncritically internalize the culture of the Britishers. This resulted in the creation of a dangerous inauthentic identity. As Roop Rekha Verma suggests—

> The unreflective or uncritical internalization of a culture is due to nontranscendental choice-closures...and the identities of individuals formed by them are inauthentic. An inauthentic identity militates against the requirements

of modernity, and consequently against those of progress too.[12]

Jemubhai realises that in trying to learn a foreign way of life he had become the mimic man, but he would not acknowledge it. When, after retiring from his job, he met his friend Bose who scathingly criticised the British, he decided to remain silent. He would not acknowledge that his exalted concept of the British had bitten the dust.

> He wouldn't tumble his pride to melodrama at the end of his life and he knew the danger of confession—it would cancel any hope of dignity forever. (208)

So he decided to buy Cho Oyu, a house made by a Scotsman and tucked away in the north-eastern Himalayas. He felt that the location of the house would give him a shelter where he could hide not only from the eyes of his fellow men, but also from himself.

> The judge [Jemubhai] could live here, in this shell, this skull, with the solace of being a foreigner in his own country, for this time he would not learn a new language. (29)

The decision is definitely an indicator of the erosion of masculinity.

In fact, after he returned from England as an ICS officer, he had a realisation of his failed masculinity. The obvious corollary is that he tried to hide his failure under the façade of hatred and fury. It is this realization that led him to take an almost misanthropic view of life. As he climbed the ladder of material success, his soul plummeted to new depths. As his creator points out—

> I think transporting a man from a poor family into a supremely wealthy society must really have an impact... must result in some kind of mental deterioration. In most cases, it is those back home who take the brunt as the power balance changes. Jemubhai's case is an extreme. I call him an ogre and believe me, there are ogres in existence.[13]

It may appear surprising that a man who could not love his wife, his daughter and his granddaughter, who had borne the brunt of a dichotomy that colonization often brought in its trail almost all his life and who had developed a "misanthropy and cynicism" over the years could love a dog to such an extent that he would move the police to search for it and beat his cook frantically for being responsible for its loss. His love for the dog and his frenzied beating of the cook are suitable indicators of his psychic status.

His relationship with Mutt is not a common relation of a man with his pet dog, nor had he an extraordinary alliance with Mutt as Jim Corbett had with Robin. A cynic as the judge was, his cynicism was further intensified as the Nepalese activists tweaked his nose. He came to the realization that an animal is better than a man. An unconscious inversion of Tennyson's concept of man as, presented in "The Lotos Eaters," as the "roof and crown of things!"

> He couldn't conceive of punishment great enough for humanity. A man wasn't equal to an animal, not one particle of him. Human life was stinking, corrupt, and meanwhile there were beautiful creatures who [sic] lived with delicacy on the earth without doing anyone any harm. (292)

Receding from humanity, he struk up a close relation with a lower animal—a definite reversal of values. Hence, he beat up the cook. The manner in which he tortured the cook is significant.

> The judge was beating with all the force of his sagging, puckering flesh, flecks of saliva flying from his slack muscled mouth, and his chin wobbled uncontrollably. Yet that arm, from which the flesh hung already dead, came down, bringing the slipper upon the cook's head. (321)

The savagery of the judge contrasted with his physical weakness creates a grimly grotesque figure that deserves, surely as the author wishes, the readers' derision than their sympathy.

The character of the cook is a paradigm of failed masculinity. He is weak, both physically and mentally. His ludicrous surrender to the GNLF activists, his superstitions and his acceptance of the fact that he had failed to play the socially sanctioned masculine roles of protector and provider reveal that he is a far cry from the traditional concept of masculinity. However, he does not become an "ogre" like Jemubhai. It is his sterling love for his son, Biju, that redeems his feeble masculinity.

The cook's love for Biju is clearly evident in the letters he wrote to his son and especially in his actions in the last chapter. The cook's sudden confession of his past crimes is not without a cause. Moreover, he was not responsible for the loss of Mutt. The wife and father of the man who was blinded by the police, stole the dog. They had repeatedly requested the judge to help them but, obviously, to no avail. They stole the dog—not in vengeance—but because they could earn some money, which would hold their body and soul together, by selling it to some fashionable people.

The cook's behaviour is apparently puzzling, but the reasons for his almost suicidal actions lie in his mental praxis. The cook is significantly given no name, just as Katherine Mansfield does not give a name to the Boss in her short story "The Fly." Of course, unlike Mansfield's treatment of the Boss's character, Desai does not use profound psychological insights to develop the character of the cook. Both the Boss and the cook represent impoverished specimens of humanity: the former standing for a type of people in whom decadent materialism has displaced the heart from its right place; the latter representing spineless, weak, and cringing individuals who enjoy a shadowy existence.

The cook's whole life centred round his son Biju who lived as an illegal immigrant in America. Once the sanguine claws of terrorism cut through the world of the hills and the entire idyllic atmosphere turned topsy-turvy, the cook grew anxious. In this predicament, he lost contact with Biju. The obvious corollary is that he was shaken to his nerves. He felt, and even started believing, that Biju had never existed and that he had only been like a dream.

> The cook didn't mention his son...he had none...he'd never had one...it was just his hope writing to him.... Biju was nonexistent.... (321)

Once, in his psyche, Biju became "nonexistent" the entire world broke down for him. He felt that he had nothing to live for. Being weak by nature, he did not have the mental strength to tide over the pessimistic thoughts, nor did he possess the mental strength—which is, of course, perverted,—to lay hands on himself. He felt, "I'd be better dead than alive" (320). In his muddled brain, which was caused by an overdose of alcohol at Thapa's Canteen and a copious dose of chhang prepared by him, he made a plan that would release him from the pains of life. So, he admitted all his faults to his master hoping that the judge would beat him to death. The cook's repeated request to the judge, "Kill me," evinces a passive effort on his part to end his existence.

Biju's rat like life in America, shifting from one restaurant to another, reflects a debilitating Indian masculinity under the pressure of the West. However, he was neither as immoral as Saeed Saeed, nor was he a "metonymy of presence" like Harish-Harry, Gaurish-Gary and Dhansukh-Danny. Biju suffered under the onus of the first world life, yet he had enough strength of character to hold up an individual identity and, hence, Desai does not anglicize his name. Biju pedaled down the proud streets of America, carrying food to the different houses from Freddy's Wok. He trembled in the cold, was torn by his worries about his father and only found peace in humming old Hindi film songs.

In singing the film songs, Biju showed enough masculine strength to hold back to the modern and integral part of India's culture. Biju's decision to return to India, in spite of the lure of lucre that had forced the "metonymies of presence" to be tied to a degrading life in the first world, was an indicator of his strength of character. On board, Biju's pledge to relinquish the life of America and begin anew an Indian life speaks volumes of firmness.

> In the mirror of this bathroom, Biju saluted himself.... Now, he promised himself, he would forget the insight,

> begin anew. He would buy a taxi.... And he'd build a house with solid walls, a roof that wouldn't fly off every season. Biju played the scene of meeting his father.... They'd sit out in the evenings, drink chhang, tell jokes. (286)

Biju's salute is to his own vigour of character. Biju holds out promises to be the modern Indian New Man who looks after the hearth and home as well as takes care of the world outside with equal diligence and responsibility.

Biju came to meet his father at Cho Oyu wearing a woman's nightgown that had been given (so thoughtfully!) to him by the anti-socials after ransacking him. Biju's dress signifies the upheaval in the social world of the hills. Dress is a social construct. A man wearing a woman's nightgown is quite grotesque in normal times. But, the manner in which Desai presents Biju in the woman's nightgown has nothing of the bizarre about it. Biju's dress implicitly asks the question, in a world that has lost its fundamental humanity, what indeed is gender?

The filial feeling of the cook, however, was not deterred by his son's uncouth dress. He was wild with joy at getting his son back. The author describes the meeting between father and son without any slips of prolixity.

> Sai looked out and saw two figures leaping at each other as the gate swung open. (324)

The verb "leaping" reflects the intense emotion that underlines the meeting. Now, the cook would wish to live again, for the very sustenance of his life, his son whom he had thought as imaginary, was near him again, throbbing and pulsating—in spite of his wretched condition. Biju, on the other hand, would bury not only the ignominy of being an illegal third world immigrant in the first world, but also the last insult that he had at the hands of the local rowdies.

Gyan, Biju's contemporary in age, represents a different dimension of postcolonial Indian masculinity. His great-grandfather was a Macho Man—what George Mosse calls "the dominant masculine stereotype"[14]—who had won laurels for his physical prowess. He was recruited as a soldier in the Imperial Army, as Desai describes, on the merit of his corporeal might.

> By and by along came the Imperial Army, measuring potential soldiers in villages all over the hills with a measuring tape and ruler, and they had happened upon the impressive shoulders of Gyan's great-grandfather, who had grown so strong on the milk of their buffalo that he had beaten the village sweet-seller's son in a wrestling match, an exceptionally glossy and healthy boy. (141)

Gyan, however, had inherited nothing of his great-grandfather's physical strength. He was satisfied with measuring the muscles of his upper arm with his fiancée, Sai.

When the GNLF movement gathered momentum, Gyan also felt the heat. However, he lacked the courage to be an active member of the movement and when his friends coaxed him to join a rally, he had to take shelter under a tale that his grandmother spun out. His only contribution to the success of the movement was his imbecile divulgence, of course under the spell of intoxicating liquor, of the fact about the weapons that Jemubhai possessed. When Sai threw this truth on his face and held the mirror up to his own frailties, he would do nothing but take recourse to one of the favourite strategies of frail masculinities: gendered violence. Gyan did not have the qualities of giving directions to his family though his parents expect it from him. He realised that he might not live up to their expectations of being a male and it worried him to death:

> He [Gyan] hated his tragic father, his mother who looked to him for direction, had always looked to him for direction, even when he was a little boy, simply for being a male. He spent the nights awake, worrying he couldn't live up to his proclamations. (260)

Gyan's promise to bring back Mutt was as hollow as his own masculine stance. Desai's insinuation does not fail to miss the mark.

> "I will find the dog. Don't worry at all.... I will find Mutt and bring her to the house."
>
> He uttered this sentence with a conviction that had nothing to do with Mutt or his ability to find her. (314)

The author's comment undercuts Gyan's pledge. This is evidence of Desai's gender-bending. Here is a subversion of the masculine stereotype. Gyan was not blind to the self-deceit that lay in his promise; he was conscious of his inability to keep the pledge. Yet, he made the promise because he did not have the psychic potency to accept his weakness.

It is significant that Desai's treatment of masculinity in the novel, thanks to her keen sense of realism and artistic fidelity, never appears to be stilted. Characters like Jemubhai, the cook, Biju, Gyan and the "metonymies of presence" do really stalk about the society. This realism is the cornerstone of the novel's appeal. Indeed, as R.A. Scott-James suggests:

> ...the novel shall not be natural history...it shall not be a mere transcript of life...it shall be something exhibited for our contemplation which is not merely "like life," but "true to life"—no "wax work figure," but the expression of a vision which has *embraced the commonness of reality, without being made common by it.*"[15] [italics mine]

This assertion of Scott-James implies that a novel must touch life, sometimes tangentially, sometimes profoundly, at various points and, yet, retain an artistic grace and an appeal that would stir the sensibilities of the readers. Kiran Desai performs this difficult task with élan in her novel.

Notes & References

1. Quoted in David Glover and Cora Kaplan, *Genders* (New York: Routledge, 2000) xiii-xiv.
2. Elleke Boehmer, *Colonial and Postcolonial Literature* (Oxford: OUP, 1995) 71.
3. Arthur C. Danto, "The Shape of Artistic Pasts, East and West," *Culture and Modernity: East-West Philosophic Perspectives*, ed. Eliot Deutsch (Delhi: Motilal Banarasidass, 1997) 338.

4. Homi K. Bhabha, "Of Mimicry and Man: The Ambivalence of Colonial Discourse," *Modern Literary Theory: A Reader,* ed. Philip Rice and Patricia Waugh (New York: Arnold, *1996*) 384.
5. Bhabha.
6. Bhabha.
7. David Glover and Cora Kaplan, *Genders* (New York: Routledge, *2000*) *ix*.
8. R.W. Connell, *Masculinities* (Cambridge: Polity Press, 1995), quoted in Avanish Kumar, "Constructs of Masculinities," 23 March 2008, <www.insightresearchnetwork.org>. I gratefully acknowledge that I have heavily drawn upon Kumar's brilliant article in Section-I of the paper. I have also made references to Mrinalini Sinha, Rosalind O'Hanlon, ICRW study and INCLEN 2000 study from Kumar's article.
9. Quoted in Lahoucine Ouzgane and Daniel Coleman, *Postcolonial Masculinities: Introduction*, 24 March 2008. <http://social.chass.ncsu.edu/Jouvert/v2i1/int21.htm.>.
10. All quotations from the novel are from Kiran Desai, *The Inheritance of Loss* (New Delhi: Penguin Books, 2006).
11. V.S. Naipaul, *The Mimic Men* (London: Penguin, 1967) 146.
12. Roop Rekha Verma, "The Concept of Progress and Cultural Identity," *Culture and Modernity: East-West Philosophic Perspectives*, ed. Eliot Deutsch (Delhi: Motilal Banarasidass, 1997) 533. Transcendental choice-closure refers to an inevitable and unopted cultural conditioning. As far as Jemubhai is concerned, he was not forced into transcendental choice-closure.
13. Maitreyee S. Ganapathy, "Never-ending Narratives," *The Hindu*, Online Edition, 05 Feb. 2006. <http://www.thehindu.com/lr/2006/02/05/stories/200602050006 0100.htm>.
14. Quoted in David Glover and Cora Kaplan, *Genders* (New York: Routledge, 2000) 59.
15. R.A. Scott-James, *The Making of Literature* (New Delhi: Allied Publishers, 2004) 373.

10

Reciprocal Relationship between Masculinity and Femininity in Thi.Ja.'s *Mogamul* and Mulk Raj Anand's *Gauri*

N. Chandra

Abstract

This article analyses Indian masculinity of the 1960s and 1970s that represent a significant period of postcolonial India. Mulk Raj Anand's *Gauri* and Thi.Janakiraman's *Mogamul* are the postcolonial texts used for the analysis. The article attempts to depict how masculinity is heterogeneous. It reveals how male characters change their masculinity based on power dynamics. The changes could also be due to the societal structures. Furthermore, the article stresses on how masculinity and femininity are interdependent and have a reciprocal relationship. Thus the study of masculinity, in a way, is complimentarily to the study of femininity.

Masculinity means "the quality of being masculine" and masculine means "having the qualities or appearance considered to be typical of men; connected with or like men" according to the *Oxford Advanced Learner's Dictionary of Current English* (Wehmeier 786). Gender studies has conventionally divided the roles of man and woman leading to strict constructions of maleness and femaleness. Connell, who mentions that men are the breadwinners of the family and the women are homemakers, substantiates this idea. Due to this division of work, as put forth by Connell, the nature of man and woman, their behaviours are ascribed different meanings.

As Beynon says in *Masculinities and Culture*, the concept of masculinity is to do with political, social, historical change and one's masculine/feminine nature cannot be constant. Masculinity is thus practiced by one's upbringing, family, work and sub-cultural influences in every society. Once consciously or unconsciously issues of masculinity are implemented in the minds of individuals, then, men start following those traits without thinking about its nature/construction and just remain masculine for their convenience. Thus men's masculinity is displayed through characteristics such as violence, aggressiveness, dominance and unemotionality while women's femininity is revealed by their passiveness, submissiveness and emotionality. Conventional masculine/feminine scales claim that men are after material success whereas women stay at home looking after the needs of the family. According to Connell, to realise masculinity and femininity, one has to remove the feminine nature from a man and the masculine nature from a woman (1995: 69). He also states that some men, being dominant, try to control women in their families and other men in the society and thus prove themselves to be hegemonic. In *Masculinities* Connell defines hegemonic masculinities by pointing out that it is—

> ...the configuration of gender practice which embodies the currently accepted answer to the problem of the legitimacy of patriarchy, which guarantees (or is taken to guarantee) the dominant position of some men over others, and the subordination of women. (77)

Further clarifying hegemonic masculinity Connell states the hierarchy of it as—

> Hegemonic masculinity was distinguished from other masculinities, especially subordinated masculinities. Hegemonic masculinity was not assumed to be normal in the statistical sense; only a minority of men might enact it. But it was certainly normative. It embodied the currently most honored way of being a man, it required all other men to position themselves in relation to it, and it ideologically legitimated the global subordination of women to men. (Connell & Messerschmidt 832)

This is possible only when someone has the power in one's hands. Without power one cannot try to control or subordinate a woman/other men. Beynon in *Masculinities and Culture* avers that "Hegemonic masculinity is established either through consensual negotiation or through power and achievement" (Beynon 16).

This article focuses on analysing and reading Indian masculinity that is obtained in postcolonial India from 1960s to 1970s by using two fictional texts, Mulk Raj Anand's *Gauri* (1976)[1] and Thi.Ja.'s[2] *Mogamul*[3] (1970), a Tamil novel.[4] Gauri as portrayed in *Gauri*, is an innocent girl, married to a peasant called Panchi. Panchi's aunt, Kesaro sows the seeds of misunderstanding between them thereby leading to their separation and broken relationship. Panchi thrives on blaming Gauri's ill-luck as the cause of his downfall and when he suspects her pregnancy, he sends her to her mother, Laxmi's place, where Gauri's uncle, Amru sells her off to Seth Ram, an old man. Later, a doctor, who comes to check Gauri in Seth Ram's house, rescues her and makes her to work at his hospital. Thus Gauri continues to lead a peaceful life by working at the hospital. When Gauri returns to her husband, Panchi's place, he does not accept her and therefore she decides to go back to the hospital and work there. *Mogamul* is the story of Babu, a young artist who falls in love with Yamuna, his family friend. Even though he is ten years younger than Yamuna he finally decides to marry her. Yamuna hesitates but finally, at forty years of age, she agrees to the alliance. Babu's story in the novel begins when he is a teenager and ends in his thirties, when he goes to North India to learn music and Yamuna waits for his consent to the marriage.

In this study, masculinity and femininity are analysed in relation to each other by analysing both men and women characters since the two gender localisations are inter-dependent. The analysis takes the men characters into consideration first as the term masculine itself refers to men. The analysis of women characters in the later part of this article shows that they are interdependent on men to remain feminine. The major men characters considered for analysis are

Panchi, the husband of Gauri in *Gauri* and Babu in *Mogamul*. Though these men do not adhere strictly to the traits of masculinity they follow some of the masculine characteristics which reveal the concept of masculinity. According to the norms prevailing in the Indian society of that period men are dominant, adventurous, ambitious, violent, intellectual, and unemotional and most of the time they act as decision-makers and breadwinners. Other than these, men sometimes reveal other characteristics such as controlling the family, becoming sexually aggressive, showing interest in other women, discussing social issues, drinking toddy, and following certain cultural codes of masculinity so as to maintain their power. In the analysis, some of these masculine characteristics are revealed by the major as well as the minor characters in the two novels.

In *Mogamul*, Babu's masculinity is shaped in different ways throughout the novel. The novel traces his transformation from an immature boy into a mature man. The novel further portrays that his father, his friend Rajam and Yamuna shape Babu's masculinity. Other than these, he faces many experiences, which also shape his masculinity. Since his childhood, he is trained by his father to attend *kacheri'* (music concerts) and to become a *vidwvan* (a classical musician) by performing *kacheris*. Thus, his father plans Babu's life and therefore, he shows no interest in college education. Later he decides to follow whatever his father tells him. Whenever Babu feels distracted, he is brought back to his senses by his father's advice. The novel traces Babu's growth from a teenager to an adult and depicts a different adult Babu—a modern man, a 'new man' who is different from other men in society and whose ideas are radical. In one of the incidents in the novel, when a groom to be married to Yamuna reveals his displeasure at the fact that she belongs to a mixed community, Babu gets upset and thinks that the groom is a fool and quarrels with him. He complains that the groom is a "beast" and therefore not a match to Yamuna. This shows that he is a 'new' man and is ready to cross the boundaries of routine masculine behaviour.

When Babu was young his masculinity was shaped by his father's example but as time rolled by his masculinity underwent many changes based on the experiences and the positions he occupied in society. He had earlier followed the hegemonic masculinity of his father and understood the power of being male and of enforcing his supremacy. Therefore as a young boy, he had tried during his school days to dominate his sister's daughter Pattu: "He showed his power over her every minute since he was two and half years older to her…" (Thi.Ja. 143). Later on he had changed his masculinity when he developed friendship with Rajam, his classmate. He stopped underestimating women as he did earlier. He began to think of women and their freedom as he states: "What freedom we're talking about? When a woman speaks loudly we don't like it, when she goes alone we don't like it" (Thi.Ja. 131). This change was also due to his infatuation with Yamuna, his family friend. Initially he was stunned by her physical beauty and then by her contradictory opinions regarding society. Though he changes some of his old masculine attitudes he is shocked when he sees the city girls, who seem to be different in their representation of femininity in comparison to the girls he has known. He feels that the city women are more masculine, which establishes that he does not want a complete change (Thi.Ja. 599).

Babu, since he is different from other men, does not like women being "gazed" by men before marriage as a part of the Indian tradition. He feels disgusted: "There's a mob to weigh the beauty of the girl. One can say they're non-sensual, since they agree to do so for the only reason he is a 'man'" (Thi.Ja. 87). Since he is a 'new' man, his views are different from other men's and that is why he is opposed to this notion of masculinity. One's masculinity does not allow one to admit one's failure. Thus, when Babu also fails to get help from Sundaram, Yamuna's step brother, he feels that it is his "maleness" that was being ridiculed. Babu and Yamuna's marriage becomes a problematic issue, because he is younger to Yamuna by ten years, which is not readily acceptable according to societal norms. One has to realise that Babu at an earlier age could not display his masculine power over others as he was still young and dependent on his father. Therefore, only when he gets a job and starts earning money, he is able to take the bold decision of marrying Yamuna despite the opposition. He replies that he would not worry about the opposition of his own parents either, when Yamuna's mother, Parvati, questions him. Thus money and power add a new dimension to Babu's masculinity.

At one point in the novel Babu states that a street dog is freer than a man because he feels that men are controlled by teacher/father/higher officials/society, and countless other agencies. Hofstede says in *Masculinity and Femininity: Taboo Dimension of National Cultures*: "Men try to bend not only women but also other men to their will. Violent actions also serve to impress women and win their sexual favors" (Hofstede 129). In another incident Babu is ready to beat a man when he talks ill of Yamuna and Parvati. Yamuna, Parvati and Babu go to a village to attend the funeral ceremony of Yamuna's father. When Babu goes out for a walk at night, he happens to overhear two men criticising the attitudes of Parvati and Yamuna. One of these men is drunk and is outrageously talking to the other man. He is stressing his masculinity by speaking ill of Parvati. He does not expect Babu to overhear him. When Babu starts beating him, he realises that he should not have spoken. He is scared because he has no power and Babu can take any action against him since he is the visitor of a rich man in that village. This episode reveals that there are two different masculinities—one displayed in front of his colleague and another in front of Babu. Therefore, power plays an important role here and Babu becomes hegemonic. Masculinity thus gets transformed in front of different men, according to the power they wield.

In *Gauri*, Panchi too, like Babu in *Mogamul*, does not display any masculinity at the beginning of the novel. He is submissive to his uncle, who brings him up and also to his aunt Kesaro. He lives with them since his childhood days without raising his voice and he is unable to oppose them at any point. He works with his uncle Mola Ram by submitting himself to his masculine role. Later when Panchi is married he wants to display to the others and his wife that he is masculine by being the breadwinner and decision-maker of the family and also to prove to the world that he is no longer under the control of his uncle. Thus Panchi begins to quarrel with Mola Ram, his guardian, and even resorts to shouting as he wishes to assert his masculinity over Mola Ram. When Mola Ram challenges him and states that he is not hard working and is irresponsible, he immediately asks for his portion of the land. As already stated, this does not happen before his marriage, but later so that he can impress his wife. Though he fails in his attempts even after selling Gauri's jewels, he does not want to compromise with Mola Ram and accept his failure. This illustrates that, in his new masculine role, Panchi desires to dominate his wife. In other words, the presence of Gauri is the trigger for him to resist Mola Ram's queries and insults and his moving away from his uncle's home. Thus by getting married, Panchi becomes an adult male and acquires a new social identity which he thought was not possible under Mola Ram's control.

Panchi soon takes over the responsibility of his family and acts as the breadwinner. He also believes that his wife is his possession and therefore when Kesaro tells him that Gauri has an affair with Rajaguru, his friend, his masculinity is hurt. But when his masculinity is not threatened he ignores other issues. For example, he does not believe in Gauri being an unlucky girl even though Kesaro tries to label her as such. He is now ready to break his friendship with Rajaguru despite his explanation that he has come to pay a friendly visit to Panchi. Panchi's masculinity also does not allow anyone even talking to his wife and at the slightest provocation he violently attacks Gauri. He often loses his control regretting taking the responsibility of the family and bringing shame upon himself. Till the end of the novel, he remains a failure and his image as a breadwinner becomes a problematic one when he has to face society. Though he appears as if he were more masculine by his behaviour towards his wife, he is submissive to other men due to the lack of economic status and power.

In his attempt to display masculine power Panchi becomes more and more violent towards Gauri. He feels he has the right as well as the reason for beating her. When he is informed by Kesaro that Gauri has uncovered her face and talked to Rajaguru, he does not try to seek any clarification from his wife. He thinks that, being a man as well as the husband, he has unquestionable rights over her. He gets angry when he learns that Gauri would stay, because he will have one more mouth to feed at home and also because Kesaro informs him that he may not be the father of the child to be born. In his anger he decides to send Gauri away and when she falls at his feet and begs with pleading hands, he feels that he has the power to get her back and also to send her away as and when he pleases. Much later, when he wants to bring her back, he comes to know that she has been sold to some one. He is upset as he feels that no one has the right to sell his wife and he complains so that he lodges a complaint with the police to get her back. Once again, through this incident, he reveals his authority over his wife.

Panchi also needs Gauri in order to prove his masculinity through his sexual prowess. Whenever he is violent towards her he tries to convince her by buying cakes of Hamam soap or food items such as mangoes for her. The novel points out this paradox by stating sardonically: "Whom he could fold in his arms at night and kick during the day that would adorn his house and help him with the land" (Anand 11). In a way, the novel reveals the animalistic masculinity of Panchi through various incidents. When Panchi is introduced in the novel he is depicted as trying to "control" it which, in a way, is symbolic of masculinity. He also does the same thing when he is pasturing the land with his bullocks. He initially tries to treat the beasts violently but when it does not work he cajoles them and the bullocks began to co-operate. He then states that is the way to do things is by force or by being affectionate, a principle which he practises with Gauri too. He beats her first and then convinces her to get satisfaction for his needs/desires: "Of prayers first, the big stick afterward so far as women were concerned" (Anand 38). He is ready to break the well established social conventions too. He readily goes with his Muslim friend, drinks with him and stays up with him, contrary to the norms of his community. Panchi resorts to thieving and gets caught and feels as though his masculinity is at stake. It is an insult to him to be caught by the servant of the landlord and to be insulted in front of other men. He feels ashamed of himself, since his masculine identity is eroded in front of the landlord and his uncle Mola Ram.

In the novel Panchi is often referred to as a "bull" and as being manly: "Panchi felt like a lucky bull going off to marry the little cow Gauri" (Anand 13). Gauri on the other hand is termed as a "cow" a feminine person: "Gauri is like a cow, very gentle and very good" (Anand 11). Thus men are expected to be strong and virile whereas women are expected to be passive and timid. Women have to submit to men's wishes and expectations. However, towards the end of the novel, interestingly enough Gauri does not revere Panchi's masculinity as she feels that he is not the sort of "bull" she has thought him to be: "He is a weak, spoilt creature! Spoilt by Kesaro. He pretended to be a lion among the men of the village. But really he is a coward!" (Anand 263). She is provoked because his masculinity got trite by harsh words such as "Tell me the truth witch?... What is the proof of your purity?" (Anand 262). Panchi, as a man, expects and forces Gauri to bear his ill treatment without protest. She, as a woman, is expected to cook/clean/please him and to suffer his physical violence. If his masculinity is questioned or provoked by Gauri, he does not tolerate it. When her patience is exhausted she says, "If you strike me again, I will hit you back..." (263). Panchi is shocked and he thinks he cannot live with her. Thus Panchi remains a part of hegemonic masculinity by beating and exercising control over his wife.

Masculinity in Other Men

Babu's father in *Mogamul* has full control over his family, especially over Babu's mother. When Babu was a young boy, his father and himself used to go home late almost everyday and his mother could not question her husband, for he was the sole decision-maker. Babu feels that the presence of his sister in a way controlled his father's masculinity. This incident again reveals that there are two masculinities—one displayed in front of the children and another in front of the wife. When his elder brother questions him whether he was bringing Babu back home late everyday, he replies in the negative to avoid problems. Even though they live at different places, the elder brother has more authority over the family. His father possessed masculinity by not dominating his son, but by being affectionate towards him. He arranged for Babu's food and accommodation, for the first of which reasons his son would be comfortable and for the other he would be in his control. Babu's father gave full freedom to him, but an unknown string has always been present, controlling Babu. Babu's father felt responsible for his son and was ambitious to make him a singer.

In *Mogamul*, Sundaram, the stepbrother of Yamuna, achieves his masculinity after his father's death. He begins to take decisions on his own and he dares stop the help that has been offered by his father to his stepmother. When Babu tries to go and get help from him, he bluntly declines to give and threatens him saying he would snatch away their house too. Since Babu is younger to Sundaram, he does not care about Babu's proposal/request. When Babu's father and other elders talk to Sundaram he agrees to offer some financial support to the family. Thus, Sundaram is forced to feel the responsibility for his stepmother's family in front of other elders such as Babu's father, but when Babu requests the same, he rejects it. He also exercises hegemonic masculinity by controlling his family after his father's death. He had remained silent when his father was alive but now he becomes the master of the house. He does not give a chance even for his mother to take decisions, and she complains to Babu that Sundaram is running the family affairs as he wishes.

Amru, in *Gauri,* is another man enjoying hegemonic masculinity. He plans to sell Gauri so as to retain his two mortgaged houses and a cow. Even though Gauri and Laxmi do not agree to this plan of selling Gauri to Seth Ram, he forces Gauri to go with Seth Ram, an old man. He sells her without her knowledge and does not worry about her any more. Although he is not the father of Gauri, he demonstrates his power over the family. He readily plays the role of Laxmi's husband and wonders who would feed Gauri, when he is already feeding and taking care of Laxmi.

As if to prove Beynon's statement that power upholds masculinity, Seth Ram in *Gauri* tries to marry Gauri and control her. By marrying a girl, a man thinks that he can control her life. When Gauri is not ready to agree to the wishes of Seth Ram, he tries to convince her by parading his jewels in front of her. Thus by the dazzling display of his material wealth man his endeavours to control woman. When Seth Ram is insulted by Dr. Mahindra, he invokes his influence on the society, but the doctor decides to save Gauri from Seth Ram anyway. Thus, in this incident Dr. Mahindra's masculinity controls Seth's power and gets back Gauri to the hospital, where she wishes to work.

Like Seth Ram in *Gauri*, a fifty-five-year old man in *Mogamul* marries a young girl named Thangam. He illustrates his hegemonic power over her by keeping her locked inside the house, while he goes to office. A shift in masculinity is revealed through Rajam in *Mogamul*. Rajam, when alone at home, tries to seduce a woman carrying a bundle of grass and invites her inside when she seeks shelter from the rain under the porch of his house. When she readily comes inside he wonders: "Are all women ready for this?" (Thi.Ja. 262). But the woman questions him: "Is it right on your part to call a woman who came for shelter?" (Thi.Ja. 262). This accusation hurts Rajam and he decides not to lust for any woman other than his wife. Thus, his masculinity metamorphoses after this incident and it becomes gentle by the shifts in masculinities. Rajam wants to put the old man, Thangam's husband, in jail for marrying a very young girl. Rajam feels if he were the monarch of the country he would punish men like the old man. When Rajam scolds the men who restrict the freedom of women he would often say: "English proverb says that man has to work and woman has to cry, but Tamil proverb says woman has to serve and man has to eat" (Thi.Ja. 100). Thus his masculinity is soft towards women and not hegemonic.

Babu's cousin Sangu in *Mogamul* is more courageous than Babu in his younger years. When he grows up, his masculinity too becomes very strong. Sangu is ready to kill a man, who talked ill of Parvati, Yamuna's mother and Babu's father. He tells Babu that he would kill him by using his knife and is ready to face the consequences. Sangu's masculinity has been growing after marriage and he often beats his wife. Thus Babu thinks that many men get married only to beat their wives. This is the evidence of Sangu's hegemonic masculinity.

In both the novels, *Gauri* and *Mugamul*, apart from the men characters some women characters too possess certain masculine traits while other women characters are completely feminine. These very feminine women in a way pave the way for the play of masculinity. As a young girl Gauri is innocent and she is often referred to as a "gentle cow" by Panchi, which means that she can be easily controlled by others. Her femininity has in fact allowed Panchi to display his rampant masculine power. She cooks, cleans and does domestic chores apart from sexually satisfying him. She learns to be passive and does not resist physical and mental abuse perpetrated by Panchi and his aunt. Even though Yamuna in *Mogamul* does domestic chores she does not draw strict boundaries between the masculine/feminine areas of operation. Yamuna questions society and its conventions and she is not ready to accept all the customs, which, being a woman, she is expected to follow. She contemplates why only women have to attend to the domestic chores, and she wishes to carry this attitude into her married life as well. Due to this kind of behaviour on her part, no man is ready to marry her. Although she is uneducated, she talks about the rights of women. She does follow certain 'feminine' conventions such as covering her head and busying herself with stitching, but later, when she is about forty years old, she has a career. Both femininity and masculinity thus get constructed equitably in the novel. As already pointed out Gauri passively submits to masculine power, yet, later in the novel, when she recognises the true meaning of free existence, she develops shades of masculine nature.

Thus the two women, when they go out and experience real life and face critical situations, unconsciously play masculine roles. Laxmi, in *Gauri*, Yamuna's mother, Parvati and her stepmother in *Mogamul*, on the other hand, suffer the masculine power exerted on them without much resistance and thus they remain feminine till the end. Although they realize it, when decisions affect them or when the men in their families take wrong steps, they do not express their feelings as it would be against the social norm. Laxmi suffers after her marriage under masculine power. She is forsaken by her husband; she is helpless and cannot lead a happy life. She is compelled by circumstances to yield to Amru and live with him. She manages to arrange the marriage of her daughter, Gauri to a poor peasant, Panchi. Although Laxmi wishes for changes in the decisions taken by Amru, she cannot voice her opinion and always agrees with him. When Gauri refuses to go with Seth Ram, Laxmi can do nothing to prevent it as she has no power over Amru and in fact her survival itself is dependent on him. Even at the end of the novel she is abused and ill treated by the policemen because she has not been living within the conventional idea of a chaste woman and her illicit affair with Amru is understood as immoral behaviour. Thus, masculinity overshadows the image of women in society. Parvati in *Mogamul* too undergoes similar treatment. In the novel she already has a daughter when she gets married the second time. Due to this she is not respected by society and especially men like Babu's cousin, Sangu, who talks ill of her.

In *Mogamul*, Yamuna's stepmother, i.e. her father's first wife, also is meted out similar tratment by society. In the beginning she is controlled by her husband and later by her son. She has no power/money even after her husband's death and she regrets this when Babu goes seeking Sundaram's help. Thus, women who readily yield to masculine power, show their disability to do things and therefore remain silent. Babu's mother too remains silent when his father controls the family and she has no say in matters of importance.

There are other women characters who do not display their femininity wholly. Kesaro in *Gauri* in her role as the mother-in-law tries to control and dominate Gauri. In *Mogamul*, Thangam tries to seduce Babu by challenging his masculinity and by teasing him that he has no courage.

In this essay the issue of masculinity has been studied from a comparative perspective in the two novels and the major as well as the minor characters have been analysed for understanding the existence and construction of masculinity/femininity in the Indian society of 1960s. Thus Panchi in *Gauri* and Babu in *Mogamul* reveal that masculinity is not rigid and that it can be dynamic because life changes. Both the men also reveal that masculinity is heterogeneous: if Babu becomes more accommodating and moves away from hegemonic masculinity, Panchi becomes destructive and resorts to not only hegemonic masculinity but also to a kind of sadism. In case of Babu, it is the time/experience which moulds him as a 'new' man and for Panchi it is his married life bringing on more responsibility that makes him vulnerable. Both Babu and Panchi feel that, after marriage, time would be enough only to look after family and wife. Babu thinks that women should be given their due respect, whereas Panchi never even considers the idea. Babu has extramarital relationship but discontinues it at some point but Panchi has no such affair. In both the novels men are shown as being interested in social/political issues while women have no such interests.

In the case of women characters, Yamuna and Gauri in *Mogamul* and *Gauri* respectively, have been shown in this study as changing their femininities. When Yamuna and Gauri are under the power of masculinity, they remain feminine and when they move away from their femininities, they move away from masculinities as well. It is, therefore, understood that femininity, like masculinity, is constructed by masculinity and one cannot give up these gender constructs easily for they are governed by social norms. Thus, in both the novels, these women try to construct a new femininity by embracing some masculine traits only after encountering bitter experiences in their lives. Thus passive/feminine nature is associated with women who stay at home and do unpaid work. Money and power change their whole character. As they become financially independent, they move from the feminine to the masculine and begin to disregard convention. Yamuna's decision to marry Babu in *Mogamul* and Gauri's decision to work in *Gauri* show them to be in control of themselves, like men.

Since these two novels were written during the 1960s and 1970s, they have discussed the masculinity and femininity that was obtained at that time. They also portray how masculinity and femininity is constructed and constantly takes on new shapes. Interestingly, masculine behaviour patterns are inherited by the protagonists of these novels from the father/guardian. It is therefore logical to conclude that, in spite of role models, all men may not have similar masculinities. Men's masculinities undergo changes as they experience life and also change partly because of the women they live with. It is also equally true that masculinity in certain cases is static and does not undergo any change (e.g. Amru in *Gauri*, and Sundaram in *Mogamul*). Most women in the Indian society are so conditioned that they readily accept these masculine power over them and they neither question it or resist it. When they do question or resist it they are immediately faulted and often enough punished by society. Once a person acquires hegemonic power, man or woman, he or she will hold on to it and soon take on the characteristics of masculinity. Thus masculinity and femininity are interdependent and exchangeable; they are mere descriptive categories and are amorphous in nature as has been amply demonstrated in *Gauri* and *Mogamul* by the experience of various characters.

Notes

1. This was first published in 1960 and titled *The Old Woman and the Cow*.
2. Thi.Ja. is the abbreviated form used to refer to Thi. Janakiraman.
3. 'Mogamul' in English can be translated as 'Thorn of Desire'.
4. The translations quoted from this text are mine.

Works Cited

Anand, Mulk Raj. *Gauri*. (as *The Old Woman and the Cow* in 1960). New Delhi: Arnold-Heinneman, 1980.

Beynon, John. *Masculinities and Culture*. Buckingham: Open UP, 2002.

Connell, R.W. *Masculinities*. Cambridge, UK: Polity Press, 1995.

____. and James W. Messerschmidt. "Hegemonic Masculinity: Rethinking the Concept." *Gender and Society* 19.6 (Dec. 2005): 829-59.

Hofstede, Geert. *Masculinity and Femininity: Taboo Dimension of National Cultures*. New Delhi: Sage Publication, 1998.

Janakiraman, Thi. *Mogamul* (Thorn of Desire). 1970. Chennai: Ainthinai Padhipagam, 1998.

Wehmeier, Sally. *Oxford Advanced Learner's Dictionary of Current English*. New York: Oxford UP, 2000.

11

Inferiority, Individual Psychology and Cultural Determinism: An 'Indian Complex' in Ra.Vi.Sastri's *A Man of No Consequence*

Rajeshwar Mittapalli

Abstract

This article attempts to assess the artistic achievement of Ra.Vi.Sastri's masterpiece *A Man of No Consequence* (*Alpajeevi*) by going into the operation of Adler's theory of Inferiority Complex in it. It seeks to prove that Ra.Vi.Sastri has nativized Adler's theory and employed it only to the extent it suited his purpose. Therefore, instead of analyzing the novel exclusively from the Adlerian perspective it would be more profitable to study it against its cultural context, and primarily as a work of art that unveils a social picture by means of plumbing into the mind of the protagonist Subbaiah who goes through intense psychological suffering unable to contend with external adversity and incapacitated by innate inadequacies and experiences in the process inferiority complex of the Indian variety. This has been termed "Indian Complex." It is finally established that the novel's true merit and significance are best understood only when it is viewed as a literary work that faithfully captures the psychological and social reality obtaining among the Telugu people at a point of time in history by fixing its attention inexorably on the mindscapes and social dynamics of its lead character.

A Man of No Consequence [*Alpajeevi*] is based on Adler's theory of Inferiority Complex. According to this theory inferiority complex sets in during one's childhood itself, and after coming of age it leads to abnormal behaviour. Adler theorized that the influence of the environment,

> especially one's family environment during the childhood years, plays a crucial role in moulding human behaviour. He suggested that in course of one's later life if a traumatic event takes place, it brings back to memory the childhood experience and enables one to fight inferiority complex by bringing about a clear understanding. The insignificant man of this novel, Subbaiah, has been moulded following the principle of inferiority complex. His getting caught in a difficult situation, his extricating himself from it, and his gaining a hitherto unexperienced self-confidence—these in short form the crux of the story.[1]
>
> —R.S. Sudarshanam

> I wanted to reserve some sympathy for the clerk [the protagonist] when I started writing the novel. But by the time I reached its end I lost much of my sympathy for him. I don't know why it happened like that.... I was surprised when *Bharati* came forward to serialize the novel. I was ashamed of and irritated with the idea of the novel appearing under my own name, and not pseudonymously. I don't use a pseudonym any more. The shame too is gone. But the irritation remained.[2]
>
> —Ra.Vi.Sastri

The protagonist of *A Man of No Consequence*, Subbaiah, has been diagnosed by critics as suffering from Inferiority Complex. It might help to clearly understand here what 'inferiority complex' primarily signifies. The term was originated by Alfred Adler, the onetime associate of Sigmund Freud and the founder of Individual Psychology. He explains in an oft-quoted passage: "The feeling of inferiority rules the mental life and can be clearly recognized in the sense of incompleteness and un-fulfilment, and in the uninterrupted struggle both of individuals and humanity."[3] *Merriam-Webster's Online Dictionary* simplifies it and defines inferiority complex as "an acute sense of personal inferiority often resulting either in timidity or through overcompensation in exaggerated aggressiveness." It is clear from these definitions that inferiority complex is basically the feeling on the part of an individual that he is inferior to others in some way. This feeling could be a result of a real inferiority in the person, such as the one stemming from an organic deformity, but most often it is purely imaginary. This feeling lies in the unconscious and directs the course of the individual's behaviour. Inferiority feeling could sometimes motivate one to achieve spectacular success but when it acts as a disincentive, one would feel greatly discouraged and retreat from the difficulties and challenges posed by life. Adler proposes two types of inferiority feeling—'primary' and 'secondary.' 'Primary' inferiority feeling is that which emanates from a child's original experience of helplessness and dependence on the adults around him. 'Secondary' inferiority feeling has to do with an adult's inability to reach his 'fictional final goal' or achieve the unrealistic subjective security. The actual or perceived distance from this exalted ideal would precipitate the original inferiority feeling. The subject then experiences a complex of these feelings as debilitating. The unconscious goal one sets to fight off the primary feeling of inferiority thus paradoxically leads to the secondary feeling of inferiority.

Subbaiah is an inferiorized and marginalized individual. His suffering has been realistically, yet artistically, portrayed in *A Man of No Consequence*. The beginning of the novel itself—the very first passage—sets the tone:

> "Subbaiah is not good-looking."
> That is Subbaiah's opinion.
> "Subbaiah is just plain no good."
> That too is Subbaiah's opinion.
> ....
> "Father is scared of mother."
> This is what his son Krishnudu has discovered.
> "Subbaiah is very inefficient."
> This is the remark the head clerk in his office often passes.
> "Subbaiah is too timid."
> This is what many people say.[4]

This beginning unmistakably establishes the severity of the inferiority complex in the protagonist. His inferiority complex is however not the same as propounded by Adler. Society as a whole, and his own wife as well, regard Subbaiah as a feckless fellow. But in reality he is a law-abiding and god-fearing man, even if unabashedly pusillanimous. He works as a clerk in a government office. He is afraid of everything and everybody around him—his wife Savitri, his brother-in-law Venkat Rao, and even his colleagues at the office. He is afraid of even himself and is greatly surprised when he inadvertently makes (what to him looks like) a bold statement. Being such a timid man, he is not efficient as an office worker. He is very slow in disposing of the files entrusted to him. For this reason he is transferred finally to the Despatch Section which is considered to be a fit place for incompetent clerks like him.

Early enough in the novel, Ra.Vi.Sastri tells us about a couple of traumatic experiences that Subbaiah had gone through during his childhood. (1) Subbaiah's mother passed away when he was a mere toddler. His father married again five years later. His stepmother was an uncouth woman and she used to beat him everyday. Luckily for Subbaiah this woman eloped with a neighbourhood gentleman within a year. (2) When Subbaiah was ten years old his father was attacked and savagely beaten by two unknown assailants. It has been suggested that these two incidents—the cruelty of his stepmother and the physical assault on his beloved father—are responsible for the sprouting and persistence of inferiority complex in Subbaiah. But there could be a host of other reasons as well, and that is what gives his complex a very 'Indian' touch. One of these reasons seems to be the unequal power relations obtaining within the families of coastal Andhra Pradesh. In this region of Andhra Pradesh, possibly because of the imperceptible remnants of a prehistoric matriarchal social order or possibly because of excessive feminization of society during the recent couple of centuries, especially among certain upper castes, women tend to be in command of family affairs, while men often play a subordinate role. Some of the important fictional works of the era, the ones that sought to depict social reality frankly and honestly and not advocate the so-called 'women are the victims' theory for the sake of being politically correct, bear out this truth beyond doubt. The women of these novels, who clearly lack in social concern and are openly money minded on top of it, often compel their men to sacrifice their individuality and that way prevent them from realising their potential as human beings and from fulfilling their social and moral obligations. In G.V. Krishna Rao's *Puppets* (*Keelu Bommalu*),[5] for example, the wealthy and well-respected village landlord Pullayya suffers a moral downfall unable to contend with his cantankerous wife Lakshmamma. Full twenty years later the situation did not change for the better for men. Thus in Vasireddy Sitadevi's *Matti Manishi* (*The Man of Soil*)[6] the manipulative and ambitious heroine, Varudhini, makes a virtual slave of her husband Venkatapathy by putting her considerable physical charms to good use, and renders her father-in-law Ooraboyina Sambaiah a pauper by appropriating his money and then investing it on highly risky ventures. She does not even hesitate to confer sexual favours on other men in the hope of furthering her business interests. In *A Man of No Consequence* too, like almost every other woman character, Subbaiah's wife Savitri is of extremely malevolent disposition. She is given to habitually belittling him by dealing countless subtle insults for not being what she expected him to be. Subbaiah has learnt to accept without protest her constant and contemptuous dismissal of him as a man utterly unworthy of her love, and to automatically treat himself as inferior to her. Thus his powerlessness at home, traceable to cultural roots, too seems to contribute in no small measure to his inferiority complex.

Because of a disagreement over sharing bribe money between two senior clerks in the office, Subbaiah is transferred from the Despatch Section to the all-important Bills Section. Passing bills filed by the contractors is now the responsibility of Subbaiah. Any other clerk managing this section stands the possibility of making huge sums of money by accepting bribes from the contractors. But, being scared of the law, and indeed almost everything under the sun, Subbaiah cannot even visualize the possibility.

Savitri and her brother Venkat Rao are confirmed in their opinion that Subbaiah is 'irredeemable' and between the two of them they trivialize him to such an extent that, except as the wage-earner, his existence has no meaning for them. But when Venkat Rao comes to know that his brother-in-law is now the clerk-in-charge of the Bills Section, he persuades Subbaiah, pleading an urgent need for money, to accept a bribe of five hundred rupees from a contractor called Gavaraiah (incidentally, five hundred rupees was considered a large sum of money during the 1950s). The moment he has accepted the bribe money from Gavaraiah and handed it over to Venkat Rao, Subbaiah loses the peace of his mind and begins to feel depressed and disoriented. He is apprehensive, against all logic, that he might be exposed, arrested and thrown into jail!

Soon however the equations change once again at the office. Subbaiah is unceremoniously sent back to the Despatch Section. He has not cleared Gavaraiah's bills yet, and Gavaraiah has thus not benefited in the least from bribing Subbaiah. He, therefore, insists, and not always politely, on Subbaiah's returning the money. When Subbaiah in turn asks Venkat Rao to do so, this unscrupulous man dodges the question and instead suggests that he should make bold to tell Gavaraiah that he would not return the money at all. Subbaiah is in a real fix, afraid of the consequences of Gavaraiah's wrath on the one hand, and cursing his powerlessness to extract the money from Venkat Rao on the other. His helplessness and the irrational fear of losing his job, getting arrested, rendering his family destitute and above everything else the increasing severity and frequency of Gavaraiah's threats subject him to an intense psychological conflict. He feels traumatized and rudely shaken by the inner turmoil. It is however not wholly true, as has been erroneously suggested by critics, that the present trauma precipitates an already existing psychological condition in him. There seems to be a deep-seated negative personality trait, an inadequacy at the core of his being, that has rendered him feeble in spirit and mind so that he finds it impossible to act resolutely even when his interests are at stake. He has been, as adumbrated earlier, thoroughly inferiorized and marginalized by all concerned, even by the unidentifiable cultural forces, and consequently his personality and self-esteem have never properly developed. His suffering is therefore infinitely greater than that of a typical victim of inferiority complex in the West where the trauma one suffers is usually of a personal nature and not culturally determined. And most definitely this trauma does not visit one for being honest and law abiding, even if incompetent. Unfortunately for Subbaiah, he is slighted, humiliated, demeaned and judged as inefficient by almost everyone for no more 'objectionable' behaviour on his part than hesitating to do things that are potentially disturbing to him.

Like Subbaiah, the other important male characters of the novel too had gone through traumatic experiences early in their lives. For example, Venkat Rao was robbed of whatever material wealth he could have inherited from his profligate father by his own maternal uncle and a long-standing employee of his zamindari household, and Gavaraiah suffered the ignominy of his wife cheating on him. These experiences, devastating as they are, instead of psychologically destabilizing these two men, only transformed them into hardened individuals. Subbaiah's experiences, naïve in comparison, have made him instead a weakling and psychological wreck. There is thus certainly something innate, and something very 'Indian' (meaning his ready acquiescence to the unfriendly social and cultural forces) in him that has subjected him to inferiority complex and made him the man he is—shy and submissive, weak and wavering, insecure and indecisive, timid and compliant, unsure of himself and uncertain in judgement, perennially plagued by doubts and fears, and generally lacking in initiative and drive.

Subbaiah is never completely relieved of his complex while it should be so in a textbook case of inferiority complex, on gaining knowledge of the underlying causes. He is not a wiser man for having gone through the recent traumatic experience either. He is intellectually and psychologically too ill equipped to derive any benefit from it. For that reason, and for several other reasons, his creator Ra.Vi.Sastri himself finds it difficult to like him. He explains in the epilogue to the novel:

> While writing the final parts of the novel I felt only disgust for Subbaiah.... I was confirmed in the belief that he was an out and out worthless nincompoop.
>
> But—
>
> I felt that gods, kings and writers should be noble and that they should show the path of righteousness to the posterity. Therefore, when I published the novel in book form I bestowed upon Subbaiah the faculty of soul-searching. He appears to acknowledge his wretchedness and mean spirit and take to the right path at the end. In the final analysis he might take to that path, or he might not. It is left to him.[7]

Subbaiah finds his deliverance from the current crisis—the need to repay Gavaraiah—not because of his own efforts, but because of a variety of forces working independently to help him out. Pothanna, the onetime all purpose man of Gavaraiah, who has some manifest courage and professes ready sympathy for Subbaiah and his family, boldly tells Gavaraiah's man that Subbaiah would not return the money any more. Blame it on his inferiority complex, but this is something Subbaiah has not been able to do in spite of his best efforts. Venkat Rao, who has drawn our 'hero' into trouble in the first place and who currently lives with Gavaraiah's estranged wife Ramayamma, threatens Gavaraiah that he would divulge the details of his failed marriage unless he leaves Subbaiah alone. Avadhani, Subbaiah's colleague, promises Gavaraiah that he would pass his bills only if he stops harassing Subbaiah. Above all, the beautiful school teacher Manorama, who unaccountably falls in love with Subbaiah and who happened to once live in the same town as Gavaraiah, pleads with him on Subbaiah's behalf and even offers to make good his loss herself. Gavaraiah finally relents and returns the promissory note that he got Subbaiah to sign under duress.

Manorama enters Subbaiah's beleaguered life like a breath of fresh air. The novelist does not tell us why she takes such a keen interest in him. Whenever a new character is introduced in his novels, it is Ra.Vi.Sastri's practice to give a detailed background of that character. But in Manorama's case he leaves it to the imagination of the readers. An atmosphere of mystery surrounds her. This being very uncharacteristic of Ra.Vi.Sastri's style of writing fiction, R.S. Sudarshanam observes:

> Ra.Vi.Sastri does not give any details about her [Manorama's] past or about her family. There lies the beauty of the craftsmanship of the writer. He portrays her only as a human being who empathizes with another human being in trouble. It is not necessary to know her past.[8]

Manorama is fully aware of Subbaiah's unenviable predicament arising out of both his short-term problems such as the ongoing conflict with Gavaraiah and the long term ones such as his incompatibility with his impolite wife and its adverse psychological impact on him. She understands that Subbaiah has been suffering from inferiority complex of a special kind and because of that nobody takes him seriously, including himself. Nobody understands him; nobody empathizes with him; and nobody loves him. Subbaiah's wife, children, relatives, colleagues (he has no friends at all) and everybody else in society regard him as a nonentity and unworthy of note. Only Manorama feels the urge to show some genuine concern for him, befriend him, and finally fall in love with him. Her love instills in him a modicum of confidence, although he continues to be beset with doubts and misgivings, and dogged by indecision and irrational fears.

Critics, including the perceptive R.S. Sudarshanam, have famously misread the novel and hastily concluded that Subbaiah finally overcomes his inferiority complex due primarily to Manorama's love for him. They seem to have been misled by a passage occurring towards the end of the novel which suggests that Subbaiah experiences a dilemma between the shadows of the past that hold him back, and the light that beckons him towards the future.

> With everyone, every minute, it has been "surrender, surrender" so far.
> Up until this moment life has been spent like that—humbly, meanly, miserably, depravedly and pathetically.

> That darkness has been holding him back.
> This light has been propelling him forward. (189)

There is no gainsaying that Manorama's love for him has a positive side to it, but to state that Subbaiah finally puts his complex behind him altogether and realizes his self-worth because of it would not be entirely correct. In all probability Subbaiah will continue with his vacillation, indecisiveness and unfounded fears because his cultural context is unlikely to change in his favour and because, above everything else, he is a moral coward, and has been so all his life. This is best established by the fact that he was not averse *per se* to accepting the bribe, but was terrified of the legal consequences and job security concerns. Adler himself has theorized that inferiority complex resolves itself if the sufferer has a developed social interest.

> If one has sufficiently sharpened one's grasp for the connections within the unity of each individual, one will easily understand how the inferiority feeling presses constantly towards its own resolution. The value and significance of this resolution rest totally in the existence and the degree of social interest which at times more strongly, at times less so, determines the fate, the failure, or the possibility for happiness of a person.[9]

Subbaiah's involvement in society is, at best, peripheral. He is, in fact, an escapist who instinctually avoids human contact, desperately tries to erect a psychological wall against the demands of community life and is deeply apprehensive about people—yes, including the kindly Manorama—who try to reach out to him. Given this state of mind, he cannot hope to achieve happiness in life since, according to Adler, "true happiness is inseparable from the feeling of giving" and—

> ...everyone who is deeply unhappy, the neurotic and the desolate person stem from among those who were deprived in their younger years of being able to develop the feeling of community, the courage, the optimism, and the self-confidence that comes directly from the sense of belonging. This sense of belonging that cannot be denied anyone, against which there are no arguments, can only be won by

> being involved, by cooperating, and experiencing, and by being useful to others. Out of this emerges a lasting, genuine feeling of worthiness.[10]

It is not surprising that Subbaiah has no idea of his worthiness or the lack of it. He does not hope to attain it. Moreover, the fertility of his imagination (which enables him to spin interesting yarns about the people passing by his house) does not impart him social interest or the strength of mind to take on the world and face its challenges courageously. It only drags him into the abysmal depths of self-doubt. Ra.Vi.Sastri himself passes the final judgement on Subbaiah.

> Cowardice and virtue are incompatible. Cowards cannot be virtuous people; they cannot stand up and be good. There is much guarantee for it.
>
> To be virtuous one needs to have a mighty heart.[11]

Subbaiah obviously does not have a 'mighty' heart. He does not even feel motivated to overcome his sense of inferiority, leave alone strive for actualizing higher aims, which he has not set for himself anyway. He is doomed to live the life of a coward, in utter ignominy, Manorama or no Manorama.

Of the seven Ra.Vi.Sastri novels, finished or unfinished, *A Man of No Consequence* is easily the best in artistic terms as well as in terms of depicting psychological and social reality. There is a perfect integration of the theme, characters and narrative technique in it. The application of Adler's theory of inferiority complex is certainly one of its strengths but Ra.Vi.Sastri has taken liberties with the theory. He used it only after his purpose and did not attempt a textbook demonstration of it. One might say that it is an 'Indian' or nativized version of the theory of inferiority complex which Ra.Vi.Sastri employs in this novel in order to enhance its artistic appeal. In the final analysis it would be better not to accord undue importance to this theory and its operation in the novel. Much of aesthetic value would emerge if the novel is studied on its own terms, as a work of art, and without elaborate reference to Adler and his theories.

Notes & References

1. R.S. Sudarshanam, *Sahityamlo Drukpathalu* (Points of View in Literature) (1968; Vijayawada: Navodaya, 1982) 243-44.
2. Ra.Vi.Sastri, "Enduku Rasenu?" (Why did I Write), appended to *Alpajeevi* (1954; Visakhapatnam: Rachakonda Prachuranalu, 2001) 199.
3. Alfred Adler, Inferiority, Answers.com, 5 July 2007, <http://www.answers.com/topic/inferiority-2>.
4. Ra.Vi.Sastri, *A Man of No Consequence*, trans. Achanta Janakiram (Calcutta: Writers Workshop, 1994). Telugu original, *Alpajeevi* (1954; Visakhapatnam: Rachakonda Prachuranalu, 2001) 4. All subsequent parenthetical page references are to this edition. Translation mine.
5. G.V. Krishna Rao, *Puppets* (*Keelu Bommalu*), trans. D. Kesava Rao (Chennai: Macmillan, 1997). Telugu original published in 1951.
6. Vasireddy Sitadevi, *Matti Manishi* (*The Man of Soil*) (1972; Visjayawada: Vishalandhra, 1994).
7. Ra.Vi.Sastri, "Akharno Mata" (epilogue), *Alpajeevi* (1954; Visakhapatnam: Rachakonda Prachuranalu, 2001) 191.
8. Sudarshanam 252.
9. Alfred Adler, "Advantages and Disadvantages of the Inferiority Feeling," *Superiority and Social Interest: A Collection of Later Writings* (1964; New York: W.W. Norton, 1979) 53.
10. Alfred Adler, from a new translation of "Individual Psychology," which first appeared in *Einführung in die neuere Psychologie* (Osterwick/Harz: A.W. Zickfeldt Verlag, 1926) in the AAISF/ATP Archives, 5 July 2007, http://ourworld.compuserve.com/homepages/HStein/qu-comm.htm
11. Ra.Vi.Sastri, "Akharno Mata" (epilogue) 191.

Selected Bibliography

General Studies: Books

Abbott, Franklin, ed. *New Men, New Minds: Breaking Male Tradition*. California: Crossing Press, 1987.

Adams, Rachel, and David Savran, eds. *The Masculinity Studies Reader*. Malden, Massachusetts: Blackwell Publishers, 2002.

Ashe, Fidelma. *The New Politics of Masculinity: Men, Power and Resistance*. London: Routledge, 2007.

Ashfield, John. *The Nature of Men: Elements of Masculine Psychology*. Adelaide: Peackock Publications, 2005.

Berger, Maurice, Brian Wallis, and Simon Watson, eds. *Constructing Masculinity*. New York and London: Routledge, 1995.

Blazina, Chris. *The Cultural Myth of Masculinity*. Westport, CT: Praeger, 2003.

Brittan, Arthur. *Masculinity and Power*. Oxford: Basil Blackwell, 1989.

Brod, Harry, ed. *The Making of Masculinities: The New Men's Studies*. Boston: Allen & Unwin, 1987.

_____, and Michael Kaufman, eds. *Theorizing Masculinities*. London: Sage, 1994.

Buchbinder, David. *Masculinities and Identities*. Melbourne: Melbourne UP, 1994.

_____. *Performance Anxieties: Re-producing Masculinity*. Sydney: Allen & Unwin, 1998.

Clatterbaugh, Kenneth. *Contemporary Perspectives on Masculinity: Men, Women, and Politics in Modern Society*. 2nd ed. Colorado and Oxford: Westview Press, 1997.

Cleaver, Frances, ed. *Masculinities Matter! Men, Gender and Development*. New York: Zed Books, 2002.

Connell, R.W. *Masculinities*. Sydney: Allen & Unwin, 1995.

Dalbey, Gorden. *Healing the Masculine Soul*. Melbourne: Word, 1989.

Edley, Nigel, and Margaret Wetherell. *Men in Perspective: Practice, Power and Identity*. London: Prentice-Hall, 1995.

Fanning, Patrick, and Matthew McKay. *Being a Man: A Guide to the New Masculinity*. Oakland, CA: New Harbinger Publications, 1993.

Fasteau, M.F. *The Male Machine*. New York: McGraw Hill, 1974.

Firestone, Ross, ed. *A Book of Men: Visions of the Male Experience*. Cambridge, MA: Stonehill, 1975.

Franklin, Clyde. *Men and Society*. Chicago: Nelson-Hall, 1988.

Gardiner, Judith Kegan. *Masculinity Studies and Feminist Theory: New Directions*. New York: Columbia UP, 2002.

Gilmore, David D. *Misogyny: The Male Malady*. Philadelphia: U of Pennsylvania P, 2001.

Gittings, C.E., ed. *Imperialism and Gender: Constructions of Masculinity*. New Lambton, NSW: Dangaroo Press, 1997.

Greenstein, Ben. *The Fragile Male*. London: Boxtree, 1993.

Haddad, Tony, ed. *Men and Masculinities: A Critical Anthology*. Toronto: Canadian Scholars' Press, 1993.

Haywood, Chris, and Mairtin, Mac an Ghaill. *Men and Masculinities Theory, Research and Social Practice*. Buckingham: Open UP, 2003.

Hearn, Jeff, and David H.J. Morgan, eds. *Men, Masculinities and Social Theory*. London: Unwin Hyman, 1990.

Hodson, Philip. *Men: an Investigation into the Emotional Male*. London: Ariel Books, 1984.

hooks, bell. *Feminism is for Everybody: Passionate Politics*. London: Pluto Press, 2000.

_____. *The Will to Change: Men, Masculinity, and Love*. New York : Atria Books, 2004..

Hooper, Charlotte. *Manly States: Masculinities, International Relations, and Gender Politics*. New York: Columbia, 2001.

Horrocks, Roger. *Male Myths and Icons: Masculinity in Popular Culture*. Basingstoke: St. Martin's Press, 1995.

_____. *Masculinity in Crisis: Myths, Fantasies and Realities*. Basingstoke: St. Martin's Press, 1994.

Johnson, Allan G. *The Gender Knot: Unraveling our Patriarchal Legacy*. Philadelphia: Temple UP, 1997.

Kaufman, Michael. *Cracking the Armour: Power, Pain and the Lives of Men*. Toronto, Ontario: Penguin, 1993.

_____, ed. *Beyond Patriarchy: Essays by Men on Pleasure, Power and Change*. New York: Oxford UP, 1987.

Kimmel, Michael S. *The Gendered Society*. New York & Oxford: Oxford UP, 2000.

_____, and Amy Aronson, eds. *Men and Masculinities: A Social, Cultural, and Historical Encyclopedia*. Santa Barbara, CA: ABC-Clio Press, 2003.

_____, Jeff Hearn, and R.W. Connell, eds. *The Handbook of Studies on Men and Masculinities*. Thousand Oaks, CA: Sage, 2005.

Kupers, Terry A. *Revisioning Men's Lives: Gender, Intimacy, and Power*. New York & London: Guilford Press, 1993.

Lash, John. *The Hero: Manhood and Power*. New York: Thames & Hudson, 1995.

Levant, Ronald F., and William S. Pollack, eds. *A New Psychology of Men*. Dunmore, PA: Basic Books, 1995.

Mac an Ghaill, Mairtin, ed. *Understanding Masculinities: Social Relations and Cultural Arenas*. Buckingham & Philadelphia: Open UP, 1996.

May, Larry, and Robert Strikwerda, eds. *Rethinking Masculinity: Philosophical Explorations in Light of Feminism*. Maryland: Rowman & Littlefield, 1992.

May, Larry. *Masculinity and Morality*. Ithaca & London: Cornell UP, 1998.

McCloughry, Roy. *Men and Masculinity: From Power to Love*. London: Hodder & Stoughton, 1992.

McLean, Chris, Maggie Carey, and Cheryl White, eds. *Men's Ways of Being*. Boulder, Colorado: Westview Press, 1996.

McMullen, Richie J. *Male Rape: Breaking the Silence on the Last Taboo*. London: Gay Men's Press, 1990.

Mendel, Matthew Parynik. *The Male Survivor: The Impact of Sexual Abuse*. London: Sage, 1994.

Messner, Michael A. *Politics of Masculinities: Men in Movements*. Thousand Oaks, California: Sage, 1997.

Middleton, Peter. *The Inward Gaze: Masculinity and Subjectivity in Modern Culture*. London and New York: Routledge, 1992.

Miedzian, Myriam. *Boys Will Be Boys: Breaking the Link Between Masculinity and Violence*. New York: Doubleday, 1991.

Morgan, David. *Discovering Men*. London: Routledge, 1992.

Mosse, George L. *The Image of Man: The Creation of Modern Masculinity*. New York: Oxford UP, 1996.

Nock, Steven L. *Marriage in Men's Lives*. New York: Oxford UP, 1998.

Pease, Bob. *Men and Gender Relations*. Melbourne: Tertiary Press, 2002.

_____. *Men and Sexual Politics: Towards a Profeminist Practice*. Adelaide: Dulwich Centre Publications, 1997.

_____. *Recreating Men: Postmodern Masculinity Politics*. London: Sage, 2000.

Petersen, Alan. *Unmasking the Masculine: 'Men' and 'Identity' in a Sceptical Age*. Thousand Oaks, CA: Sage, 1998.

Pittman, Frank S. *Man Enough: Fathers, Sons, and the Search for Masculinity*. New York: Putnam, 1993.

Pringle, Keith. *Men, Masculinities and Social Welfare*. London: UCL Press, 1995.

Rosen, David. *The Changing Fictions of Masculinity*. Urbana, IL: U of Illinois P, 1993.

Ross, John Munden. *The Male Paradox: Why Men Feel Like the Weaker Sex and How the Struggle Between Sexuality and Aggression Shapes their Identity*. New York: Simon & Schuster, 1992.

Ruxton, Sandy, ed. *Gender Equality and Men: Learning from Practice*. Oxford: Oxfam GB, 2004.

Segal, Lynne. *Slow Motion: Changing Masculinities, Changing Men*. London: Virago, 1990.

Seidler, Victor J. *Transforming Masculinities: Men, Cultures, Bodies, Power, Sex and Love*. London: Routledge, 2005.

Silverman, Kaja. *Male Subjectivity at the Margins*. New York: Routledge, 1992.

Simpson, Mark. *Male Impersonators: Men Performing Masculinity*. New York: Routledge, 1994.

Snodgrass, Jon., ed. *A Book of Readings: For Men Against Sexism*. Albion CA: Times Change Press, 1977.

_____. *Refusing to be a Man: Essays on Sex and Justice*. CA & Suffolk: Fontana/Collins, 1990.

Stoltenberg, John. *The End of Manhood: A Book for Men of Conscience*. New York: Dutton, 1993.

Stott, Sarah. *Out of the Shadows: Help for Men Who Have Been Sexually Assaulted*. Lyme Regis: Russell House, 2001.

Sullivan, Robin, ed. *Focus on Fathering*. Melbourne: ACER Press, 2003.

Sweetman, Caroline. *Men and Masculinity*. Oxford, England: Oxfam, 1997.

Tacey, David. *Remaking Men: The Revolution in Masculinity*. Ringwood, VIC: Viking, 1997.

Thomas, David. *Not Guilty—In Defence of the Modern Man.* London: Weidenfeld & Nicolson, 1993.

Whitehead, Stephen M. *Men and Masculinities: Key Themes and New Directions.* Cambridge: Polity Press, 2002.

Whitehead, Stephen M., and Frank J. Barrett, eds. *The Masculinities Reader.* Cambridge: Polity Press, 2001.

Zilbergeld, Bernie. *The New Male Sexuality: The Truth about Men, Sex, and Pleasure.* New York: Bantam Books, 1992.

General Studies: Journal Articles & Book Chapters

Archer, John. "Origins of Male Domination." *New Behaviour* 2.5 (1975): 166-96.

Bazelon, David T. "Strong Women, Weak Men—or Unisex." *Review of Existential Psychology and Psychiatry* 9.3 (1972): 130-43.

Bouma, Donald H. "From Female Superiority to Male Chauvinism." *Intellect* 103 (Dec. 1974): 166-69.

Brickell, Chris. "Masculinities, Performativity, and Subversion: A Sociological Reappraisal. Men and Masculinities" 8.1 (2005): 24-43.

Chopra, Radhika. "Retrieving the Father: Gender Studies, 'Father Love' and the Discourse of Motherhood." *Journal of the Women's Studies International Forum,* UK 24.314 (2001): 445-55.

Collier, James Lincoln. "Are Men Really Men Anymore?" *The Reader's Digest* (Aug. 1972): 154-58.

Connell, R.W., and J.W. Messerschmidt. "Hegemonic Masculinity: Rethinking the Concept." *Gender Society* 19.6 (2005): 829-59.

_____. "The State, Gender, and Sexual Politics: Theory and Appraisal." *Theory and Society* 19.5 (Oct. 1990): 507-44.

Cottle, Thomas, et al. "The Relationship of Sex Role Identity and Social and Political Attitudes." *Journal of Personality* 38.3 (1970): 435-52.

Courtenay, Will. "Constructions of Masculinity and their Influence on Men's Well-being: a Theory of Gender and

Health." *Social Science and Medicine* 50.10 (2000): 1385-1401.

DeGoglia, Rick. "Thoughts on Men's Oppression." *Issues in Radical Therapy* 1.3 (Summer 1973): 14-18.

Dubbert, Joel. "Progressivism and the Masculinity Crisis." *Psychoanalytic Review* 61 (Fall 1974): 443-55.

Falabella, Gonzalo. "New Masculinity: A Different Route." *Gender and Development* 5.2 (1997): 62-64.

Ferreira, Allen. "The Male Dilemma." *Contemporary Education* 46.1 (Fall 1974): 68-70.

Flood, Michael. "Men, Gender, and Development." *Development Bulletin* 64 (March 2004): 26-30.

Gagnon, John H. "Physical Strength, Once of Significance." *Impact of Science on Society* 21.1 (1971): 31-42.

Gilder, George. "Why Men Marry." *Village Voice* 19 (Dec. 1974): 16-18.

Gold, Herbert. "The Masculine Malaise." *Saturday Review* 6 June 1970: 31-48

Green, Robert-Jay. "Traditional Norms of Masculinity." *Journal of Feminist Family Therapy* 10.1 (1998): 81-83.

Hacker, Helen Mayer. "The New Burdens of Masculinity." *Marriage and Family Living* (Aug. 1957) 227-33.

Harlow, Robert G. "Masculine Inadequacy and Compensatory Development of Physique." *Journal of Personality* 19 (1951): 312-22.

Kaufman, Michael. "The Burden of Pleasure: Men and Sex." *Cracking the Armour: Power, Pain and the Lives of Men*. Toronto, Ontario: Penguin, 1993.

_____. "The Construction of Masculinity and the Triad of Men's Violence." *Beyond Patriarchy: Essays by Men on Pleasure, Power and Change*. Ed. Michael Kaufman. New York: Oxford UP, 1987.

Komarovsky, Mirra. "Cultural Contradictions and Sex Roles: the Masculine Case." *American Journal of Sociology* 78.4 (1973): 873-84.

Marecek, Jeanne. "Men, Masculinity and Feminism." *Feminism & Psychology* 10.4 (Nov. 2000): 505-10.

McCracken, S. "From Performance to Public Sphere: The Production of Modernist Masculinities." *Textual Practice* 15.1 (Spring 2001): 47-65.

Miller, Thomas W. "Male Self-esteem and Attitudes toward Women's Roles." *Journal of College Student Personnel* 14.5 (1973): 402-06.

Morton, Charles W. "Twilight of the He-Man." *Atlantic* 219 (Feb. 1967): 111-12.

Plumb, J.H. "A Return to Manliness." *Horizon* 9 (Winter 1967): 100-01.

Plummer, Ken. "Male Sexualities." *The Handbook of Studies on Men and Masculinities*. Ed. Michael Kimmel, Jeff Hearn, and R.W. Connell. Thousand Oaks, CA: Sage, 2005.

Pogrebin, Letty Cottin. "Do Women Make Men Violent?" *Ms.* 3 (Nov. 1974): 49-55 & 80.

Rasmuson, Marianne. "Men, the Weaker Sex?" *Impact of Science on Society* 21.1 (1971): 43-54.

Ruthven, K.K. "Male Critics and Feminist Criticism." *Essays in Criticism* 33.4 (Oct. 1983): 263-72.

Sanderson, Linda. "Men: Dispelling the Masculinity Myth." *Minnesota Daily Complement* 78.143 (April 1977): 13-16.

Sattel, Jack W. "The Inexpressive Male: Tragedy or Sexual Politics?" *Social Problems* 23 (April 1976): 469-77.

Schwartz, Tony. "Women and Men: No More Absolutes." *Change* 6.8 (Oct. 1974): 24-28.

Steinem, Gloria. "The Myth of Masculine Mystique." *International Education* 1 (1972): 30-35.

Stevens, Barbara. "The Sexually Oppressed Male." *Psychotherapy, Theory, Research and Practice* 11.1 (Spring 1974): 16-21.

Tavris, Carol and David Pope. "Masculinity: What does it Mean to be a Man?" *Psychology Today* 9.10 (March 1976): 58-67.

Tipton, Robert M. et al. "Invasion of Males' Personal Space by Feminists and Non-feminists." *Psychological Reports* 37 (1975): 99-102.

Wandachild, Gary Mitchell. "Complacency in the Face of Patriarchy." *Win* 12 (Jan. 1975): 4-11.

White, David. "Male Backlash." *New Society* 13 July 1972: 64-65.

Woods, Sherwyn M. "Some Dynamics of Male Chauvinism." *Archives of General Psychiatry* 33 (1976): 63-65.

Indian Masculinity: Books

Banerjee, Sikata. *Make Me a Man! Masculinity, Hinduism, and Nationalism in India*. New York: State U of New York P, 2005.

Chopra, Radhika, ed. *Reframing Masculinities: Narrating the Supportive Practices of Men*. Hyderabad: Orient Longman, 2007.

_____, and UNIFEM South Asia Regional Office, New Delhi. *From Violence to Supportive Practice: Family, Gender, and Masculinities in India*. New Delhi: United Nations Development Fund for Women, 2002.

_____, Caroline Osella, and Filippo Osella, eds. *South Asian Masculinities: Context of Change, Sites of Continuity*. New Delhi: Women Unlimited, 2004.

Dernâe, Steve. *Culture in Action: Family Life, Emotion, and Male Dominance in Banaras, India*. New York: State U of New York P, 1995.

_____. *Movies, Masculinity, and Modernity: An Ethnography of Men's Filmgoing in India*. Westport, Conn. Greenwood Press, 2000.

Jeffrey, Craig, Roger Jeffery, and Patricia Jeffery. "Degrees without Freedom: The Impact of Formal Education on Dalit Young Men in North India." *Development and Change* 35.5 (Nov. 2004): 963-86.

Kakar, Sudhir. *The Inner World: A Psycho-Analytic Study of Childhood and Society in India*. Oxford and New York: Oxford UP, 1978.

Monti, Alessandro, ed. *Hindu Masculinities Across the Ages. Updating the Past*. Torino: L'Harmattan Italia, 2002.

Mulchandani, Sandhya. *The Indian Man: His True Colours*. New Delhi: Picus Books, 1999.

Nandy, Ashis, *The Intimate Enemy Loss and Recovery of Self under Colonialism*. Oxford: Oxford UP, 1983.

_____. *The Illegitimacy of Nationalism* (Delhi: Oxford UP, 1994).

Ravindra, R.P. et al., eds. *Breaking the Moulds: Indian Men Look at Patriarchy Looking at Men*. Delhi: Books for Change, 2007.

Ray, Sangeeta. *En-gendering India: Woman and Nation in Colonial and Postcolonial Narratives*. Durham, N.C.: Duke UP, 2000.

Sinha, Mrinalini. *Colonial Masculinity: The 'Manly Englishman' and the 'Effeminate Bengali' in the Late Nineteenth Century*. Manchester: Manchester UP, 1995.

Srivastava, S. *An Education of the Passions: Sexuality, Consumption and Class in India*. London: Routledge, 2007.

Vanita, Ruth, ed. *Queering India: Same-Sex Love and Eroticism in Indian Culture and Society*. New York: Routledge, 2002.

Indian Masculinity: Journal Articles & Book Chapters

Alter, Joseph, S. "Indian Clubs and Colonialism: Hindu Masculinity and Muscular Christianity." *Comparative Studies in Society and History* 46.3 (July 2004): 497-534.

Basu, Subho and Sikata Banerjee. "The Quest for Manhood: Masculine Hinduism and Nation in Bengal." *Comparative Studies of South Asia, Africa and the Middle East* 26.3 (2006): 476-90.

Chakravarti, Uma. "Inventing Saffron History: a Celibate Hero Rescues an Emasculated Nation." *A Question of Silence?*

The Sexual Economies of Modern India. Ed. M.E. John and J. Nair. New Delhi: Kali for Women, 1998. 243-68.

Chopra, Radhika. "Invisible Men: Masculinity, Sexuality, and Male Domestic Labor." *Men and Masculinities* 9.2 (2006): 152-67.

_____. "Muted Masculinities: Introduction to the Special Issue on Contemporary Indian Ethnographies." *Men and Masculinities* 9.2 (2006): 127-30.

_____, et al. "Indian Masculinities." *Men and Masculinities* 9.2 (2006): 127-225.

George, Annie. "Reinventing Honorable Masculinity: Discourses from a Working-Class Indian Community." *Men and Masculinities* 9.1 (2006): 35-52.

O'Hanlon, Rosalind. "Issues of Masculinity in North Indian History: The Bangash Nawabs of Farrukhabad." *Indian Journal of Gender Studies* 4.1 (1997): 1-19.

Osella, Filippo, and Caroline Osella. "'Ayyappan Saranam': Masculinity and the Sabarimala Pilgrimage in Kerala." *Journal of the Royal Anthropological Institute* 9.4 (2003): 729-54.

_____. "Migration, Money and Masculinity in Kerala." *Journal of the Royal Anthropological Institute* 6.1 (Mar. 2000): 117-33.

Roy, Parama. "Meat-eating, Masculinity, and Renunciation in India: A Gandhian Grammar of Diet." *Gender & History* 14.1 (April 2002): 62-91.

Sinha, Mrinalini. "Giving Masculinity a History: Some Contributions from the Historiography of Colonial India." *Gender & History* 11.3 (Nov. 1999): 445-60.

Srivastava, Sanjay. "The Order of Men: the Nation and the Metropolitan Imaginary at an Indian Public School." *Australian Journal of Anthropology* 4.3 (1993): 163-83.

Verma, Ravi K. et al. "Challenging and Changing Gender Attitudes among Young Men in Mumbai, India." *Reproductive Health Matters* 14.28 (2006): 135-43.

Yim, Jennifer Young, and Ramaswami Mahalingam. "Culture, Masculinity, and Psychological Well-being in Punjab, India." *Sex Roles* 55. 9-10 (Nov. 2006): 715-24.

Masculinity Studies in English Literature: Books

Armengol, Josep M. *Re/Presenting Men: Cultural and Literary Constructions of Masculinity in the U.S.* Saarsbruck: VDM Publishing, 2008.

Barsham, Diana. *Arthur Conan Doyle and the Meaning of Masculinity*. Aldershot, England: Ashgate, 2000.

Boheemen, Christine van, and Colleen Lamos, eds. *Masculinities in Joyce: Postcolonial Constructions.* Amsterdam; Atlanta: Rodopi, 2001.

Cannon, Kelly. *Henry James and Masculinity: The Man at the Margins*. New York: St Martin's Press, 1994.

Clark, Keith, ed. *Contemporary Black Men's Fiction and Drama*. Urbana: U of Illinois P, 2001.

Clifford, Stephen P. *Beyond the Heroic 'I': Reading Lawrence, Hemingway, and Masculinity*. Bucknell UP, 1999.

Crane, Susan. *Gender and Romance in Chaucer's Canterbury Tales*. Princeton: Princeton UP, 1994.

Greiner, Donald J. *Women Enter the Wilderness: Male Bonding and the American Novel of the 1980s*. Columbia: U of South Carolina P, 1991.

Low, Jennifer A. *Manhood and the Duel: Masculinity in Early Modern Drama and Culture*. New York & Basingstoke: Palgrave/St. Martin's Press, 2003.

Patai, Daphne. *The Orwell Mystique: A Study in Male Ideology*. Amherst: U of Massachussetts P, 1984.

Pleck, Joseph H. *The Myth of Masculinity*. Cambridge: MIT Press, 1981.

Rosen, David. *The Changing Fictions of Masculinity*. Champaign, IL.: U of Illinois P, 1994.

Sedgwick, Eve Kosofsky. *Between Men: English Literature and Male Homosocial Desire*. New York: Columbia UP, 1985.

Wells, Robin Headlam. *Shakespeare on Masculinity.* Cambridge: Cambridge UP, 2000.

Masculinity Studies in English Literature: Journal Articles & Book Chapters

Appelbaum, Robert. "'Standing to the Wall': The Pressures of Masculinity in *Romeo and Juliet.*" *Shakespeare Quarterly* 48.3 (Fall 1997): 251-72.

Armengol, Josep Maria. "Gendering Men: Re-Visions of Violence as a Test of Manhood in American Literature." *Atlantis* 29.2 (2007): 75-92.

Armengol, Josep Maria. "'Attention, attention must be finally paid to such a person': A Men's Studies Rereading of Arthur Miller's *Death of a Salesman.*" *Revista de Estudios Norteamericanos.* 10 (2004): 21-46.

Billingham, S.E. "Fraternizing with the Enemy: Constructions of Masculinity in the Short Fiction of Timothy Findley." *Yearbook of English Studies* 31.1 (Jan. 2001): 205-17.

Bromley, Roger. "Rewriting the Masculine Script: The Novels of Joseph Hansen." *Gender, Genre and Narrative Pleasure.* Ed. Derek Longhurst. London: Unwin Hyman, 1989.

Buchanan, B. "'An Anthropomorphic Insolence of Short Duration': Oedipus, Masculinity, and the Death of 'Man' in the Work of Samuel Beckett." *Men and Masculinities* 4.4 (2002): 357-67.

Bullock, Chris J. "Men and Depression: Saul Bellow's *Seize the Day.*" *Journal of Men's Studies* 4.2 (Nov. 1995): 153-68.

Clabough, S. "Negotiating the Afterglow: Masculinity in Willa Cather's *A Lost Lady.*" *Women's Studies* 32.6 (2003): 719-34.

Claridge, Laura, and Elizabeth Langland, eds. *Out of Bounds: Male Writers and Gender(ed) Criticism.* Amherst: U of Massachusetts P, 1990.

Del Gizzo, Suzanne. "Hemingway's Theaters of Masculinity." *Mfs-Modern Fiction Studies* 51.3 (2005): 679-83.

Dudley, John. "Henry James and the Suspense of Masculinity." *American Literature* 77.1 (2005): 188-89.

Fasick, Laura. "Authorial Angels: Writing and Masculinity in Thackeray's *The English Humourists of the Eighteenth Century*." *Nineteenth Century Prose* 26.1 (Spring 1999): 100-17.

Fiedler, Leslie. "The Male Novel." *Partisan Review* 37.1 (1985): 74-89.

Filene, Peter. "Manhood in the Twenties: Was it so Great to be Gatsby? *Ms.* 11.12 (June 1974): 12-18.

Gollin, Rita K. "Understanding Fathers in American Jewish Fiction." *Centennial Review* 18 (Summer 1974): 273-87.

Heilbrun, Carolyn. "The Masculine Wilderness of the American Novel." *Saturday Review* 29 (Jan. 1972): 41-44.

Hinz, John. "Huck and Pluck: 'Bad' Boys in American Fiction." *South Atlantic Quarterly* 51 (Jan. 1952): 120-29.

hooks, bell. "*Malcolm X*: The Longed-for Feminist Manhood." *Essays in Context*. Ed. Sandra Fehl Tropp and Ann Pierson-D'Angelo. New York: Oxford UP, 2001. 714-24.

James, Pearl. "History and Masculinity in F. Scott Fitzgerald's *This Side of Paradise. Mfs-Modern Fiction Studies* 51.1 (2005): 1-33.

Power, William. "Huck Finn's Father." *University of Kansas City Review* 28 (Winter 1961): 83-94.

Riemer, James D. "Rereading American Literature from a Men's Studies Perspective: Some Implications." *The Making of Masculinities: The New Men's Studies*. Ed. Harry Brod. Boston: Allen & Unwin, 1987.

Traister, Bryce. "Sentimental Medicine: Oliver Wendell Holmes and the Construction of Masculinity." *Studies in American Fiction* 27.2 (Fall 1999): 205-27.

Contributors

Alterno, Letizia. Department of English and American Studies, The University of Manchester, M13 9PL, Manchester, UK.

Bedjaoui, Fewzia. Department for Foreign Languages, Université de Sidi-Bel-Abbès (Djillali Liabès), BP 89 Sidi Bel Abbès 22000 Algérie (Algeria).

Chandra, N. Department of English, Pondicherry University, R.V. Nagar, Kalapet, Puducherry-605014 India.

Chatterjee, Purnendu. Department of English, Rabindra Bharati University, 56A Barrackpore, Trunk Road, Kolkata-700050, West Bengal, India.

da Silva, Stephen. Department of English, Brookhaven College, 3939 Valley View Lane, Farmer's Branch, Dallas, TX 75244 USA.

Ganapathy-Doré, Geetha. UFR de Droit, Sciences politiques et socials, Université de Paris 13-99, avenue, Jean Baptiste Clément 93430 Villetaneuse Cedex, France.

Gasparini, Adalinda. via Pratese, 56-50145 Firenze, Italy.

Karekatti, Tripti. Department of English, Mekelle University, P.O. Box No. 3118, Mekelle, Ethiopia.

Mittapalli, Rajeshwar. Department of English, Kakatiya University, Warangal-506009, Andhra Pradesh, India.

Roye, Susmita. Department of English, University of Bristol, 3/5 Woodland Road, Clifton, Bristol BS8 1TB, UK.

Sundaram, Aparna. Department of English, Ethiraj College for Women (Autonomous), Ethiraj Salai, Egmore, Chennai-600008, Tamil Nadu, India.

Viswamohan, Aysha. Department of Humanities & Social Sciences, Indian Institute of Technology Madras, I.I.T. Post Office, Chennai-600036, Tamil Nadu, India.